from

kauri
trees to
sunlit seas:

D0317818

from

kauri trees to sunlit seas:

**shoestring
shipping
in the
South Pacific**

DON SILK

First published 1994 by
Godwit Publishing Limited
P.O. Box 4325, Auckland 1
New Zealand

© 1994 Don Silk (text and photographs)
© 1994 Dennis C. Williams (illustrations)

ISBN 0 908877 49 8

Design and production by Orca Publishing Services
Cover design by Christine Hansen
Cover photographs by Glenn Jowitt

CONTENTS

CONTENTS

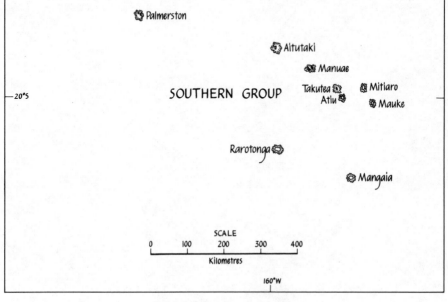

-10°S

Penrhyn

Rakahanga
Manihiki

Pukapuka

Nassau

NORTHERN GROUP

Suwarrow

Palmerston

Aitutaki

Manuae

-20°S

Takutea
Atiu

Mitiaro

Mauke

SOUTHERN GROUP

Rarotonga

Mangaia

SCALE

0   100   200   300   400

Kilometres

160°W

Map of the Cook Islands

CHAPTER ONE

ESCAPE TO PARADISE

It was at Opononi that the truck fell on me. During my last fleeting moments of consciousness I wondered which world I would wake up in. When I opened one flickering bloodshot eye and got things into focus, I was in a white room. An angel in white with bright, mischievous eyes stood at the foot of the bed. 'Thank God, it's heaven,' I whispered.

'No,' said the Angel, 'you can thank Nurse Puru. And it's Rawene Hospital.' I started to laugh, but it wasn't funny, laughing with three broken ribs.

Lying in bed convalescing gives one time for reflection. I'm convinced we should do more of it — reflection, that is. Here I was, the local country carrier, trying to make a living in Godzone. Talk about blood, sweat, toil and tears! I'd been kicked by horses, gored by bulls, bitten by dogs, shat on by bobby calves, abused by cow cockies for leaving freight behind, fined by traffic cops for overloading; the list was endless. Now a truck had fallen on me! But that wasn't the half of it. All that was the easy part. Try running a small business in New Zealand in the 1950s where officials of one sort or another controlled every detail of your public and private life! With one person in five working for the Government (one in four if you included local bodies), it didn't leave many of us to get on with the real work. And by the time one had satisfied the bureaucrats with their never-ending streams of application forms for permits for this and licences for that, one had to work far into the night to get anything done at all — and there was a fine for driving long hours as well. Also, if one wanted to carry something more than 80 kilometres parallel to a railway, there was a special permit required for that too, issued by — you guessed it — the Railways Department. No wonder the place was described as the most over-governed, over-regulated country in the world, outside the Communist Bloc. (Only in Sri Lanka, 35 years later, did I realise that the bureaucrats in New Zealand were bungling amateurs by comparison.)

Then there was the vicar's piano, which had led to my present predicament. The vicar in Kaikohe had asked me if I could bring his piano from Auckland next time I went as he didn't want to trust it to the tender loving care of the New Zealand Railways. I had been only too happy to oblige, for surely by helping the vicar I would be getting God on my side, and that couldn't do any harm. So the piano had been duly loaded behind six tonnes of beer for the Opononi pub, and on the way through Kaikohe at daylight next morning, I backed down the vicar's driveway to unload the instrument. Nobody told me the driveway was built over the septic tank ...

It took three hours to extricate the truck. The local traffic cop, who had been trying to nail me for some time over these illegal trips to Auckland, could scarcely believe his good fortune when, driving to work, what should he see but six tonnes of beer on the vicar's front lawn and a large tractor pulling my truck out of the septic tank.

The piano survived the ordeal and the beer was finally delivered to the pub at Opononi, by which time I realised the truck had a broken spring. I was replacing this spring when the truck fell on me. I was beginning to wonder whose side God was on.

I did some thinking, lying there with the Angel waiting on me hand and foot. There were two things I had long wanted to do. One was to sail a boat around the South Seas. The other was to go to Canada, to live. These things were going through my mind as the Angel was giving me a sponge bath, and I suddenly realised there was a third thing I'd like to do — take her with me.

Later, when I told my mother I was going to build a boat and sail to Canada, she said I was crazy. Then I told her I was going to marry a Catholic. That rocked her to her Protestant core. When I said that the Catholic was also Maori, I thought she was going to faint. I might have fainted myself if I'd known I would be sleeping with a direct descendant of Willi Tawhai, the last convicted cannibal in New Zealand.

Despite the episode with the piano, I still managed to make the odd trip to Auckland undetected. The system of Railways protection was so unjust

10

that everyone was igoring the rules. 'Licensed lawbreakers' one judge called us. During one of these trips I spent some time nosing around Okahu Bay, looking at the cruising yachts on the hard. A young bloke was doing some repairs to the bowsprit of a neat little nine-metre ketch. It looked about the sort of boat I had in mind. It turned out he had built it himself; he didn't tell me he was planning to sail around the world in it. I asked him where I might get plans for such a boat and he said, 'Go and see old Bert Woollacott over at Devonport.' The young bloke's name was Tony Armitt, and he and Tig Loe became the first New Zealanders to sail their boat around the world, earning the New York Cruising Club's coveted Blue Water Medal for the most outstanding small boat achievement of the year. (This was before the Americans became less keen about awarding any kind of yachting trophy to New Zealanders.)

Bert Woollacott showed me the plans of *Marco Polo*. I asked him about building it myself, as I had never built a boat before. He scoffed at any hesitations I might have. 'That's what they all say! But they all manage to get it done!' Bert proved to be a marvellous old gentleman, everybody's friend, and through him I met a few other amateurs building their dream boats to his designs. It was like belonging to a club, and Bert was its guru. Long since retired, Bert now made his business his hobby and he was always ready with advice and a helping hand.

Even in the land of kauri trees, good kauri timber wasn't easy to come by, so I scouted around the local bush and picked a likely tree. A price was negotiated and it didn't take long with a chainsaw to terminate a thousand years of growth. Getting it to a road was another matter, for all the 'easy' timber had long since been worked out, but, with the help of a skilled and friendly bulldozer driver, it was brought down the side of a mountain and loaded on a truck and trailer for the 50-kilometre haul to the sawmill. Bert helped me draw up a milling list so that as the boat was constructed all the correct-sized timber was to hand. This saved a lot of wastage later.

While the timber was seasoning, I prepared the builder's yard. I had a one-room cottage at Opononi, what they call a bach in New Zealand, and the first job was to knock out one wall and double the size of the building. This gave me sufficient floor space to lay down the full-sized 'lines plans', the cross-sectional drawings from which exact patterns were made for all the sawn frames, a process known as lofting. Then, by extending the roof in another direction I had an open lean-to under which the actual construction was to take place. It wasn't far to go to work; in fact it was more like living in a boatyard, surrounded by sawdust and shavings, and the smell of red-lead and linseed oil, and freshly sawn kauri timber.

The keel, the stem and the stern-post were shaped from the heavier timbers and fastened together with copper bolts made on the job. Next came the floor timbers, bolted through the keel, and to these were fastened the transverse frames, carefully shaped from the lines plans lofted on the bedroom floor. Once these were erected at one-metre intervals, and a few fairing battens nailed on fore and aft, I had what began to look like the skeleton of a boat, and I had to spend time in my 'thinking chair' figuring out what came next. The reader may well ask how I came to know how to do all this, never having built a boat before. The answer is, I didn't, but I learned mainly by studying books on the subject, the most useful of which was *Boatbuilding* by Howard Chappell. The actual shaping and fitting of the timbers didn't present too much of a problem for I had had to use my hands as a lad on the farm and had always enjoyed woodwork.

All this took a lot longer than it takes to tell, for I had other things to do at the same time — like marrying the Angel and starting a family, not to mention making a living as a country carrier. This last really bugged me, for it was interfering with my main purpose in life. I was trying to sell the business so I would have the necessary time and money, but it was taking a while. Then came a major setback.

Having finished the lofting, I turned the loft into a bedroom. One night, after making wild passionate love to the Angel, I awoke from an exhausted sleep to hear glass falling from the kitchen windows. I leapt up and was greeted by a burst of flame as I opened the kitchen door. There was an 800-litre water tank on a stand outside the window, and with the aid of a couple of buckets we got the fire under control before it reached the linseed oil and shavings and freshly sawn kauri timber. We may have made history as the first naked fire brigade in the Hokianga. The boat was unscathed, but half the bach had to be rebuilt.

I closed the whole boatbuilding operation for over a year and concentrated on making money with the truck. Olly, the Angel, was a great help, doing all the bookkeeping and often driving the empty truck home at night while I stretched out asleep on the seat. This was much to the chagrin of my friend the traffic cop, who thought he had me for driving too-long hours. It must have ruined his night when he pulled up the truck and this diminutive little Maori girl peeped out the window from behind the wheel, wanting to know what his problem was.

Olly had to give up for a while when her time approached. One day I came home early and just happened to see a stray tomcat sneak under the house. I had been after this noisy beggar for some time, so I grabbed the .303 from the shed and crawled under after him and let him have it right between the eyes, not realising that Olly was asleep right above me. It was with some trepidation that we awaited the birth of our baby to see if it was going to have two heads or something, but Patsy Jean came into the world as a normal, healthy baby girl. It seemed a good omen, and a nice name for the boat, if it ever got built.

I wrote to my old mate, Bob Boyd, and told him I could do with a hand to build this boat, perhaps even to sail it. Bob and I had already had a few adventures together as Boy Scouts. He was a pretty handy all-round bloke and not too hard to get on with. In some ways we complemented each other. For instance, I was still struggling with my overpowering, inborn sense of shyness, while Bob was always the hail-fellow-well-met, the life of the party, always dominating any conversation that might get started. It took a while for him to get my letter, for he was signwriting his way around outback Australia on a motor-bike and side-car, but he came back quick as a flash, just in time to help put in the ribs, or steam-bent frames.

We got stuck in, first building a steam box. After about 20 minutes in the steam box these ribs were sufficiently pliable to bend to the sharpest curve required, without breaking. While hot, they were placed in the boat at 15-centimetre intervals and secured with a few nails and C-clamps until they cooled and set to shape. Then came the planking, with every plank full length. Each plank was fastened to every rib with two copper nails, each nail fitted with a copper roove and riveted on the inside. We became the best pair of riveters in Opononi by the time we had done 4000 nails.

Now she was starting to look like a boat, but there was plenty to do yet. We were fast learning the right terminology, and words like carlins, stringers and clamps slid off our lips like we were seasoned boatbuilders, while heads, knees and buttocks assumed new meanings. Deck beams, coamings and hatch frames all had to be made and fitted; surely a boat was a complicated thing. Then came the big job of melting down three tonnes of scrap lead and casting it in one piece for the keel; that's when we found we had plenty of willing helpers amongst our friends.

At last she was ready for the water. We built a big sledge from old bridge timbers, firmly bolted together, and began the two-kilometre haul to the launching site. For this I had to borrow my truck, now sold, and with a few tonnes of sand on the back she handled it without any problem. That is, until we hit the short stretch of tarseal in front of the pub, by which time the sledge runners had worn down to the stage where the bolts were sticking through a few centimetres. That didn't do the tarseal any good, and of course it had to be the day for the weekly visit to Opononi by my old sparring partner, the traffic cop, who quickly had the county engineer on the scene. I offered to pay for repairs to the tarseal, but in fact I never got the bill.

Launching day came, and two tractors edged her down the beach to the low-tide mark. It was the biggest day in Opononi since Opo the dolphin had died, for it was the first boat built in the vicinity for 50 years. A great crowd assembled from all around to see which way up she would float, if at all, for since when did a local country carrier know anything about building a boat?

The tide crept in, and a hangi was prepared — pork, chickens, kumara and vegetables cooked in the ground in the Maori custom — helped down with the aid of the odd 80-litre keg, another Maori custom. When the tide reached a small platform near the bows, Olly, having been well instructed by Bert Woollacott who presented the champagne, said, 'I name thee *Patsy Jean*' and broke the bottle with such force that as much splashed on her as it did over the boat. Shortly, with much pushing from the shore and pulling from an anchor laid out, and amid much cheering, *Patsy Jean* slid off her cradle and into her natural element for the first time.

It would be nice to say that she motored off quietly to an anchorage, but that would be simplifying things too much. Instead of standing proudly at the helm of my new ship, waving to my friends ashore, I was down below doing battle with the auxiliary motor which was getting hotter than it had ever done in its 20 years' service as a power plant in one of Mr Ford's small cars. I had installed the water-cooling system back to front. It wasn't the last time I was to have trouble with the plumbing on an engine installation.

With the help of many friends, the rigging was completed and we soon moved on board. Patsy was 20 months old and adapted to life afloat as if she had never known anything different.

Having taught myself how to build a boat, the next thing was to learn how to sail it, and in the process we also learned the whereabouts of many sand bars in the Hokianga Harbour, which hadn't been surveyed

Launching the *Patsy Jean*, 1958

since the last square-rigger sailed with kauri logs for Australia. On one occasion both anchor cables parted in a storm and we spent a few hours on the beach. Another time, in front of a good crowd of holidaymakers, we got swept by the tide under the Opononi wharf. One of the onlookers was heard to say, '… and they're going round the world in that thing!' And another, '… that little girl, what's she going to do when it gets rough?' We were the best spectator sport that people had seen since the time I backed the cream-truck over a Volkswagen Beetle outside the pub one Christmas Eve.

Years before, prior to taking up truck driving, as a sailor at sea in the mid-Atlantic I had had the unpleasant experience of seeing a shipmate suffer from a burst appendix. It was the one thing that really worried me about our proposed venture, so one day we all marched up to Rawene Hospital and asked to have our (perfectly good) appendixes out. The doctor was a bit taken aback, but he had a young intern there who needed some practice. I had mine out first, then watched carefully while Bob had his taken out. Now that I knew how it was done, I thought I could probably do Olly's, but she preferred to have it done by the young intern, which I took as a personal affront.

Olly was still in hospital when one morning Bob and I woke to find the Hokianga Bar as calm as a tropical lagoon. Just what we had been waiting three weeks for, so, not wishing to add to the list of the 13 ships wrecked on the bar so far, we lost no time weighing anchor and heading to sea.

When we slipped quietly out of Auckland on 20 April 1959, only a handful of people knew we were bound for faraway places. I didn't want any publicity in case we came to grief up the coast and then we'd look foolish, and the doubters would say 'I told you so'. Better to send word back after we had accomplished something.

It was a leisurely cruise to the Bay of Islands, giving ourselves plenty of time to attend to the last-minute things that always crop up, and to make sure we hadn't forgotten any of the thousand and one things that one thinks are needed for a major ocean crossing, some of which actually *are* needed. Many friends came from Opononi to see us off when we sailed from Russell, some of them convinced this would be the last they would see of us. Missing in the crowd was my old mate the traffic cop, who I'm sure would have dreamed up another ticket to hand-deliver to me if he'd known it was his last chance. I missed his red hair and smirking face.

We sailed under almost perfect conditions, with a light southwesterly breeze that quickly carried us away from the coast. We carried a spinnaker for two days under freshening conditions; in fact the wind got fresher and fresher, until we were soon shortening sail. Still it blew stronger, and still we shortened sail, until there came a point when there wasn't any sail left to shorten. Still the wind got stronger, the seas higher and steeper. It wasn't fun any more. It became harder and harder to control the boat as we ran on under bare poles. As each wave approached, a great wall of water would stand poised behind us until the *Patsy Jean* threw her stern in the air and the sea would break under us with a thunderous roar. Then the odd extra large waves started to topple forward as they approached and would break on board, also with a thunderous roar.

Every cruising yachtsman who ever wrote a book describes these conditions, and all of them seem to try the textbook methods of riding out a gale in a small yacht at sea. These methods vary. There is heaving-to under a storm-jib; inevitably the storm-jib blows out and you are left with the bolt-ropes. There is the employment of a sea-anchor; this usually turns out to be too small, or, if it is big enough, the gear chafes through and carries it away. You can try towing warps and drogues behind; this usually results in the same as the sea-anchor tactic, except you are doing it from the opposite end of the boat.

The most dangerous tactic would appear to be to keep going in these extreme conditions, resulting in the vessel pitch-poling, or else broaching, and rolling through 360 degrees; either way the boat stands a good chance of getting dismasted. After trying some or all of these things, the crew are exhausted and collapse into their bunks, lashing themselves in, then poke their heads out three days later to find the boat has looked after herself perfectly well. Of course, if you are stuck for sea room you must try something, but we had 6000 miles of ocean ahead of us, so the sensible thing seemed to be to take the line of least resistance and give up right away. This we did, and it worked out all right, but it was not an enviable experience. As Bob said, 'This is not what I signed on for!'

As we lay in our bunks listening to the approaching roar of a breaking wave, bracing ourselves for the moment when the boat would be hurled sideways, I kept telling myself that of course she could stand up to it. Hadn't I followed old Bert's instructions to the letter? Hadn't I used all the specified fastenings — if anything, bigger than specified? Wasn't she built of the finest boatbuilding timber in the world? Those stories I had read about riding out gales, hadn't those guys all come back to tell the tale? Of course they had, otherwise I wouldn't have read about them. But what about the ones who hadn't come back? Well, I hadn't thought about them. Perhaps we would break up and sink. Perhaps I should have stayed in Rawene hospital. But at least we wouldn't die of a ruptured appendix.

And what about that little girl? What's she going to do when it gets rough, the critics had wanted to know. Well, that little girl was doing very nicely thank you, playing with her toys and her colouring books in

'What's that little girl going to do when it gets rough?' — Patsy Jean at sea.

her quarter-berth, never missing a meal, which was good for morale as it shamed the rest of us into struggling up and getting something to eat.

Like all storms, it eventually passed. No doubt many yachts have experienced worse storms, but for us it was the worst weather we were to have in thousands of miles of cruising, and I consider we were extremely fortunate in striking it as early as we did, for now we knew what she could take and were perfectly confident that, as long as she had deep water around her, *Patsy Jean* could handle whatever came along.

I never regretted not having a radio transmitter, for I believed, and still do, that unless you have very good equipment and are skilled in the operation and maintenance of it, you are better off without it on an ocean passage of this nature. This way, nobody sparks off a search-and-rescue operation just because he heard there was some bad weather and you didn't report in. On the other hand, cruising yachtsmen who are radio hams can make a lot of friendly contacts as they go along, especially with the large number of yachts cruising the oceans today. But then today it's a whole new ball game, as the Americans say. What with plastic boats, plastic sextants and global positioning systems, is it the same challenge any more?

We lay becalmed in the channel between Tahiti and Moorea all night, inhaling the scent of frangipani, vanilla and copra, and watching the lights of Papeete over the reef. In the morning the pilot launch came out to meet us and we were soon tied stern first to the main street amongst yachts from half-a-dozen countries. There were many formalities and a seemingly endless request for lists in triplicate, quadruplicate and quintuplicate, but the officials were most courteous and helpful. Gigi Grand, the Capitaine de l' Immigration, even lent us 1000 francs to buy some fruit for lunch. Gigi was the yachtsman's friend and never forgot a face.

People say Tahiti is not like it used to be. People are saying it now, they were saying it then, and Captain Cook said as much on his second voyage. I believe any time is the best time to see Tahiti, the sooner the better, for it certainly won't be the same again, ever. We were perhaps lucky seeing it before the major changes of the sixties, before the airport, before the big hotels, and before *la bombe* and the Foreign Legion. It's still a nice place, but not like it used to be.

In 1959 Tahiti was like a little bit of France tucked away in the South Pacific, with a bit of Saigon thrown in for good measure. There wasn't any place in the world quite like it, and small wonder many cruising yachtsmen never got any further (not that the French made it easy for them to stay). Two such yachtsmen were Bill Baker and Roger Gowan, who, with three other ex-constables from the Rhodesian police force, had set out from England in their yacht *Si Yi Pambili*, Zulu for 'Go forward'. They went forward as far as Tahiti, by which time the other three crew members had fallen by the wayside at various ports. Bill and Roger fell by the wayside in Papeete, and left only when the French kicked them out. They returned from New Zealand the next year, and once again stayed until the French kicked them out. The next year they were back again, and this time while doing a charter trip to the Austral Islands they lost their yacht on a reef in Rurutu. 'The best thing that ever happened to us,' Roger told me years later, while sipping Hinano in his Paul Gaugin Restaurant in Tautira. 'With no means of transport, it wasn't so easy to kick us out.' Eventually they both got French passports, married into local families and became successful businessmen.

When we arrived there were about 30 yachts in port, and they varied in size from *Patsy Jean* to Sterling Haydon's ex-pilot-schooner *Wanderer* from San Francisco. Watching Sterling stroll along the waterfront with his easy, rolling gait and lopsided smile, you automatically glanced down to see if he was wearing his six-guns. To be a Hollywood film star, own a magnicent sailing vessel like *Wanderer* and sail it yourself to Tahiti would surely be many people's dream. But Sterling, too, had his problems. In the throes of a divorce back home, he was wanted for abducting his own children and was trying to figure out where next he could sail to without getting extradited back to the States. *Wanderer* was moored next to us, and we saw a lot of Sterling; a really nice ordinary bloke.

Another New Zealand yacht in port was the *Drifter*, sailed (or drifted?) single-handed by Bill Moore of Wellington. Bill was a radio ham but this hadn't been much help to him when a fuel line broke and he couldn't charge his batteries. Without radio he had no time signals; his first landfall, instead of Tahiti, was Mangareva, 800 miles away, where he found his chronometer was six minutes slow. Bill was on his way to Canada, but suddenly changed his mind and headed for Rarotonga, and back to New Zealand. When he hadn't been heard of six months after leaving Rarotonga, his yacht club friends in Wellington discussed which wall of the clubhouse would be suitable for a memorial plaque for him, but before they got around to erecting it the *Drifter* sailed into Auckland, not much the worse for wear. Bill explained he had had 'a funny experience' and forgot how to navigate.

New Zealand was well represented along the Papeete waterfront. *Nereides* was a beautifully appointed ketch from Auckland, owned by Ted Copsey, and navigated by Tig Loe of *Marco Polo* fame. Although I had met Tony Armitt, the owner of *Marco Polo* (and indeed, had I not chanced on him that day in Okahu Bay, a boat quite different from *Patsy Jean* might have been built), I had not met Tig, who sailed around the world with him. When we mentioned to Tig we were thinking of making a trip to some of the Tuamotu Islands for a couple of weeks while waiting for the July celebrations in Papeete, he was keen to come, and this suited us fine as he had been through those tricky waters in *Marco Polo*. Besides, he had forgotten more about sailing than we were ever likely to learn, and there was a chance some of his knowledge would rub off on us. A large, easy-going Kiwi with a quiet sense of humour that enabled him to see the funny side of most situations, Tig fitted in well and was a great asset.

It took half a day to get through the formalities of leaving port but, once away, we soon picked up the trade winds and made good time to the phosphate island of Makatea, 120 miles to the north. Approaching the island in the dark, we headed for the lights of the town, only to realise after a while that they were moving, and weren't the lights of the town at all but the lights of the French ship *Oiseau des Iles*. Having sorted that out, we closed the coast and made fast to one of the large mooring buoys offshore.

Daylight revealed surf breaking on the reef a few hundred metres away. Close beyond was a beach, fronting a narrow strip of land, and behind that rose almost vertical cliffs 100 or so metres high. The only break in the reef was at a small manmade boat harbour, where a crane was installed for lifting lighters. Nearby could be seen the huge cantilever construction built to carry the bulk phosphate to ships which moor to the buoys while loading, the water being far too deep to anchor.

Presently a launch was lowered into the water and several officials and an interpreter came out. We were invited ashore and conducted to the offices of the phosphate company on top of the cliff, access being by cable car. The manager gave us a cordial welcome and arranged a guide to show us over the diggings after lunch. In exchange we were to carry mail for the island of Tikehau, about 80 kilometres away.

We strolled around the village while we waited. The island consists almost entirely of dead coral, or 'makatea', for it was once beneath the sea. Since being raised by underwater eruptions eons ago, it had been covered to a depth of almost a metre with the droppings of seabirds over countless centuries, droppings which had reacted with the coral stumps to form guano, or phosphate. Most of the guano had by now been removed and the resultant surface was rough and deeply pitted. The village was like a wild, untended park with comfortable modern bungalows tucked away picturesquely among the trees. These houses were rented to the workers at a nominal fee. Each had a big concrete water cistern, for water was precious on the island, there being no streams, and each also had flowers growing in half-drums of soil placed around the house.

All this was very nice, but the most remarkable thing was to be greeted in English by the workers, all of whom seeemed to own Norman bicycles with little New Zealand flags on them. It was not until we were asked into a house for cool drinks that we learned that many of the people came from the Cook Islands and were working here on contract. The company preferred Cook Islanders but this was to be their last year, for the French Government had decreed that in future only French nationals could be employed. These Cook Islanders appeared to be friendly, and hospitable to a fault, and told us much about their homeland. We decided it must be worth a visit.

For our tour of the diggings we climbed aboard a small train, riding on a short platform on one of the wagons. After meandering through the village picking up the workers, we headed across to where the phosphate was currently being worked, about eight kilometres away, rattling along at 25 to 30 kph. For Patsy, this was the highlight of the day. Who would have thought she would have her first train ride on a remote Pacific atoll?

The men worked in pairs, one at the bottom of the crater-like hole, which might be three metres deep, fossicking the stuff out with a mattock and filling a bucket which his mate hauled to the surface and emptied into a wheelbarrow. After being run across planks with the wheelbarrow, the guano was then tipped onto a conveyor belt which carried it some hundreds of metres to an elevated hopper above the railway line, from where it went to the drying plant at the coast. The men were paid on a production basis and really worked hard in the sweltering heat. Some of this phosphate was shipped to New Zealand and in our minds we had visions of a Fletcher top-dressing aircraft skimming over the hills of Hokianga, phosphate streaming from its belly, while on the ground tip trucks and mechanical loaders worked without effort. Another vision was of my father in earlier times trudging across the fields spreading it by hand from a knapsack.

We called at some of the more typical atolls in the Tuamotu Archipelago, anchoring at different villages in the clear sheltered waters of the lagoons. The smaller the village, the greater the hospitality. Cruising yachts were still something of a novelty in some of these places, for most of them seemed to head straight for Papeete and then Moorea, Raiatea and Bora Bora. To my mind they missed some of the best of Polynesia, for while the high volcanic islands look spectacular, some of the best anchorages, the best underwater viewing and the friendliest people are to be found in the low-lying atolls, dangerous though they may be to the navigator.

At one such village local fishermen came out and helped us anchor in a snug little cove on the edge of the pass, right beside the village, mooring us fore and aft in the current, thus avoiding the problems of swinging at anchor and getting our chain caught around the coral heads.

Two youths claimed the honour of taking us for a guided tour, and most of the kids followed us, so we made quite a procession. The village was built around a small lagoon of brackish water, so the only street was circular. Many of the houses were of coconut thatch, but there were also many with wood or concrete walls and iron roofs. The iron roofs didn't look so picturesque, but were no doubt more practical when it came to collecting rainwater. As we made our way along the street, many of the mamas would come out to greet us with 'Iaorana' or 'Bonjour' and occasionally would hang a necklace of shells or 'hei pupu' around our necks and give us each a kiss on both cheeks. 'Iaorana' is not so different from the New Zealand 'Kia ora' and Olly soon found she could sometimes get by speaking Maori, which was much better than my French.

It began to rain and we took shelter in a Chinese shop — not that we really needed to, for it was warm rain. Our audience had grown by now and the little shop was full to overflowing. Patsy enjoyed being the centre of attention amongst the kids, while we sat on empty milk-powder boxes chatting to the storekeeper. Someone reminded the children that school had long since started, so they all took off down the road, but were soon back, saying teacher had declared a half holiday.

It cleared, and we progressed along the circular street. At the chief's house we were asked in after the chief had changed his only garment, a pair of shorts. A big, well-built man, he spoke no English, but with a mixture of French and Maori we were able to answer his many intelligent questions about our travels. His wife, a jolly woman of ample proportions, favoured us with more hei pupus and kisses, while one of our guides was sent up a tree to knock down some fresh coconuts.

The crystal-clear waters of the lagoon teemed with fish and it was no trouble to spear our breakfast each morning; it was more a matter of choosing which fish it would be. There were a few sharks around, but they didn't bother us until one day Tig speared a fish that a shark had apparently lined up for itself. The shark grabbed the fish and a tug-of-war followed, with Tig deciding discretion was the better part of valour and abandoning his spear. On another occasion a boy got a nasty row of gashes on one knee from a shark which was probably going for fish the boy had on a string, rather than for the boy himself. Olly was able to call on her nursing skills and, with the help of antibiotics and dressings from our medical kit, the wounds soon started healing.

Now she was quite the heroine and this warranted another tour of the village, this time on the island's only vehicle, a pre-war Citroën truck, probably of about ten horsepower originally, but many of the horses had since been put out to graze. The truck was a push-start job, and the trick was for the pushers to jump on the moment she roared into life, for she had neither clutch nor brakes. Many stops were made to call upon relations, where we dined on watermelon and cake, washed down with fresh coconut milk, then it would be a push-start again and on to the next place. A major hazard presented itself when school came out, with as many kids leaping onto the truck as space would permit. The whole thing was getting out of hand, so there were no more stops, and after two final circuits of the village, during which we actually reached top gear, we arrived back at our starting point and the elegant old vehicle was parked in its shed, perhaps to await the next big event.

We announced our intending departure the following day, and that evening there was an even bigger 'himene' and 'hula hula' than usual. Part of the street was swept clear of small 'kirikiri' or pebbles, and Bob and Tig were kept on their feet by the local maidens, to the music of the island's only accordion and as many ukeleles and guitars as could be pressed into service. Although nobody in the village professed to speak English, it was surprising how many English songs they could sing, mostly cowboy songs, of which Bob had an endless repertoire. 'Imene Bob!' they would keep shouting every time he looked like flagging. Then there was that Tahitian favourite, 'Une puaatoro Hellaby', being a ballad sung in a crazy mixture of French, English and Tahitian about Mama waiting for Papa to come back from the store with a tin of Hellaby's for supper, but Papa comes home drunk, without the corned beef.

The whole village came down to see us off in the morning. We swept out through the pass on the four-knot current and within a couple of hours the tops of the palm trees had sunk below the horizon.

At Rangiroa we met up with the French naval auxiliary ketch the *Zelee*, surveying the atoll. Her master, Lt Anglejan, came on board and was able to point out several errors in our charts, including the position of the atoll, which was four miles further east than charted. The lieutenant and his engineer, a Tahitian named Louis Wohler, were friendly and hospitable, and so were their ladies. Mme Wohler was a jolly, laughing woman, while Anglejan's girlfriend Teura was absolutely gorgeous, so much so that the tight T-shirt she wore interfered with my breathing. I stole a surreptitious glance at Olly and wondered if perhaps I had brought coals to Newcastle so to speak, but it was only a fleeting thought. The *Zelee* had finished her survey and was about to sail for Papeete. Because it was a naval vessel, the girls had to be left behind; they were to travel on the next copra boat, the *Popoua*, due in a few days.

Back in Papeete things were warming up for the fête. Rows and rows of stalls were being built along the waterfront by various sponsors; all the major firms were represented, as were most of the bars including Quinn's, the Bar Lea and the Pu Offi, the favourite haunts of the yachties. Merry-go-rounds and a ferris wheel were springing to life and Patsy thought it was going to be the biggest Christmas ever.

Then one day we had a visit from Lt Anglejan. He had been worried about the girls, as the *Popoua* was long overdue. The missionary schooner *Paraita* had been out to all the islands that she was supposed to call at, and searched south towards Tahiti without success. The warship *Lotus* had had a look around with her radar and still there was no sign. A plane search was instituted and the *Popoua* was at last located and towed into port. Then it was discovered the girls weren't on board anyway. The ship had broken down soon after leaving Rangiroa and some of the passengers had taken to a boat and returned to the island. Teura was competing in the 'Miss Tahiti' contest and Lt Anglejan offered us 10,000 francs if we would go and fetch her in time.

Not only was the 10,000 francs pretty tempting, but the thought of having the beautiful Teura at close quarters for a few days was even more so. However, we had a problem in that our engine was ashore for overhaul and we really needed it if we were to be sure of making it back in time for the beauty contest. Happily, an alternative presented itself. The sleek 16-metre yawl *Westward Ho* lay near us, and Taffy and Barbara Sceva, who owned her, were very keen to go to the Tuamotus after hearing of our exploits there, but they were just a bit hesitant on account of the dangers described in the *Pilot Book*, and indeed the *Pilot Book* would put anybody off. I most generously offered my services as navigator if they would only agree to pick up a couple of passengers at Rangiroa and get back in time for the fête. They couldn't agree quickly enough, and invited Olly and Patsy as well, although they hadn't figured in my plans.

The sight of Teura stepping on board at Rangiroa clad in a pareu took my breath away again, and I was really looking forward to the trip back — it could take as long as it liked. Taffy and Barbara gave up their owner's cabin to the girls, and being typical Polynesian travellers, that was the last we saw of them until they surfaced in Papeete two days later. Teura made it to the competition and must have taken the judges' breaths away too, for she was crowned 'Miss Tahiti', winning a trip to Paris. She won Anglejan as well, for they got married there, and I never saw either of them again, although I was to meet Mme Wohler a few years later.

CHAPTER TWO

BOATBUILDING IN THE TROPICS

We spent a few wonderful weeks cruising the beautiful islands of Moorea, Raiatea, Tahaa and Bora Bora, but we couldn't get out of our minds the friendly Cook Islanders we had met in Makatea, plus others in Tahiti. We decided a call to Rarotonga was a 'must', even if only for a weekend. It was to be some weekend.

It was a boisterous five-day run from Bora Bora and it was almost dark as we came into the lee of Rarotonga. We crept slowly into Avarua Harbour, just making out the reef on either side in the light of the pale new moon. The 25-metre inter-island trader *Dobiri* lay on one side of the finger jetty and it seemed reasonable to assume that there was enough water on the other side for *Patsy Jean*, but as we glided towards the berth a pyjama-clad figure called out from the *Dobiri*, 'Can't go there, water too shallow, come beside me!' So we did, and 'pyjamas' introduced himself: 'Williams, Captain Hugh Williams, from Sydney, but living here now, doing a bit of island trading, no money in it of course, only doing it for the good of the people really. Got this ship in New Guinea, like her? I've sent a boy up to get the Customs man.' All this in one breath at staccato pace almost without pause. We were to get to know Williams, best described as 'a brisk little man of 60', and we usually set our ears into 'receive' mode and left them there, for there was seldom time to transmit once Hughie got going. Others just put up a mental barrier, but he could be quite interesting if you had the patience to listen. Certainly one had to admire his guts and determination when one learned how he and his engineer friend, Les Livingstone, another non-smoking Australian teetotaller (unique in the South Seas, surely), brought an ancient Brixham trawler out from England and made a go of shipping in the islands, against all odds.

The crew of *Patsy Jean* on board, arriving at Rarotonga.

The Customs man, a Kiwi expatriate, arrived and came on board. After a goodly chat about the islands, and things in general, he excused himself, as 'the missus will have tea waiting'. As he got up to go he pulled his packet of Greys tobacco from his hip pocket. 'I'll just jot down your names. Come over to the office on Monday and we'll get you cleared in.'

Well, if this was bureacracy à la Cook Islands, it would do us.

We wandered ashore. A number of people had come down to the wharf; obviously yachts didn't arrive every day of the week. Everyone had a friendly 'hello' or 'kia orana'. This latter delightful greeting, meaning literally 'long may you live', was also found to be used, and still is, by most long-term expatriates. It is a courteous way to answer the telephone, although occasionally, after realising who is calling, one may feel that 'e mate koe' — 'drop dead' — would have been more appropriate.

Across the little bridge there were many people milling around, for the pictures were about to start at the Victory Theatre. At the shop opposite, Island Merchants, the proprietor, Dick Brown, a large, well-padded, slow-speaking Cook Islander (but with a mind as sharp as a sail needle) introduced himself and wanted to know all about our travels. Dick had his own schooner and traded around the islands, buying copra and pearl shell and selling general merchandise. He explained that there was no bank here but we would be able to change our travellers cheques at the Treasury on Monday. 'Meanwhile, here's ten pounds. You can pay me back next week.'

Next morning at the office of the Union Steamship Company we found Tekeu Framhein and told him we had a birthday cake for him from his aunty in Tahiti. We didn't tell Tekeu that we were glad to get rid of this blasted cake, but it was a fact, because we had nowhere stow it. Having got rid of the cake, we thought that was that, but that wasn't how things were done in the Cook Islands apparently. A quiet, unassuming young man of part-European extraction, married to the daughter of a Tahitian family, Tekeu insisted on us meeting his family and driving us around the island in a borrowed pickup, during which time we visited his orange plantation and were loaded up with wonderful sweet oranges.

A couple of Kiwis came and took us to the Sailing Club where a variety of craft of vastly different sorts, all locally built, including canoes with homemade sails, competed over a hazardous course amongst the coral heads on Muri lagoon. Even more hazardous was the social gathering in the clubhouse afterwards. There was no bar as such, for the sale of liquor was prohibited in the Cook Islands except on production of a doctor's certificate saying you required it on medical grounds. By an ingenious system of coupons it seemed everyone in the club qualified, but then we found that the chief medical officer who issued these certificates was the club commodore. While most of the blokes were 'papa'as', or Europeans, most of the females (wives or girlfriends, we weren't sure which and it didn't seem to be of importance) were locals. One thing was certain, everyone knew how to enjoy themselves. A fire was lit on the beach and out came sausages and chops — and ukeleles.

Sunday saw us in the LMS (London Missionary Society) church listening to the choir, which was marvellous, and the Boys' Brigade band, which was pretty dreadful. Stuart and Tereapii Kingan asked us home to their place to watch a movie. Stuart was a scientist and ran the Ionosphere Station for the New Zealand Department of Scientific and Industrial Research. He had built his own house out of ten car cases (he never did say what he had done with the cars). The movie projector was a museum piece, driven by a sewing machine belt held together with a safety pin which had a habit of parting when the action got a bit exciting.

Altogether a fabulous weekend.

On Monday Bob and I were walking back to the harbour after collecting our Customs clearance to leave for Apia where friends were expecting us. I said, 'Let's go and have another look at the *Siren*'. The *Siren* was a wooden ketch, 13 metres long and as beamy as a Samoan mama, that had been wrecked on the reef just outside Avarua Harbour. Dick Brown had bought the wreck and dragged it ashore onto the beach next to the Island Merchants store where, over the years, an attempt had been made to repair her, using second-rate materials and third-rate carpenters. Lying on her side under a purau (hibiscus) tree, stripped to a bare hull and with rainwater rotting her decks, she looked a sorry sight — but repairable.

'I wonder if Dick would sell her?' I said.

'Yeah, I wonder what he'd want?'

'Let's go and ask. We owe him ten quid anyway.'

We gave Dick back his ten pounds, talked about the weather, and asked how business was.

'Well, not so good. It's the Government. Now they have introduced income tax, and *that's* no good for business.'

'And what is the rate of tax, Dick?'

'Oh, I don't know. Last year I had to go to New Zealand. They made me put up a bond of ten thousand pounds before I could go. They said when they worked out how much tax I owed they'd give me a refund. Never got any refund yet!'

'That's hardly fair. By the way, what are you planning to do with the *Siren*?'

'Well, there was a Chinaman going to come down from Tahiti to buy her. But he hasn't showed up yet. You know, the engine and sails and everything's round in my shed. Shall we have a look?' So we piled into Dick's Bel-Air Chev and drove in low gear around to the shed.

'Nice car, Dick.'

'Yeah, it's okay, I suppose. One of my shell buyers sent it down from the States for a present for me. This stupid Government wants to tax me

Siren as she came off the reef

on that too.' We learned later that Dick used the Bel-Air only in the mornings. In the afternoon he drove to work in the Chrysler. Mrs Brown drove separately, in the Holden. (According to a sticker on the rear window of the Holden, it had been protected for life with Proofcote, but you could stand on one side and see clear through both doors and out the other side, there was so little metal left.) Anyway, there in the shed was all the gear for the *Siren*, and heaps of other gear besides, salvaged off various ships over the years. And a Ford Zephyr.

Back in Dick's office we sat in silence. Dick said, 'I wonder who's going to speak first? Are you going to tell me how much you want to pay, or am I going to tell you how much I want?' I asked how much the Chinaman was going to pay, had he come.

'Oh, at that time we were talking about two thousand pounds.' This sounded about right, but was way beyond our means.

'Oh,' I said, 'I would have thought two hundred would be more like it.'

'Okay. I'll sell you the *Siren* for two hundred pounds.' I nearly fell off the beer crate.

'All right,' I said, 'but I've only got one hundred in travellers cheques. I'll have to get some money from New Zealand.' (What money in New Zealand, Bob was thinking.)

'That's all right. You give me the hundred pounds now and the other hundred when you get your money from New Zealand.'

We walked back to our ship to have a closer look, then back to *Patsy Jean* to tell Olly she needn't have stowed everything so carefully as we weren't going anywhere. She thought that was a marvellous idea. That night we had a celebratory dinner on board (there being no restaurants ashore) and faced up to the real reason we had bought the *Siren*; we needed an excuse to stay in this delightful place which had as much as Tahiti to offer, but without the French.

Rebuilding the *Siren* proved to be quite a formidable task. Dick Brown found us a 'boy' to assist. Miringa Vaevaeongo was a local fisherman, a Mangaian like Dick. Fortunately we were able to call him Miri for short. Middle-aged and energetic, his rugged, weatherbeaten face was always ready to break into a smile, especially at the first sign of disaster. As honest as the day is long, he never ceased to remind us to 'not trust

Boatbuilding in the tropics: *Siren* 1961

these bloody Maoris'. (Actually the 'bloody Maoris' never seemed to be a problem.)

First we borrowed a couple of timber-jacks from the Electric Power Supply and stood the boat upright under the purau tree. All the patchwork repairs were torn off, as was the decking, for freshwater had started some rot. From this demolition we salvaged enough decent timber to put up a builder's shed, and with electricity connected, we were able to use a borrowed Skilsaw and other tools.

It was obvious we were going to need a lot more timber than at first thought, and where would we find that in this remote South Pacific island? The answer was staring us in the face. Out on the reef, not half a mile away, was the wreck of another of Dick Brown's ships, the 400-tonne *Rannah*. Built in Tasmania of huon pine and Australian hardwood, she provided us with all the timber we needed for deck beams, steam-bent ribs, stringers and floor timbers, plus copious quantities of bronze and galvanised fastenings. For actual planking we went to the Public Works Department and, lo and behold, they had 36-foot lengths of 8' x 2' Oregon pine specially imported from North America for roof trusses on water-catchment tanks. These were not for sale, but it so happened that the chief clerk of Public Works, Tim Perry, a part-Maori, came from Hokianga too, and somehow these special lengths of beautifully clean timber became available. Short and rotund, Tim always tried to keep the wind on his port side, so that the few remaining wisps of hair would remain swept across his scalp. His wife Lani was taller, but weighed much less than half her husband. Lani didn't drive, so the only time Tim's Austin A35 left home, Tim was at the wheel, and the car had a list to starboard. The list eventually became permanent, even when the car was parked.

We had to pay for the timber of course, so the problem of money had to be addressed. Mana Strickland, a local headmaster, made us a loan, for which we mortgaged the vessel to him, making out the mortgage documents ourselves, there being no lawyer on the beach in those days (now there are 40 of them!).

To bend the planks into shape we built a steam-box from sundry bits of timber and hose. The boiler was a 200-litre drum, and when steam was raised it was quite an impressive performance, much enjoyed by passing spectators. When the plank was judged sufficiently 'cooked', it was hauled from the box and quickly slapped into place with clamps and wedges. It even looked as if we knew what we were doing and Miri would adopt a very nonchalant attitude if he thought any of his fishermen friends were watching.

However, it wasn't all hustle and bustle, and much time was spent sitting under the purau tree, gazing out over the reef and listening to the juke-box in Taripo's store across the road blasting out *Heartaches by the Number* (top hit), or *Danny Boy* (a close second), while we speculated what we would do with the fortune we were bound to make when we finished rebuilding the *Siren*.

'You know, Bob, they say Dick's schooner *Tahitien* was wrecked right here in Avarua Harbour.'

'Yeah, supposed to have sunk over there on the western side of the harbour. Can't be very deep. The keel must be still there.'

'That's right. Ship that size must have had a hundred tonnes on the keel. Maybe lead?'

'Let's ask Dick.' So we asked Dick if the *Tahitien* had had a lead keel. Dick pushed his hat back on his head (he never ever took it off) and said, 'Oh, yes, they say it was a lead keel.' So we spent some more time under the purau tree figuring out what 100 tonnes of scrap lead would be worth and what tackle would be required to haul it ashore with the island's heaviest piece of machinery, a vintage D4 bulldozer.

On the first calm day we snorkelled around the harbour and, sure enough, there was the keel. Bob dived with a hacksaw to get a sample to test for purity. His face was a picture of dismay when he surfaced. 'Bloody concrete!' he yelled. Dick must have chuckled to himself over that one.

The weeks slipped by. We were faced with what to do with *Patsy Jean* in the approaching hurricane season, for there was no safe harbour and no means of lifting her out of the water. Also, we needed to raise some more money to finish the *Siren*, so we decided to sail to New Zealand at the end of November. The Resident Commissioner asked us to secure the *Siren* against any possible hurricane, so we lashed her to the purau tree with wire rope borrowed from the PWD. (Fortunately there wasn't any hurricane that year: when one did come a few years later the purau tree went through Taripo's store, and that was the end of *Heartaches by the Number* and *Danny Boy*.)

Back in New Zealand it was pleasant enough living on board in the Town Basin at Whangarei. Bob went back to his old trade of sign-writing in Dargaville, Patsy stayed with grandparents, Olly worked at the Commercial Hotel, and I got a job driving what was then the biggest road tanker in New Zealand, but we were glad when the time came to head back to the islands.

There were several cruising boats in the basin sitting out the hurricane season including a couple of Woollacott ketches. Selwyn Matheson and Peter Ashcroft were back from Tahiti and were fitting out *Kehua*, for another cruise to the Islands. Bert Woollacott had also designed *Kehua* but the builders had committed the unforgiveable sin of changing the design a bit as they went along, so she wasn't truly a Woollacott, although Selwyn and Peter liked to think so. They were itching to get away again and we convinced them that Rarotonga should be their first stop.

Another Woollacott ketch in port was the ten-metre *Nina*. Theo and Mary Buckthought had bought her in Australia and, with their hard-case sons of six, five, four and three years, were also persuaded to head for Rarotonga. The first New Zealand-Rarotonga race was on! Theo and Mary had their hands full, what with four mischievous kids, so Bob offered to crew for them, about which Patsy was pretty indignant. We took on board *Patsy Jean* a couple of old mates, Keith Saul and Glyn Fell. Glyn was a farmer from Opononi who had put in many hours helping to build *Patsy Jean*.

Bert Woollacott, now in his seventies, came from Auckland to see us off. It was the first time he had seen the *Kehua*. Selwyn was very proud of their boat and asked Bert what he thought of her. 'Son, you should take an axe to it!' he said as he turned away. Selwyn was devastated.

It was glorious weather as we sailed together through Whangarei Heads on the last day of April 1960, but it didn't last and we soon got separated in strong head winds. In *Patsy Jean* we found ourselves pushed well to the north of our track, passing close by the Kermadec Islands, 600 miles northeast of Auckland.

I had long been fascinated by tales of Raoul, or Sunday, Island told me by Arthur Dyke, grandson of Tom Bell, an adventurous New Zealander who with his wife and children settled there in 1878. From the very start the family had had to live the life of true desert islanders. The captain of the schooner which brought them to the island sold them food which proved to be rotten, and never returned. It was to be a year before they saw anyone from the outside world. But they survived, raising

a family of ten, and were finally evacuated by the New Zealand Government in 1914 when German raiders were prowling the Pacific.

Although the Bells lived through some grim times, nothing matched
those experienced by two part-Samoan, part-European families who
lived there for a while in the 1860s, making a living supplying produce
to passing whalers. In 1863 the Peruvian ship *Rosa y Carmen* called there
with 300 Polynesian slaves on board, mostly from the northern Cooks
and Tokelau, plus some from Easter Island. Disease had broken out on
board, and the ship was desperately short of food and water. The slaves
were put ashore in order to recuperate while the ship was cleansed, but
many of them, over 100 it is believed, died ashore or on board. The ship
pillaged all available food and sailed off to Peru, and the settlers and a
few survivors reached Apia on a whaling ship that called in shortly after.

Now the island is uninhabited except for a New Zealand meteorological station, and at the risk of losing the race, for which the first prize
was a case of beer, we decided to call in for a few hours. Anchoring near
North Beach in the early hours of Sunday morning (surely an auspicious
day to be visiting Sunday Island), under the lee of the cliffs and out of
sight of the hostel, we couldn't see how to effect a landing through the
surf or how to attract attention ashore, so Keith swam to the beach through
the breakers. We imagined him knocking on the door of the met. station
and blandly asking for a weather report, but we had been observed from
the clifftop and by the time Keith shook the water out of his hair a tractor
full of bearded men had burst through the undergrowth to welcome him
ashore. Arrangements were quickly made to get the rest of us ashore and
we were signalled to proceed along the coast to Fishing Rock, where a
boat was lowered down a flying-fox from the top of the cliff, about 125
metres up, to an area of flat rock below. It was then launched from a
derrick and in no time the officer in charge, Colin Clarke, was on board,
offering the use of his men to look after the yacht while we stretched our
legs ashore.

The lads had been there almost a year, having been left by the *Holmglen*
on one of her last trips before she mysteriously foundered with all hands
off the New Zealand coast. They hadn't seen another soul since landing,
and Patsy was believed to be the first child to step ashore since the Bell
children lived here, and Olly only the second woman. The hospitality
was overwhelming, and it was three days before we were able to tear
ourselves away. There were nine of them altogether, and they seemed to
fit in well together under Colin's leadership.

Raoul is a pretty island, most of it mountainous and bushclad, but with a few fertile valleys where fruit trees from Tom Bell's plantings were still bearing, as was a grove of oranges planted during an abortive attempt to settle Niue Islanders there. The meteorological teams over the years had established fresh orchards and gardens, and a small dairy farm. From the rocks, or offshore, fishing was fabulous, so it really was a nice place to spend a year. Frequent earthquakes added a little spice to life. At one place where the road ran along the clifftop it was possible to look down at the surf on the rocks on one side and a beautiful green lake on the other, while across the lake could be seen signs of recent volcanic activity, with trees devastated and mud and stones in all directions.

Of course we lost the race, but it's an ill wind that blows no one any good. *Kehua* and *Nina* arrived at Rarotonga within 12 hours of each other, both in time to get thrown ashore by a tidal wave the following night. *Kehua* got dismasted, and another yacht, *Tahiti*, was holed and sunk, while we rode it out safely at sea. We had met *Tahiti* in Papeete, with single-hander Lorin Smith, who claimed to be 'on vacation, since 1945'. The crews of all three yachts, with much assistance from the locals, including members of the Sailing Club, and some railway lines borrowed from the Union Company wharf, built a slipway. Each boat in turn was hauled out and repaired over a period of several months.

Back on the job with the *Siren*, we pressed on with renewed vigour. The first job was to completely overhaul the Lister engine, and we stripped it down to the last nut and bolt — but how to put it back together again? By a stroke of luck Charlie Withers, the Ministry of Transport mechanic at Aitutaki, had the misfortune to break his leg and was in Rarotonga convalescing. He needed something to do, so we built him a nice comfortable chair at Dick Brown's shed where he could rest his leg and supervise the assembly of the Lister, an engine he was particularly familiar with as the Ministry had three of them as generating sets at Aitutaki.

Then one day the *Waitemata* arrived from San Francisco, and on board was a great baulk of timber for our new mainmast, the original having been broken during the salvage of the vessel from the reef. To get it ashore we simply threw it overboard and floated it right in to our shipyard. Bob was pretty handy with the adze by this time and in a few days he had it shaped into an elegant professional-looking mast.

One of the few visiting yachts to call in at this time was a converted lifeboat by the name of *Readwill*. Without an engine and with a broken mast, she was a sorry sight as she came into Avarua. The crew of six had been divided into two watches, three bailing while the other three slept. They had bailed so hard and long they had worn away some of the ribs, while the heads of the keel bolts were shiny from the passage of feet. She hit the reef coming in and got towed into shallow water where she quietly sank, never to sail again. Teariki Tuavera bought the hulk for use as a lighter at Aitutaki, and we offered to convert it for him on condition we kept the surplus bits and pieces. We finished with sundry rigging, a compass, navigation lights, a fibreglass dinghy and a beautiful cabin top and coamings, built of solid teak, which just happened to fit our recently drawn plans for the *Siren*.

We experienced other distractions from time to time. There being a chronic lack of shipping in the area, we were asked to do occasional mercy missions with *Patsy Jean*, to pick up patients (always described as 'sick' patients) and deliver medical supplies. One trip we did was to take examination papers to Mauke where the Resident Agent was sitting a university degree. The Resident Commissioner, Mr Neville, always took an interest in these little ventures and wrote us some great commendations on behalf of the Government. We started to feel 'we were only here for the good of the people', as Hugh Williams liked to say.

On another occasion we got called to Mitiaro to pick up Brian White and his crew. Coming down from Bora Bora in his eight-metre cutter *Margaret* (another Woollacott design), they had piled on to the reef in the middle of the night. He and his two crew scrambled ashore and up the makatea cliffs, and by daylight his yacht was reduced to driftwood, while they were left in the clothes they stood in, which for two of them amounted to the clothes they were born with. (Only the lead keel remained intact, but we had gone off salvaging lead keels by then.)

Brian stayed on in Rarotonga for a while. There was already a Brian White working in Customs, so the locals soon dubbed this new one 'Brian Teatea', 'teatea' being Maori for white. (They were good at these nicknames; Gordon Saywell became 'Tuatua Meitaki' — 'talk good'.)

In order to continue his cruising, Brian chartered *Patsy Jean* for a trip to Honolulu. There wasn't any money in the charter for me as it was mate's rates, but I did ask him to try to sell the boat there if he could, as it didn't look as though we would ever be continuing our voyage to

Canada. Brian eventually did sell the boat, but first he met this curvaceous young blonde, Bev Hale, who he thought might be a suitable contender for the position of the future Mrs White. Just to check her out he took her for a shakedown cruise (if that's the right term) to Fanning Island and back. Once at sea they must have been too busy shaking down to sail the boat, or perhaps the sex in sextant got used in the wrong perspective. Anyway it took them 54 days to reach Fanning, by which time there was a Coastguard alert out for them. (Later, Brian muttered something about contrary winds and strong currents, but we all said we had heard all about them before.)

When they got back from their adventure Bev did in fact become Mrs White. *Patsy Jean* was sold, and made further headlines when the new owners sailed her into the Johnston Island atomic-testing zone. The Coastguard seized the boat and towed it to Honolulu where the crew were thrown into jail.

Hugh Williams had been trying to sell the *Dobiri* to Dick Brown, but Dick wasn't having any, even with Hugh's usual promise never to return. Dick said it was too difficult to find good captains and engineers these days. Hugh thought maybe if he could find a captain and an engineer, Dick might be persuaded to buy the ship. He invited us along for a trip to Mangaia.

'We'll get away Friday afternoon, be back Sunday. Bring Bob and the missus. There's an empty cabin.'

Meanwhile we got invited for the evening to his house, a rambling dilapidated place behind St Joseph's School. Inside, it was like a museum, crammed with the most incredible collection of junk imaginable, picked up from bazaars in ports around the world. Stuffed parrots and alligators jostled for position with wood carvings and tapestries. A moth-eaten tiger-skin rug adorned the floor in front of an old pianola, still in working order. Perhaps the most incongruous of all was his collection of battery-operated, remote-controlled Japanese toys. Hugh made no secret of his ambition to find a 16-year-old girl to become his life's companion, and amongst his colour slides which we were obliged to watch were shots of one or two toddlers taken in the Northern Group which he wanted our opinion on as to whether we thought they looked like him. All this in front of his current 16-year-old, who didn't seem at all fazed by the performance.

We were looking forward to the break, so we reported on board, along with what appeared to be half the population of Rarotonga. The 'empty cabin' had long since been taken, so we staked our claim to a section of the hatch, under the canvas awning. It was all very cosy until we cleared Matavera Point and stuck our nose into a good stiff southeast trade wind. The ship had been built in Noumea in 1941 and used on the rivers of New Guinea. Broad-beamed with a shallow draft, she was inherently 'stiff', with a rolling period of about four seconds. It wasn't the degree of roll so much as the sudden whip-back at the end of it that gave her such a diabolical motion; she didn't roll so much as lurch and shudder. She would take a portion of the wave over the bows and climb through the rest of it, crashing down on to her flat bottom, quivering to almost a stop while she gathered momentum for the next one.

Bodies started to slide to and fro across the hatch, which by now was well lubricated with whatever the passengers had eaten at their last meal, or perhaps a few meals before that. Because of the rise in the deck, the bodies tended to work their way aft as they slithered from side to side, so that those at the after end would drop off and have to go right up to the forward end to find room to climb on again. Thus everyone got a turn at the forward end, which was the wettest end.

The ship staggered on into the night with its deck-load of human misery. In the middle of the night there was a great commotion and I could hear Hugh giving orders and telling someone they 'might as well piss on it!' This wasn't like Hugh, so I investigated and found the crew were trying to prime the deck pump, an antiquated affair that looked as if it might have been the village pump from some place in the New Guinea Highlands.

Hugh said, 'Oh, Don, you're just the man we need — you and Bob — seafaring types — don't mind giving us a hand. Making a bit of water in the engine-room — but Les'll have the pumps going shortly. Just a bit of a problem at the moment.' I went below to see what the bit of a problem was.

The floor plates were awash. Crew and passengers had formed a bucket brigade led by Joe, the bosun, a tall powerful Fijian, a seaman if ever there was one. I found the engineer, Les Livingstone, trying to fit a pulley to a pump shaft; the shaft was too big for the pulley, plus Les didn't have enough hands. We squatted on the floor plates, Les filing away at the shaft while I held the pump between my knees. The bilge water was up around our waists as the ship rolled, but it was warm, and also clean, for half the Pacific had been through the ship by now. After a couple of hours filing, we got the pulley to fit, with the aid of a heavy hammer. Les coupled up the pump and it worked fine. I staggered on deck and spewed my heart out.

I had already suggested to Hugh that if he turned back and ran before it, the ship wouldn't make nearly so much water, but he wouldn't hear of it.

'We're halfway now — no use turning back — be there in the morning!' In the morning Hugh had his sextant out.

'How are we doing, Captain?'

'Oh, great — nearly halfway already — not bad considering the weather. Thanks for helping out last night — knew I could depend on you. Can always depend on real seamen.'

With these words of encouragement, I went in search of breakfast. The saloon was deserted, although it hadn't been deserted during the night judging by the amount of vomit on the floor. Hugh came in, still in his pyjamas.

'Oh, blast! I see the fridge has gone out again — bit of a nuisance these kerosene fridges — the lamp is inclined to go out in heavy weather.' Whereupon he got down on his hands and knees, lit the lamp, wiped his hands on his pyjamas and lined up for breakfast. 'Good little ship, this,' says Hugh. 'Many a ship would have had to turn back in weather like this.' I had to agree that many a ship would have turned back. That afternoon Hugh got another sight which showed us halfway to Mangaia. We made it the following day. The following week, back in the shelter of Avarua Harbour, divers went down and hammered caulking into the seams and nailed on more copper sheets to hold it in.

If only half the stories told about Dick Brown were true, he would still be one of the greatest characters of his era. Dick never talked much about himself and any stories he did tell were usually against himself in the guise of 'I'm just a poor dumb Mangaian'. Dumb he certainly wasn't. In fact, under the Administration's newly formed Legislative Assembly, the forerunner of self-government, Dick had been elected the Leader of Government Business, and it was generally assumed he would become the country's first Premier, and no doubt would have, but for the return from New Zealand of Albert Henry, who ran a professional election campaign and took the wind completely out of Dick's sails.

When the Americans built their bases and airstrips on Penrhyn and Aitutaki during the war, they cabled Willie Watson in Rarotonga for hula skirts to stock their PX canteens. By the time Willie got the message, Dick had been around the island and bought every hula skirt that wasn't being worn, and probably a few that were. It was said that Dick's brother worked in the telegraph office, but that could have been just a malicious rumour.

Ventures like this soon convinced Dick that being an island merchant beat the hell out of working in the taro patch so, armed with a bagful of US dollars, he arrived in Auckland after the war looking for a ship to further his merchant adventuring. After several false starts he sailed for Rarotonga, the proud owner of the ancient schooner *Tahitien*. They arrived in Rarotonga in April 1946.

Built in 1923 and formerly owned by Maxwell and Company in Papeete, the *Tahitien* had really seen better days and probably the most important pieces of equipment on board were the three gasoline-powered portable bilge pumps. Even these were having the greatest difficulty keeping her afloat one trip coming back from Aitutaki in heavy south-easterly weather. With the engine broken down, and headed by the wind, she got further and further down to leeward. The weather was heavily overcast and the captain, Willy Schutz, was unable to establish his position. Having passengers on board and in real danger of sinking, he sensibly called for help. The only vessel able to go to his assistance was A.B. Donald's schooner *Tiare Taporo*, which Donalds offered to send, but only to take off the passengers. They had no interest in trying to save the ship.

By this time there was doubt as to the *Tahitien's* position. A Catalina flying-boat was called in and searched all day without success. A second Catalina joined in, and after 52 hours the ship was found. The crew got her back to Rarotonga and beached her in Ngatangiia Harbour for repairs. Jim Price, an American who had arrived from Honolulu in September 1946 on *Myrtle S*, the first yacht to call at Rarotonga after the war, repaired the engine but refused to return it until he was paid. Meanwhile the ship, after hull repairs had been completed, was towed round to Avarua Harbour, where she went aground in a blow and broke up and sank on 23 November 1949, by which time Dick had already secured a replacement vessel, the *Mahurangi*.

The *Mahurangi* was obtained on charter with an option to purchase. A Fairmile built in New Zealand during the war, she was long and lean, rolled like a barrel and had little cargo capacity. On one of her first trips, in April 1949, she sailed for the Northern Group and got so far off course she finished up in Apia instead. But one of the best stories was told to me by Jim Price of a trip to Manihiki when he sailed as engineer. He told Dick they needed lube oil and Dick said not to worry, they would pick some up in Aitutaki. There wasn't any oil in Aitutaki but Dick said they had some in Manihiki. At Manihiki Dick bought a load of pearl shell. Some of the traders were a bit doubtful of his ability to pay, but he waved a post office money-order for six thousand pounds and said not to worry, just get the shell on board, then he'd go to the post office and cash the money-order and they'd all get paid. They loaded the shell, but of course when Dick went to cash the money-order the post office didn't have that much money, so he had to take the money-order back to Rarotonga — and the shell too, which was already on board.

They sailed for Rarotonga, still without any oil, and Jim could see they were going to run out, so he ran the engines at reduced speed to cut down consumption. However, Dick was in a hurry as he had already sold the shell as having been shipped on the *Waitemata*, which was shortly due in Rarotonga, so each time Jim went to sleep, Dick would speed up the engines, and every time Dick went to sleep, Jim would slow them down. There was a fearful row and passengers reported that Jim pulled a gun on the captain, Willy Schutz, saying, 'Bastards like you should be shot!'

With both engines dangerously low on oil, Jim stopped one and drained the oil into the other; they continued on one engine. It still wasn't enough. They melted down dripping from the galley but that only clogged up the filters. The remaining engine gave up and the ship drifted helplessly on the ocean. It didn't look as though they would ever connect with the W*aitemata*.

But Dick wasn't beaten yet. A call for help went out — and guess what ship was the only one in the area? The *Waitemata*, which obligingly came to their rescue with two drums of oil. Jim in his dry drawl said, 'If that wasn't the funniest goddamned thing! Here was this huge ship towering over us, lowering a couple of barrels of oil in a cargo net. We rolled the barrels out of the net and you should have seen the passengers jump into it. As they heaved the net back up, there were arms and legs sticking out in all directions and the priest upside down with his cassock over his head. You never saw such an entanglement.'

Well, they cranked on the knots and got into Rarotonga the day after the *Waitemata*. Dick's gang packed shell all night and loaded it in time for sailing next day. Running on dripping apparently hadn't done *Mahurangi's* engines much good and one of them had to be replaced. Dick still had the *Tahitien's* engine in his shed, so they installed that, although it was a terrible mismatch. The original engines were a handed pair, so that the two propellors were counter-rotating. This fact was overlooked and they finished up with two right-handed engines but one propellor left-handed and the other one right-handed. This problem was overcome by running one engine full ahead and the other full astern.

Having so much trouble with his ships, Dick decided he'd better have another one if he was going to keep ahead of Donalds in the pearl-shell game. In Auckland he bought the *Karoro*, a wooden vessel built as a tug for Gisborne. She had a powerful Fairbanks-Morse engine and a reasonable turn of speed, although not much cargo capacity. She was fitting out for the delivery voyage to Rarotonga, lying at the Western Viaduct, and berthed close by was A.B. Donald's *Charlotte Donald*, also preparing for the voyage to Rarotonga. The *Mahurangi* meanwhile was away in Suva for lengthy repairs, so, instead of waiting to fill the *Karoro* with cargo, Dick wasted no time and sailed almost empty, making good time on the voyage and arriving in Rarotonga on 9 April 1950. She sailed thence straight to Manihiki, beating the *Charlotte Donald* to the pearl-shell harvest, which she then took to Apia for trans-shipment overseas.

Shortly after leaving Apia for the return voyage, they had the misfortune to break *Karoro's* main-engine crankshaft. Nothing daunted, Dick had a replacement engine shipped to Apia, and after fitting it they sailed for Rarotonga via Pukapuka and Suwarrow, arriving in September. However, *Karoro* had a short history after that. She left Aitutaki on the evening of 6 January 1951, under the command of Captain Wrigley, an experienced mariner but without much local knowledge. The captain set course for Rarotonga, neglecting to make allowance for the fact that he should first steer southwest to clear the reef at Maina Island. She ran onto the reef and, although Dick went over in the *Mahurangi* to try to pull her off, became a total loss, only nine months after her arrival in the Cook Islands. Worse, the ship was not insured, although that didn't worry Dick too much as she was well paid for out of the load of pearl shell.

The *Mahurangi* wasn't all that suitable for the trade; plus she was also soon due to be handed back to the owner, in the same condition as when she came on hire. This was likely to pose a problem, for she was getting a bit shaky and tended to follow the shape of the waves as she went along. Dick started looking around for another ship, and in 1953 purchased the *Rannah*, which at 400-tonnes was a bit big for the job, especially as she couldn't get into the harbour. Arriving from Auckland on 6 October, her first job was to tow the *Mahurangi*, which had broken down on a voyage from Atiu to Mangaia.

Four months later Dick had a load of aviation gasoline to take to Aitutaki for the flying-boat, and there were a lot of passengers wanting to go to Aitutaki as well. The av-gas was loaded on the *Mahurangi*, while the passengers were ferried to the *Rannah*, it being against the rules to carry them on the same ship, although it wasn't like Dick to be so pernickety about regulations. This time it was just as well, because when the *Mahurangi* neared Aitutaki it was found she was taking on water. She sank in the lee of the island, not far from the wreck of the *Karoro*, which had by now been joined by the *Alexander*. (The latter wasn't one of Dick's ships but by coincidence had the same previous owner as *Karoro*.)

The *Rannah*, following close behind, was able to pick up the crew, as well as the drums of av-gas, which floated to the surface. Dick cabled off to the insurance company ... I asked Dick did he claim salvage on the drums they picked up with the *Rannah*. He hadn't thought of it. 'But that would have been dishonest, wouldn't it?' he asked with a straight face.

There was a lot of speculation at the time that the whole thing was a put-up job but an inquiry ruled out barratry and the insurance claim was paid. If it was barratry, and Captain John Blakelock would have had to be a party to it, it misfired, because the insurance was paid to *Mahurangi's* owner, not to Dick.

Captain Blakelock took over command of the *Rannah,* but her career soon came to an end also. Anchored outside Avarua Harbour, her engine dismantled for repair, she dragged her anchor in a northerly blow and finished up on the reef on 8 November 1954. Dick cabled the insurance company. 'And you know what they did?' he said. 'Instead of sending their cheque, they sent an assessor to investigate. I don't know, these insurance companies are not like what they used to be.' But in the end he did get his twenty thousand pounds.

Finding another ship wasn't so easy, and it was to be another 17 months before the arrival of the *Taveuni*, a 24-metre wooden ketch. Built for Burns Philp in 1947 by the Whippy yard in Suva, she carried about 70 tonnes and a dozen passengers in cabins, plus an unspecified number on deck. She arrived with an all-Fijian crew; Malcolm Sword was the mate and Emori Waka the engineer. Captain Archie Pickering joined the following year. All three raised families in the Cook Islands and never got around to leaving. Neither did the *Taveuni*.

We just about had the *Siren* ready for painting when Public Works advertised an auction of surplus inventory, including paint. Bob was our auction man and went along. Most of the paint was in rusty 22-litre pails, colour unknown. There was only one other bidder, and he soon pulled out. Bob finished up with the lot, far more than we could possibly use, so he sold half to the other bidder for the total price paid! At the price, we couldn't be fussy what colour it was. It turned out to be all grey, and that's the colour the *Siren* remained for the rest of her days.

When she was ready for launching we got some old bridge stringers and built a big sledge, joining the timbers with old keel bolts from the *Readwill*. Using the timber-jacks, again borrowed from the Electric Power Supply, we lowered the boat to the sledge, first placing tyres so as not to damage our expensive paint. However, we misjudged, and she was too far to one side. Moving her sideways wasn't so easy as the tyres really had a grip. It was Saturday morning and a large crowd soon gathered to watch this event. We pushed and heaved and got nowhere. Then Miri spotted Old Joe in the crowd, and had a quiet word with him. Old Joe was more or less in charge of the airport, not such an onerous task as there weren't any aeroplanes, although he did have to keep the pre-war fire-engine mobile. But Joe was a leader of men. Joe took charge. His stentorian voice brought everyone to attention. What he probably said in Maori was, 'Let's show these silly papa'as how to do it!' Next thing twenty or thirty willing helpers got their shoulders under the boat and with Joe calling 'Tai, Rua, Toru, A', the job was done before the next rendering of *Danny Boy* on the juke-box.

We had borrowed a brand-new coil of wire from PWD which we ran from the sledge to a pulley block on the end of the jetty and back to the D4 on the beach. The bulldozer pulled, the boat moved, but only as far as the soft sand, where the sledge bogged down, and with a loud report the wire broke at the pulley; both ends came flying back but by great good fortune no one was decapitated.

I had to see the Superintendent of Works, Evan Lewis, about the wire. Like most of the Kiwi expatriates working for the Administration,

Evan was friendly and co-operative, and a credit to the Administration that recruited him. (What was less of a credit to the Administration was the fact that they had to keep recruiting expatriates instead of training locals who, it was later proved, were quite capable of doing the same job, and who, later again, performed many of the Public Works functions as private enterprise.) Anyway, Evan wasn't too happy. They had one more length of wire, and if we broke that we had to pay for it. 'No problem,' I said, thinking of our few remaining pounds in the Post Office Savings Bank. I knew the trouble was caused by the faulty block we had borrowed from the Union Company, and next time we got it right and the job was completed without a hitch.

As expected, *Siren* floated very high in the water, and on her side, for she had been designed to have all inside ballast, and that wasn't in yet. We had five tonnes of it waiting on the wharf, mostly old crusher jaws from the quarry and discarded machinery from PWD, and once all that was stowed in the bilges she looked pretty trim. Next came the engine, hoisted in with the aid of the Union Company derrick on the end of the wharf, and the mainmast the same way. We towed her to Avatiu Harbour for final fitting out. Then some Public Works mechanics arrived, looking for the back-end of their Fordson tractor, and we had to go right through the ballast looking for it. We didn't find it.

Two 200-litre drums were installed for fuel tanks and two more for fresh water. Plumbing for engine water-cooling and exhaust was all done in galvanised pipe with flanged joints. It came time to start the main engine. (It sounded more ship-like to call it the *main* engine, even though it was the only engine we had.)

'Oil in the sump?'

'Yes.'

'Fuel in the tank?'

'Yes.'

'Bled the injectors?'

'Yes.'

'Got compression?'

'Yes.'

'Should go!'

So we cranked her over and she almost went, but died after just a few revolutions. We checked everything again, and cranked some more. The sweat poured off us, to no avail; she would always die after just a few revolutions. I consulted Evan Lewis.

'Have you got compression?'

'Yes.'

'Have you got fuel at the injectors?'

'Yes.'

'Have you checked the timing?'

'Yes.'

'Well, she should go. Maybe you're not cranking her fast enough!'

I reported back to Bob, 'Maybe we're not cranking her fast enough!'

We cranked that bloody engine for two days. Then Evan came down and watched our efforts. 'Sure the exhaust line is clear? Have you got a hole in the gasket in that flange there?'

'Of course there's a hole in it,' I said. 'I put that one in myself, but I'll make sure.' And sure enough, there wasn't any hole in the gasket. Bob made some rather scathing remarks about my ability as an engineer — but his turn was to come.

The New Zealand yacht *Tempest* was tied alongside us and we were having a few drinks on board after work on Saturday. It turned into quite a few drinks, with girls arriving, ukeleles playing, singing, and more drinks. One of the boys went on deck for a leak and called out, 'I say, *Siren* seems rather low in the water!' A quick look showed water to be nearly to the top of the engine. Our ship was sinking! There was a quick sobering up and we soon had a bucket brigade organised, girls and all, and before long had the water down to where we could see the problem. Bob had been installing a sink bench and had neglected to put a hose clip on the sink fitting, with the result that the hose had popped off and water was pouring in through a 25-millimetre hole. Sunday was spent stripping the engine and cleaning the mess. There wasn't a word said all day about the gasket with no hole in it.

CHAPTER THREE

ISLAND TRADERS

During the final fitting-out we checked with the Resident Commissioner as to what regulations we would have to comply with if we were to operate the *Siren* commercially. It seemed the only legislation was the old Inter-Island Boat Travelling Ordinance, aimed at controlling open-boat voyages between islands, whereby a declaration had to be made before sailing to the effect that there was sufficient food and water on board and that a compass was carried. However, the Resident Commissioner could make any rules at any time, and he ruled that in our case we must carry radio equipment to the satisfaction of the Superintendent of Radio. It looked as though it was going to be much easier to get into shipping in the Cook Islands than into trucking in New Zealand.

We checked with the Superintendent of Radio, who thought yachties were the scourge of the Pacific. He said we would need to be able to transmit on the two international distress frequencies, 2182 and 8198·1 kHz. We had lots of friends in the Administration by now and we called on Allen McQueen. His ancient Ford 8 had carried many improbable loads for us, but this time we needed his help as a radio technician. We explained about the radio equipment we were going to need. We had a transistorised receiver, but we needed a transmitter capable of sending on 2182 and 8198·1. Allen scratched his head and cleaned his glasses.

'Well, there is an old army ZC1 set lying around somewhere. We can modify that for you, but finding a crystal for 8198·1 is going to be impossible. Anyway, what good is that going to be to you? There is no listening watch on that frequency!'

We questioned the Superintendent about the need for 8198·1. 'Oh yes,' he said. 'You'll need 8198·1 if you are going to the Northern Group; you won't get through on 2182 from the north. Not in daylight.'

'But how are we going to get through on 8198·1 if there's no listening watch?'

'Oh, you'll be able to attract attention somehow! Call us the night before and arrange a sked.' So if we were to have an emergency in daylight, we had to arrange it the night before. We went back to Allen with this illogical argument.

'We'll just have to make a crystal then.' And he did, grinding a crystal of a lower frequency by hand, for hours on end, until he got it just right.

In June 1961 we were ready for our first trip, which was to be a load of general cargo to Atiu, returning with oranges for the juicing factory. There was a delay getting a berth at the Union Company wharf and it was Sunday before it became free. While there is no law against loading ships on Sundays in the Cook Islands, it wasn't the done thing. However, since the oranges were already picked and waiting for us, we thought we would give it a go and see what happened.

What happened was we had the ship about half loaded when church came out. A deputation of white-suited deacons came marching down the wharf. Glassie Strickland demanded to know who was in charge. Being a very live coward, I pointed to Bob who was down the hold and hadn't seen them yet. Bob explained that we had oranges rotting in Atiu and that really we were only trying to help the people. That didn't cut any ice with Glassie. A big, imposing man, he would have made a good drill sergeant. He said we must stop immediately, forthwith. Rather than offering to pray for us, as one might expect of a good Christian on the way home from church, he threatened to see us in court on Monday, for he was a Justice of the Peace as well as the secretary of the LMS Church. We stopped immediately, forthwith, for Glassie's wrath knew no bounds when it came to defending the sanctity of the Church. We recalled the beauty contest.

Someone had hit on the idea of a beauty contest to raise money for a charity. The contest was advertised and the girls were to appear on stage, first in a pareu, and then in a swimsuit, something unheard of in the Cook Islands. Well, what a furore! The Catholics were forbidden outright to participate in this demoralising performance, while the LMS pastors preached loud and long from the pulpits. Glassie wrote a full-page letter to the press, denouncing the contest and everyone associated with it.

'What disgusting degradation of our young womanhood. How could any decent girl of Christian upbringing even think of parading her body in public in such a manner? With only a thin piece of kakau between her private part and the public gaze? And I mean *the* private part! It reminds me,' he wrote, 'of my missionary days in Papua, where all that the girls wore was a cork and a piece of string.' The reader was left wondering just where the girls wore the cork and how Glassie was able to see it.

This tirade and others like it inhibited a lot of would-be contestants, but there were still enough to hold the competition. It was deservedly won by 16-year-old June Taringa, who braved the wrath of the priests as well as her college principal. In fact, June told me years later that she wouldn't have bothered to enter if they hadn't been so bloody-minded about trying to stop it. So began what was to become a popular annual event, with the beauty queens travelling to other contests in various parts of the world. June's daughter Tania became one of the models for Silk & Boyd's 1987 calendar. But I digress.

The *Siren* performed beyond our expectations. She had a reasonable turn of speed under sail, considering her somewhat bulky dimensions, and with the Lister ticking over she went to windward like a witch. Miri had never been to sea before but he became just as good a seaman as he had become a boatbuilder and barber — and he was still a good fisherman too. Our other crewman, Peter Nelson, a blown-away Kiwi from the middle of the North Island, was, at 25, already an old hand around the Islands, and had been to many exotic places and had some exciting experiences, including getting washed overboard from the topsail schooner *Te Vega*. Peter had been working on Walter Johnson's schooner *Tiare Maori*, and Walter had left him in Penryhn to run a store while he made a few runs with drummed fuel from Tahiti to Rarotonga. The *Tiare Maori* never came back for she caught fire and burnt to the waterline in Papeete Harbour and Peter was stranded in Penrhyn for a year. Short and stocky, Peter was never short of a tale to tell or a joke to crack.

One of our first trips was a charter to the island of Manuae, which had been run for years as a copra plantation under the managership of Karlo Andersen, who claimed to be a Danish count. People said he was mad, but on a trip there in *Patsy Jean* one time we had found him to be a pleasant, hospitable old gentleman, if perhaps a little eccentric. 'I veel haff no liqueur on zee island!' Our crew were entertained ashore like royalty, enjoying a tour of the plantation (where hardly a blade of grass was out of place) and the barracks (where the workers' beds were neatly made with military precision), all this conducted by Karlo in his pith helmet and white uniform. At the administration centre was Karlo's workshop, with an impressive array of tools, all arranged on a shadow board in perfectly straight lines, and a dental clinic with a genuine dentist's chair. The radio room sported an equal array of equipment, with dials and gauges enough to confuse any ignorant yachtsman. (One of our crew on the trip was Allen McQueen, not so ignorant. Allen took a surreptitious look behind the switchboard and reported later that many of the dials weren't connected to anything.) The tour ended with a banquet-style luncheon, where waiters were summoned by a handbell and the chicken drumstick ends were wrapped in silver foil. Coconut water was served in crystal glasses and the silverware bore what was assumed to be Karlo's family crest. (Some jealous critic later suggested he had probably bought it at an auction.) We liked Karlo, and were a little unhappy about the circumstances of our charter.

While Karlo was away on furlough the lease of the island had been bought by the Co-operatives for some two thousand pounds. The Registrar of Co-operatives, C.J. Joannides, was very anxious to take over before Karlo returned to uplift his considerable personal possessions. This Joannides was a Greek Cypriot, who had come to the Cook Islands from Ghana, where he had spent 12 years in palm-oil production.

Anyway, money was money, and we didn't let scruples about doing business with Joannides get in the way. It was a hell of trip. There was a strong northeasterly wind, dead against us, and without any cargo *Siren* bounced all over the place. Joannides got sick as a dog and was panic-stricken the whole way. The wind headed us off towards Aitutaki and we decided to run there for shelter until the wind blew itself out. We were sympathetic towards Karlo so we secretly listened to the shipping skeds and when we heard the *Dobiri* was well on the way to Manuae (with Karlo on board) we decided the weather had moderated sufficiently to continue the voyage. Joannides was furious when we got to Manuae and found Karlo had already been and gone, with all his private possessions.

Several of our early trips around the Southern Group were to Mangaia to pick up tomatoes for trans-shipment to New Zealand. The local coast station, Rarotonga Radio or ZKR, was known in the South Pacific as the Tomato Station. The operators had standing instructions during the season to listen for any ship in the area and to ask them to call for tomatoes. All sorts of ships were asked, including cruise liners and warships, but the system worked remarkably well and it was surprising the variety of vessels that answered the call. (One time Olly and the kids got a ride to Auckland on the *Port Adelaide* when she made a tomato call.) It would be panic stations for the islanders to get the tomatoes ready once a ship had agreed to call, so we would sometimes sail for Mangaia at very short notice.

Mangaia had the best lighterage operation of any island. Their lighters were up to 12 metres long and they could fill the *Siren* in a couple of trips. Rowed by 12 men, they made a magnificent sight coming out of the harbour when the sea was breaking right across the passage. Sometimes they would meet us miles out at sea at daylight and the crews would fight to get the cargo out of the ship, for they were paid by the ton and each lighter was owned by a separate village. They often had more tomatoes than we could carry and it always seemed a shame to leave them behind to rot. We would load what we could and sail with cases of tomatoes stacked on deck, around the engine and in the cabin until there was scarcely room for the crew. We were paid by the case.

All this was very interesting, and profitable, but the real lure was the pearl-shell diving season at Manihiki. The lagoon had been closed for four years to conserve stocks and now it was about to open again. The thing to do seemed to be to run a store in Manihiki and trade goods for shell. Money to buy goods was the problem, so we had a chat to Neil Mortimer of Cook Islands Trading Company. We proposed that he sell us a load of goods on credit. We would take the goods to Manihiki and trade them for pearl shell, which he could sell for us on commission. Then we could pay for the goods. This sounded okay to Neil, so we sailed for Manihiki loaded to the gunwales with flour, rice, sugar, cabin bread, bully beef, pareu cloth, transistor radios and a thousand and one other things from peanuts to panties, plus enough timber and roofing iron to build a store. On deck we had, besides our own boat, Bob's five-metre catamaran (carried in from Muri on the roof of Allen McQueen's car) and Akeau Kairua's boat, plus Akeau and his brother, plus 20 drums of benzine and kerosene. She was a full ship, but we had good weather and made the 650-mile voyage in four and a half days.

The lagoon opened on 1 August, the day we arrived, and the villages seemed deserted except for old people and young kids. Akeau allowed us the use of a bit of land at Tukao to build a shop on, and the use of his partly finished house in the meantime.

Manihiki is one of the most beautiful atolls in the South Pacific. There are dozens of motus surrounding the lagoon and several in the lagoon as well, each one a picture to behold with its countless coconut trees, thick as hair on a Fijian's head, the outside ones leaning out over the water for breathing-space. The Resident Agent's bungalow was situated beside the lagoon in Tauhunu and S.G. O'Brien, known as Don Bryan, became a good friend. Don was born in the Islands and spent practically all his life here, except for a spell away with the New Zealand Expeditionary Force in World War II, most of which was spent in a POW camp. Jocular and portly, Don was good company and I always tried to spend a night ashore with him and his charming wife Mii when weather permitted.

It is sometimes said of bungling bureaucrats that 'he couldn't run a two-hole toilet!' Don was by no means a bungling bureaucrat, but he actually had a two-hole toilet. Perched on stilts over the water beneath a pandanus tree, it was a perfect grandstand (grandsit?) to watch the cutters beating out to the diving grounds in the early morning, or flying back before the wind towards sunset.

Leaving Bob to mind the shop, I sailed on to Penrhyn to see if I could buy copra while he was trading goods for shell. The RA at Penrhyn, Jock MacCauley, came out in the Administration launch to escort us into the lagoon, for, unlike Manihiki, there is a wide passage into the lagoon here and sizeable ships can anchor inside. Penrhyn is much bigger than Manihiki and in many ways quite different. I found the village of Omoka to be rather dirty and derelict-looking and the people dour and difficult to get on with, a contrast to the happy-go-lucky Manihikians. They were certainly difficult to get on with when it came to buying copra. There were endless hassles over the price, and even when the price was agreed on you had to have your wits about you to see that it was all copra in the gunnies and not a few rocks as well, and that they didn't have their foot on the scales as you weighed it.

Sitting on Jock's veranda, gazing out over the lagoon, we yarned far into the night. One of the most interesting bits of history about Penrhyn is the slave trade of last century, which must have a big bearing on why many Penrhyn people differ so much from other Cook Islanders. In 1864 most of the adult population was recruited for work in Peru, lured by the promise of high wages, easy work and a speedy return, and encouraged by the missionaries to earn money for a new church. They were sold as virtual slaves when they got there and most of them died of smallpox or pneumonia. The situation was brought to the attention of foreign consuls in Peru and pressure was exerted to make

The two-hole toilet

View from the two-hole toilet

the shipowners take back the survivors. There were not only Penrhyn Islanders involved, but other islanders as well. Of about 470 Penrhyn Islanders taken to Peru, none returned, but 111 survivors from the Gilbert Islands (now Kiribati) were returned on the *Ellen Elizabeth* and dumped in Penrhyn. The influx of over 100 adult Micronesians, mainly men, into a population which by now was down to 88 (plus 130 living in Tahiti) had an obvious effect on the physical appearance and culture of future generations.

Jock had his own story to tell. Coming from New Zealand with his wife to take up his appointment, he joined A.B.Donalds' schooner *Tiare Taporo* in Rarotonga for the passage to Penrhyn. On the way they experienced heavy weather and the ship developed a very serious leak, so bad that before they reached Penrhyn the crew and passengers were completely buggered from bailing the ship. The boats were swung out in readiness for abandoning ship, but the Penrhyn Islanders saw their lights and came out to meet them. With a fresh gang on the pumps and buckets, they kept her afloat and reached the shelter of the lagoon. After temporary repairs the ship reached Tahiti, where she was hauled out on the slipway.

These Resident Agents of the time mostly did a remarkably good job, each in his own way. They were the buffer between the real people and the buffoons of bureaucracy. In later years under self-government the position was localised, and the title changed to Chief Administrative Officer. These CAOs were politically appointed, and consequently had a difficult job, as sometimes at least half the island would be working against them. Also, under self-government, there tended to be more bureaucracy rather than less. The huge staff in Rarotonga accumulated like a fungoid growth, with departments sprouting new sections which broke away and became divisions of their own, and spawned sub-divisions. Albert Henry didn't like to see anyone unemployed, particularly anyone who might vote for his party.

Several divers in Penrhyn asked for passage to Manihiki, but I was adamant: 'No passengers'. However, on the way out across the lagoon I spotted a foot sticking out from under the lifeboat. I got the boys to suddenly lift the boat, and when the bloke sprang to his feet I pushed him overboard. The last I saw of him he was striking out for Omoka, loudly abusing me because his tobacco was getting wet.

Much later I questioned my own motives for chucking this poor fellow overboard when all he wanted was to get to Manihiki and he wouldn't have been any trouble on board. Was it because he was challenging my decision not to take passengers, or was I feeling bloody-minded because the Penrhyn people had tried so hard to put it across me one way and another? Whatever it was, my action didn't seem to cause any ill will; they were still laughing about it next time I called.

In my younger days I had aided and abetted a stowaway. It was on the *Port Alma* and we had put into Durban for engine repairs. The crew were all Pommies except for the Australian chippy and myself. Being the only colonials on board, we always teamed up and got into mischief together.

We met this young bloke from Southern Rhodesia who was recovering from a massive stomach operation — at least it looked massive by the fresh scar that stretched clear across his belly. A baker by trade, he couldn't get a job as the laws had just been changed allowing black Africans to be engaged in the baking trade, and they were paid a mere pittance by comparison. He was desperate to get to some place like Australia, and since we were bound for Adelaide it seemed a humane thing to do to help him on his way.

We were to sail in the evening, so during the afternoon we had him on board and hid him in the funnel. Port Line ships always sported a big impressive stack, which was mostly for show, as inside were only the exhaust pipes from the main engines and auxiliaries. There were gratings and ladders for maintenance, and for access, which was from inside the engine-room.

Just prior to sailing, the police searched the ship, looking for some army deserters. They had been informed by the ship's quartermaster that there was still one visitor on board, so they made a pretty thorough search, going through the cabins and looking in wardrobes and under bunks, but they never thought of looking in the funnel.

Next morning I climbed up inside the funnel with some food and water to see how our friend was getting on. He wasn't getting on too well; the heat was appalling and he looked a wreck, especially with all the soot and exhaust fumes falling on him. It had been planned that he remain hidden for 24 hours, but he couldn't take any more, so as soon as I was safely back at my job he climbed down, ready to give himself up, whatever the consequences. Word soon got to the Old Man, who exclaimed, 'I don't want to know about it! Tell me tomorrow when we're 24 hours out of port.' This was to avoid having to turn back to land him, which he was loath to do, having lost three weeks already with our engine repairs.

We got Bruce cleaned up and lent him some clothes. He was badly dehydrated and all he wanted was to drink gallons of cold water, which we foolishly allowed him to do, for he broke out in a mass of blisters and became very ill. The ship's doctor confined him to the hospital for several days until he was well enough to assume the duties he had been given by the captain — 'Since you seem to like engine-rooms you can help the engineers.'

Bruce turned out to be a good worker and was popular with both crew and passengers, all of whom chipped in with clothes, so that by the time we got to Adelaide he was the best dressed bloke on board. On arrival in Adelaide he was arrested as an illegal immigrant, but the Old Man went to court and told the judge what a fine young man he was, just the type of immigrant Australia was looking for. The judge fined him ten pounds, with a month to pay, and ordered the Clerk of the Court to see that a suitable job was found for him. Later that year, when I was working on the three-masted schooner *Reliance* out of Port Adelaide, I met him again, working for the city council, happy as a koala in a gum tree.

There was a shortage of fuel in Rarotonga, largely due to the loss of the *Tiare Maori*, so we planned a trip to Tahiti to buy some. Money was less of a problem now and I arranged for two hundred pounds to be cabled via New Zealand to the Bank of Indo China in Papeete. In addition I took one hundred pounds with me in ten-pound notes, and a few hundred cases of tomatoes for sale or trade. It didn't appear that there would be any problem paying for a load of fuel. But I reckoned without the bureaucrats.

Because of foreign exchange regulations the bank in New Zealand could send the money only in the form of French francs, not good old Kiwi pounds. The oil company in Papeete could sell to a foreign customer only in foreign currency; French francs were not acceptable by law. The New Zealand ten-pound notes I had with me could not be changed outside New Zealand — it was illegal to take them out of the country. Before I could sell the tomatoes the buyer had to get an import licence, a condition of which was he had to pay for the tomatoes in foreign currency, by way of a draft through a bank in New Zealand. This was the sort of bureaucracy I had left New Zealand to get away from.

After many days on bended knees before numerous officials, I was allowed to cash the draft for the tomatoes into francs, convert the francs into pounds, and pay the oil company. Meanwhile my finances were in sore straits. Fortunately I ran into Mme Wohler of *Patsy Jean* days. She was about to leave for a trip to New Zealand and mentioned the trouble she was having getting New Zealand currency, owing to exchange control regulations.

'How would you like some New Zealand ten–pound notes?' Suddenly I was a black marketeer of currency, which troubled my conscience so badly I spent the proceeds on provisioning the ship and the balance on some trade goods for Bob in Manihiki. Having got all that sorted out, I sailed *Siren* across to the oil dock to load the drums of fuel. There I was met by a burly policeman who said I had to get permission before I could move a ship in the harbour. (At least we were recognised as a ship.) I sailed back to the quay and tied up again with all the yachts. Permission was readily granted, so back to the oil dock again.

Apart from the bureaucratic hassles, I found that Papeete was still fascinating, but what a change had come over the place! What with the airport and the tourists, hotels and traffic, it just wasn't what it used to be, as Captain Cook said. One of the few things that hadn't changed was the Capitaine de l'Immigration, Gigi Grand, affable as ever, and asking how was the missus, and that little girl on *Patsy Jean*?

With all the wheeling and dealing out of the way, we set sail for Rarotonga, where we sold the petrol for five shillings and ninepence a gallon, having paid three francs a litre for it in Papeete, then sold half the diesel for the equivalent of what we had paid for the whole lot in Papeete. The rest kept the *Siren* going for the next six months.

At the end of the diving season Bob came back to Rarotonga to continue his courtship of one of the sisters at the hospital. I mean the sister was at the hospital; the courting occurred in all sorts of places. A part-Maori from New Zealand, Della was about the same height (five-foot nothing) as Olly, and they became great mates. When Della and Bob got married we always seemed to go everywhere together and newcomers often got confused as to which wife was which. We had a lot of fun keeping them confused. The courtship had been a close thing, for there was stiff competition in the form of Colin Clarke, formerly the leader of the team at Raoul Island, who was now working for the Administration as an instructor in the use of heavy plant, a job which he found not very demanding.

By this time we had been blessed with a new Resident Commissioner. Ollie Dare arrived full of enthusiasm and grand schemes, all of which had to be implemented immediately if not sooner, whether they were practical or not. He did have some good ideas and at least he wasn't afraid of making decisions or stepping on people's toes in the process.

Ollie asked us why didn't we try long-line fishing with the *Siren*? The Japanese were long-lining in our waters and if they could do it, why couldn't we? Well, the why was that we were having a heap of fun making money at what we were doing and fishing looked like too much hard work, but we didn't want to tell the RC this, so we said we didn't have the gear, didn't know where to get it, couldn't afford it, et cetera, et cetera, otherwise we would have been only too happy to have a go, at least on an experimental basis, because yes, it was a damned shame to see these foreigners taking fish out of 'our' waters when we could be catching them and making all the money ourselves.

'Oh, that's jolly good,' he said. 'In that case I'll get Fisheries to get some gear down from Japan. I'm authorised to spend up to five hundred pounds without reference to Wellington. Ron Powell knows all about long-lining. He's just had an article published. I'll get him to help you rig it all up.'

So we became commercial fishermen. They were long, hard days, sailing at 4 a.m., setting two miles of line, patrolling it all day, pulling in mainly sharks and swordfish by hand, and returning to the harbour in the evening. We caught very few tuna, but we always sold all the fish we caught, including the sharks and swordfish.

Ron had arrived from England by yacht in 1939 and hadn't got around to leaving yet. Now married with seven children, it didn't look as though he was in too much of a hurry to do so. For all his skills and wide experience (fisherman, boatbuilder, cabinetmaker and all-round handyman), Ron was quietly spoken and an absolute gentleman. There was plenty of time for telling yarns while patrolling up and down the setline all day, and Ron had some interesting tales.

One day he asked me if I used star sights for navigation and I said yes, whenever possible. He related an incident on the yacht *Vagus*, a 15-metre cutter, which his friend John Pratt had sailed single-handed

We became commercial fishermen

non-stop from Panama to Rarotonga, arriving in January 1942. When John asked where Ron was, he was told, 'Oh, Ron's in Palmerston Island, chasing Elizabeth Marsters.' After John reached Palmerston, Ron told him it was a bit risky hanging about in the hurricane season; he had better go and lay up in Penrhyn until the end of March. Ron offered to go with him, and they thought they would call at Suwarrow on the way.

Neither of them had ever learned to do star sights, so when they failed to raise the island by dusk, they turned back on their track. The following evening, the same thing happened, and they turned back again. On the third day they made it, and entered the pass shortly before sunset. Ron said there was a huge swell running, so high that when they were in the trough, they couldn't see the trees ashore. Once inside, it was calm enough, but the coast-watching team that was stationed there told them that the daddy of all hurricanes was on the way and they should put to sea. However, it was now too late to negotiate the pass before dark, so they put out two anchors and moved ashore for the night, or so they thought. The hurricane struck and the yacht was never seen again. (Pearl-shell divers found the keel 25 years later.) Huge seas swept clear across the island and they only escaped with their lives by tying themselves to some tamanu trees in the centre of the island. After the hurricane they survived on coconuts and the odd tin of food dug out of the sand, plus any crabs and shellfish that they could find.

The first vessel to arrive was the *Taipi*, a 10-metre ketch sailed by old Captain Cambridge, which leaked so badly that they had to tear up their shirts and caulk her from the inside. Ron made a bilge pump out of a few boards and the upper of an old boot, and they pumped their way to Rarotonga. In a report written to the Resident Commissioner on the loss of his yacht, John Pratt described the voyage on the *Taipi* as more harrowing than the hurricane itself.

'If only we had known how to do star fixes,' said Ron, 'we would have been in and out of Suwarrow long before the hurricane struck.'

Even with Government supplying us with all the gear as well as Ron Powell and a couple of Fisheries staff, there was no money in fishing. The *Siren* was not suited for the job, and Bob said it wasn't his idea of a game of soldiers — 'We'd best get back to trading and freighting' — so we did.

There was a bit more competition now. Hugh Williams sold the *Dobiri* to the Co-operatives, which now set up the Co-operative Shipping

Company. To become a shareholder all you had to do was ship some cargo on the *Dobiri*; you got a ten per cent discount on the freight rate and at the end of the year you stood to share in the profits which would be paid out pro rata to the amount of cargo you had shipped. Like the co-operative village stores, it was meant to be a great means whereby the people could help themselves. The people helped themselves all right, without waiting for the end of year. The Administration had written the Act so that only the Registrar could audit the books. With Joannides auditing the books and juggling the accounts between the 60 or so co-operatives, nobody knew what was going on.

Meanwhile Hugh had purchased the old *Apanui* from the Northern Steamship Company of New Zealand. At 400 tonnes, she was, like the *Rannah*, too big to berth in the harbour and had to anchor outside, lightering the cargo to and fro in lifeboats, a time-consuming and labour-intensive exercise. One night a couple of the lifeboats drifted off, never to be seen again, and this, coupled with the fact that he couldn't get to the pictures, made Hugh very despondent, so he sold the ship to Dick Brown, with the usual promise never to get into Cook Islands shipping again, ever. Dick never had much joy with *Apanui*, although he did manage to get her in and out of Avarua Harbour. (Dick was a great ship-handler.) The ship was underpowered, and the old Allen engine was always breaking down. On one occasion she took 12 days from Rarotonga to Tahiti with a tere party (a group of people travelling from one island to another) of 90 people on board. The passengers had planned to pay for their trip from the proceeds of the cargo of tomatoes they were carrying, but by the time they arrived in Papeete the tomatoes had all been eaten.

Another time they were on a trip around the Southern Group and had put all their passengers ashore at Atiu for the weekend. On the Sunday-evening radio sked they got a call from the *Taveuni* coming back from Palmerston Island (where they had spent a week trying to get a handful of cargo ashore in bad weather) to say they had a broken gearbox and needed a tow. Leaving the passengers ashore, *Apanui* headed to her assistance and both ships arrived back in Rarotonga at the end of the following week. The Union Company launches took the *Taveuni* into Avatiu Harbour, while the *Apanui* berthed in Avarua. That night there was a bad blow from the north. The *Apanui* tried to put to sea but didn't have the power to get out the passage. Overcome by the force of the waves, she was driven back into the harbour and, in spite of letting go both anchors, she finished up on the sea wall in front of the hotel (now the Banana Court).

Next day Dick went round the island with a few cases of corned beef and rounded up all the football teams. Although it was Sunday, they all got stuck in and bodily pushed the ship back into the water. What they didn't realise was that she had been holed when she ran over her own anchors. She managed to float on her tank tops and went off to Pago Pago for repairs, while the passengers sat waiting in Atiu, eating their hosts out of taro and chickens. The *Tiare Taporo* was away on survey and the *Taveuni* was still awaiting spares.

It was 1962 and shipping in the Cook Islands was at a low ebb. But worse was to come.

One night in July, the *Taveuni*, now mobile again, was in Avarua Harbour, together with the *Dobiri*, when the wind, which had been blowing a strong easterly for nearly three weeks, switched to the north. Both ships broke adrift and went aground. Although both vessels were refloated without too much trouble, the *Taveuni* had lost her rudder and broken her stern-post. After three months in port they rigged a jury rudder and sailed for Pago Pago with Captain John Blakelock in command. The *Dobiri* leaked worse than ever.

The *Apanui* had meanwhile come back from Pago Pago and completed her Southern Group voyage, to the relief of the Atiuans and their few remaining chickens and pigs. Shortly after that she sailed for the Northern Group with Dick Brown as captain. Two days after leaving Manihiki for Penrhyn, a distance of less than 200 miles, Dick asked for a radio bearing from Rarotonga. He reached Penrhyn two days after that and kept radio silence for some days, until a call came from Rakahanga requesting urgent medical assistance. Then it transpired that the *Apanui* had major engine problems and would be staying in Penrhyn until spare parts arrived. Don Bryan made the hazardous 25-mile journey across to Rakahanga in an open boat in rough seas and brought the patient, a girl, back to Manihiki, where it was found she had a fractured spine. At the request of the Chief Medical Officer in Rarotonga, Dr T.T. Romans (himself gravely ill), an RNZAF flying-boat was despatched from Fiji, but arrived in *Manihiki* just as the girl died. The same day the RNZAF sent a DC6 from New Zealand to Rarotonga to pick up Dr Romans; unfortunately he also died, after reaching New Zealand. (Although these two mercy missions failed, the RNZAF carried out many successful flights of this nature over the years and saved numerous lives.)

About this time the *Tiare Taporo* arrived back from Auckland where she had been given a clean bill of health by a marine surveyor, and she did indeed look pretty good. What couldn't be seen, however, was the dry rot inside the mainmast, which broke at deck level while under full sail in fresh conditions, about 350 miles north of Rarotonga, on the way to Pukapuka. Archie Pickering had just relieved Andy Thomson as captain, Andy having at last retired. It was an anxious time, with the 30-metre mast still standing, supported by the rigging, which was now hanging loose in festoons like a clothesline, allowing it to wave around like a drunk finding his way home. They managed to hold everything together and limped back to Rarotonga where the mast was removed. *Tiare Taporo* spent the rest of her days as a one-masted schooner, finally burning to the waterline in Port Vila in 1968.

The *Apanui's* extended sojourn in Penrhyn was causing problems. Trapped in Penrhyn were several VIP passengers, some of whom were expecting to join an RNZAF Hastings aircraft from Rarotonga to Auckland on 23 December. Other passengers for the same flight were stranded in Aitutaki. Meanwhile the *Taveuni* had left Pago Pago with spares on board for the *Apanui* but had to turn back because of further problems with her own machinery. The *Dobiri* left for the Northern Group but had to turn back, leaking so badly that the Administration decreed she could leave port only if headed for a slipway. This order was later revoked to enable her to help out with the pineapples from Mangaia, but passengers were not allowed. This order too was changed, to allow her to go to Aitutaki to uplift the passengers for the RNZAF Hastings. She left on 19 December and should have been in Aitutaki next morning, but instead was only 45 miles north of Rarotonga, drifting with a broken rudder. The crew were trying to rig a jury rudder to enable them to get back to Rarotonga.

That same day we left for Aitutaki in the *Siren* with a load of general cargo. The weather was lousy, with a strong easterly wind and a heavy northerly swell, giving us one of the worst trips we ever had. At Aitutaki the passage was very bad and one of the lighters, while being towed in by the launch, overturned and was swept out to sea, the crew clinging to the bottom and most of the cargo trapped underneath. We took a second lighter to assist it, and with the help of the launch managed to turn the first one over and salvage some of the cargo. Items like roofing iron and bicycles had gone to the bottom, but sacks of flour, cartons of cigarettes and bolts of material floated long enough to be retrieved.

Siren under sail

In worsening weather the lightermen refused to make further trips, so we took the *Siren* up the passage, something not usually possible while still partly loaded, but the high seas from the storm created sufficient depth for us. We were glad to be in sheltered water when that evening a hurricane warning was broadcast.

Meanwhile, the *Dobiri* wasn't faring too well. Next day Captain Peter Scott reported that all attempts to rig a jury rudder had failed, as had attempts to steer the ship without it. Some of the women and children on board were in weak condition. The ship was behaving very badly (I could believe that!) and he requested immediate assistance. He needed further material to make a jury rudder and he needed fuel. Preferably he needed a tow. There was no way we could tow him, but we rustled up the material and some drums of fuel in preparation for going to his assistance, which was impossible until the huge seas stopped breaking across the entrance to the passage. Besides, he looked by now to be lying right in the path of the hurricane, and it would be impossible to reach him before it struck.

Rarotonga Radio had been putting out a general alert to shipping in the area, and the *Athel Princess*, a large cargo ship, answered the call. Then began many long hours of sending messages back and forth while Joannides haggled over the cost of salvage, while on board the *Dobiri* they spent the most terrifying night imaginable, surviving the storm. The worst was over by the time they were taken in tow under a Lloyd's Open Salvage Form (no cure, no pay). They reached Rarotonga on Christmas Eve, much to the relief of everyone, including 23-year-old Captain Scott. By this time the RNZAF Hastings aircraft from New Zealand had been to Aitutaki and Penrhyn, uplifted the VIPs and departed for Auckland. Also, the *Taveuni* had reached Penrhyn with the spare parts for the *Apanui*.

After rigging a jury rudder, the *Dobiri* sailed for Suva, never to return.

That year there was one shipping disaster which did in fact bring good fortune to Rarotonga, if not to the owners of the vessel. In September a Japanese long-liner, with 80 tonnes of tuna on board, ran onto the reef at full speed, just opposite the Sailing Club. Once the crew got safely ashore in the early morning, with the aid of a breeches buoy, the Government claimed the wreck and organised the salvage of fish for the government freezer. Anyone else was forbidden to touch anything, but nevertheless tuna began appearing ashore all round the island, out of canoes, on shoulders, on bicycles, cars and trucks. There were tuna astride horses cantering through the bush, and there were two Public Works trucks loaded with tuna that left for destinations unknown. With every fridge and stomach on the island bursting at the seams, tuna still rotted in the holds, and oh the aroma!

It seemed there was never a dull moment in 1962.

With all the excitement going on around us, life on the *Siren* was almost boring by comparison, but we had to think about cleaning and painting the bottom after a year in service. There was no slipway, and no crane capable of lifting her out, nor was there enough tide to be of any use, so we careened her in the harbour. First removing the five tonnes of ballast, we then attached blocks and tackle to the mast hounds and hove her down to a bollard on the jetty until the keel was clear of the water. The sight of the *Siren* lying on her side startled people at first, thinking she had capsized, until we explained what we were doing, and how clever we were. We didn't let on we got the idea from Lord Nelson.

In May 1962 the Manihiki lagoon opened again and so did Bob's store. The harvest was not nearly as good this time, as the divers were now working in deeper water and mostly using diving machines. These antiquated pieces of equipment depended on two men continuously working a hand-pump to supply air to the man below, who would spend an unspecified amount of time at an unspecified depth. Diving tables and rates of ascent were unheard of, and attacks of the bends were not uncommon and were usually treated with whisky. Aqualungs were outlawed as being too efficient.

Bob was still able to sell trade goods and buy copra so I was kept quite busy keeping him supplied from Rarotonga. He prided himself on being able to sell anything, so one trip I took him a few dozen brassieres, these being a new line in Manihiki. I was hardly back in Rarotonga before a telegram arrived: 'Send more bras'. There was much speculation as to whether Bob was offering personal fitting as part of the service.

It was almost always a good sail to Manihiki and back; this was yachting at its best, straight across the warm trade wind, and we made some great passages. There was the odd time when it was a hard slog back home, with the wind in the south-south-east, but even the worst trip beat the hell out of driving trucks in Hokianga.

It was always good to get ashore and have a yarn with Don Bryan in Manihiki, or Jock MacCauley and Phillip Woonton in Penrhyn. Phillip claimed to have been born in Penrhyn in 1886, but there was some rivalry between him and Andy Thomson as to who was the older, and a year or two was probably added by one or the other, or both of them. A big bombastic man with a voice like a foghorn, Phillip had been brought up on the shores of Auckland's Manukau Harbour, and had run away to sea at 14. He recalled crossing the Hokianga Bar in a scow with a deck-load of sawn kauri which broke loose when they got swept by a huge sea. 'Christ! There were 12 x 1s as far as the eye could see!' Back in the Cook Islands he ran a store in Penrhyn and got into the shell-diving business, having one of the first diving machines in the Cooks. Now he had three machines and nine children and 'I don't know how many grandchildren. I haven't got a family, I've got a herd!' Actually, he lagged behind Dick Brown, who told me he had 62 children.

There was a lot of activity in Penrhyn in those days, for the Americans had set up a monitoring station to observe the bomb tests on Johnston Island, 1800 miles to the north. This observation station was no mean affair. A huge tank-landing ship arrived one day and disgorged more construction material than Penrhyn had seen since the war. There was even a bulldozer for levelling the site (although Penrhyn is dead level anyway) and a Priestman excavator for loading shingle from the beach (although there was an abundance of labour available at 12 shillings a day), plus a transporter to get the bulldozer and the Priestman from the landing to the site, on the edge of the old wartime airstrip. The main camp consisted of a dormitory, a kitchen and a recreation hut, all air-conditioned. The PX canteen contained all the necessities of life, including cold beer. Films arrived weekly by plane, some not yet released in the States. In the kitchen were rows of refrigerators and deep-freezes, and a huge gleaming electric stove. Fresh water was distilled from seawater and electricity was supplied by a bank of generators.

At the other end of the airstrip was a canvas marquee where two British scientists were making similar observations. Twice we were present during the count-down for a test, but on one occasion it was aborted and on the second the bomb failed to explode. However, one night at sea just south of Manihiki we did see one go off and it was a truly awesome sight. The after-glow was seen as far south as New Zealand. One only hoped they knew what the hell they were doing.

In July 1961 Donald Gary Silk had arrived into the world and our children doubled in number overnight. It really was time I paid some attention to my homelife, so at the end of the 1962 diving season when Bob came back to Rarotonga he ran the *Siren* for a while so that I could build a house. I managed to borrow twelve hundred pounds from the newly created Housing Authority, and we were fortunate to get a piece of land at Pue, close to the sea. (Too close to the sea during hurricanes, it later turned out.) Employing local labour, I had aggregate carried from the beach and concrete blocks made one by one in a mould. The floor was a concrete slab, the cement being mixed by hand with shovels, and the roof was of corrugated iron, pre-painted with three coats of paint, followed by another two coats after installation. All joinery was made on the job. A wide veranda faced the sea and became the main living area, while out the back was a workshop and carport, which became a small boatyard from time to time.

We moved in just before Christmas, and held a house-warming party on New Year's Eve. It was also a party to introduce our third child, Karen Anne, four weeks old. It was a great party, and she has liked parties ever since. Some guests never made it home; the Resident Commissioner got the Wolseley bogged down to the Gold Crown in the sand, while the Judge, driving under the influence of his wife, backed into the graveyard next door.

CHAPTER FOUR

THE TEN COMMANDMENTS

One day Ollie Dare called us into his office. We couldn't think what misdemeanour we had committed this time, and waited for him to tell us. He explained that Wellington was getting rather concerned at the state of local ships and the so-called service they were providing. Sooner or later there was bound to be a tragedy, as there had already been in Western Samoa with the disappearance of the *Joyita*.

The *Joyita* was a twin-screw wooden fishing boat, 21 metres, owned in Honolulu but on charter to a Captain 'Dusty' Miller of British nationality. The Tokelau Islands were badly in need of food and medical supplies and the District Officer, Mr R.D. Pearless, tried to get the Government to charter the *Joyita* for a voyage, or several voyages. The ship had been lying idle in Apia for five months and was in poor condition. Captain Miller was unable to produce all the ship's papers and the proposal was dropped. The District Officer then encouraged a private company to charter the vessel and she left for Tokelau with a full load of cargo and 25 people on board, including the District Officer, a doctor and a dispenser, all employees of the same government that had declined to charter the ship because of lack of papers.

They never reached Tokelau, 270 miles away. Thirty-eight days later the ship was found in a waterlogged condition near Vanua Levu, Fiji. There was no sign of the 25 people and a subsequent inquiry failed to establish why or how they had abandoned ship. Certainly they hadn't taken to the lifeboat, for there wasn't one. At the inquiry officialdom ducked for cover. It was stated that the Administration had no legal powers over the vessel or the charter because she was foreign-owned. Most of the responsibility was laid at Miller's door, and some with the

District Officer, neither of whom was there to speak for himself. The whole sad affair was embarrassing to Wellington, particularly in view of the worldwide publicity it created.

What Wellington now proposed for the Cook Islands was legislation requiring ships to be of a certain standard: steel ships, classed with Lloyd's or a similar body, of a minimum capacity of say 100 tonnes, plus cabin accommodation for a dozen passengers, and so on. If two shipowners could be found who would each put such a vessel into service, then the Government would licence inter-island shipping and restrict the number of licences to two. Moreover, Wellington was prepared to pay each shipowner a subsidy of three thousand pounds a year for the first three years, providing the ships were maintained in Class. Would we be interested in such a licence? We assured him we would, and would present him with a proposal as soon as possible.

We had already been giving some thought as to whether we should be getting into shipping seriously. The desire to move on from Rarotonga was fading, if indeed it had ever existed. If we could make money with a small ship, couldn't we make more money with a bigger ship? (This theory sank without trace in later years.) We knew there were coasters for sale in Europe, although not with passenger accommodation. The alternative would be to build a new ship, and Hong Kong seemed to be the place for that. In a surprisingly short time we had General Arrangement drawings and a draft contract from a shipyard in Hong Kong to build a ship. The cost was to be about twenty-five thousand pounds, a colossal amount of money.

We took the plans to the Resident Commissioner, and Ollie promised to set up a meeting with the Minister of Island Territories, Mr (later Sir) Leon Gotz, who was due to arrive on the next boat.

It was with some trepidation that we awaited this very important meeting, which we felt could be the turning point in our careers. Anxious to make a good impression on the Great Man, we dressed in long trousers and shoes, much to the astonishment of the locals. The time came, and we were ushered into his presence, clutching our proposal in a brown manila folder. Gotz presented a quite formidable appearance with his one arm and one eye, and fierce expression. He glanced cursorily over the papers and said, 'Oh, I don't know anything about all this. I'll leave it up to Mr Dare.' Five minutes later we were back into shorts and jandals.

We were granted a provisional licence, along with A.B. Donald and Dick Brown, making three altogether, which we all thought was too many, but no one objected, fearing that the objector might be the one to be eliminated — or perhaps the others didn't take Silk & Boyd seriously.

The first thing we needed was money, lots of it. We once more looked to our friend Neil Mortimer of the Cook Islands Trading Company. He suggested we wait for Neil McKegg to arrive on the following boat. Neil, a son of Boss McKegg, the founder of CITC, had his own law practice in Auckland and, owing to the untimely death of his older brother Henley, was now the managing director of 'The Company', as it was known. He was later to shed his suit and tie to live full-time in Rarotonga. We proposed to him that CITC take a 25 per cent share in Silk & Boyd, which he agreed to. His only request was that we name the ship *Tagua* after CITC's graceful old schooner of the same name. Seized from the Germans in Samoa during World War I, the *Tagua* was famous throughout the Pacific. She was operated by CITC until World War II, when she was requisitioned by New Zealand for the purpose of supplying coast-watching stations around the Pacific.

At this time CITC was itself undergoing an expansion, and had just sold 25 per cent of its shares to Jardine Matheson of Hong Kong, so with names like these to bandy around, we anticipated an aura of respectability attaching itself to a couple of beachcombers named Silk and Boyd.

It was decided I should fly to Hong Kong and discuss details of the proposed ship with Cheoylee Shipyard and at the same time get an alternative quote from another yard. Cadging a lift to Auckland on a visiting Air Force Hercules, I caught the BOAC Comet to Sydney, and a Qantas DC8 to Hong Kong. I had joined the jet set, but I didn't like it, and have remained allergic to flying ever since.

I found my way by bus and taxi to Cheoylee's yard in Ngau Chi Wan. What a shambles; there was a vast conglomeration of lean-to sheds in all directions, with hundreds of workmen scurrying all over the place. Most of the craft being built were yachts for the American market but there was the odd small steel ship on the ways. The whole place seemed to be a scene of total chaos. The yard engineer, Mr Mak, took me into his tiny office (he was pretty tiny himself) and over a bottle of Coca Cola we went through the plans and the proposed contract, making alterations here and there. It was all very amicable and I promised to give him a definite yes or no as soon as I got back to the Cook Islands.

Next morning I phoned Hong Kong and Whampoa Dockyard from my hotel and explained that I represented one of Jardine's associate companies and was interested in discussing the building of a ship for the Islands. They sent a Daimler to pick me up.

In the plush, carpeted offices of the commercial manager, over glasses of ice-cold beer, we went over the details of the proposed ship. At lunch time I was introduced to the executive officers of the company, and treated to lunch in the panelled boardroom where a white-coated flunkey stood behind every chair. (I was glad I had had the forethought to wear my wedding suit.) The menu was incomprehensible to me so I just ordered the same as the fellow sitting next to me. These executives were really nice chaps, all British of course, and they seemed rather fascinated with my tales of the Cook Islands. By the third glass of wine I was getting rather fascinated myself.

I told them I would get back to them when I had consulted with my 'principals' in Rarotonga. They insisted on taking me to the airport, where more drinks were pressed upon me in the airport lounge while the public-address system announced the final call of the Qantas flight. It wasn't until they paged 'passenger Silk' that I was allowed to go. On the flight I got really crook and at Manila a doctor was called on board to check me out. He wanted to take me ashore, but I would have none of it, as the flight was the last chance to connect with the *Moana Roa* from Auckland to Rarotonga.

In Auckland I found that I was only wait-listed on the *Moana Roa*, along with a dozen others. My plea that I was travelling on a matter of national importance didn't seem to carry any weight at all. What was of national importance was that the Minister and Secretary of Island Territories and an entourage of bureaucrats and politicians, accompanied by the media, were travelling to Rarotonga to sort out the constitutional future of the Cook Islands, the people of which were quite unaware they were about to take a flying leap into the twentieth century. It would be a month before the next sailing.

Rather dismayed, I went on board and had a yarn to Tony Thomson, the mate. Tony said, 'Hell, you just have to get back! Look, why don't you just happen to be on board when the ship sails and let things sort themselves out after that?' So I went down and had a yarn to the cook. He also agreed I just had to get back. I should just sit in his cabin until the ship was clear away.

So I sat in his cabin, but the ship didn't get clear away. The first thing that happened was she ran aground pulling out from Marsden Wharf. While a Harbour Board tug was getting organised there was a lot of chiacking from the crowd on the wharf, among whom was the cook's gay lover, hand in hand with yet another lover. Cookie was beside himself with grief at this blatant betrayal, and by the time we got clear and were on our way down the harbour in the dark, his emotions just got too much for him and he jumped overboard, determined to swim ashore and sort out this sordid triangle. Of course, I wasn't aware of all this as I sat in his cabin listening to the commotion on deck. 'Man overboard! Throw a lifebuoy! Launch a boat!'

They soon had the cook back on board, wet as a *Dobiri* deck passenger. I heard the patter of footsteps coming down the companionway, and dived into the wardrobe out of sight. It was Kim, the stewardess, looking for a change of clothes for Cookie. Others were behind her. She opened the wardrobe door and, stifling a scream, grabbed a handful of clothes and slammed the door shut again. Nobody else saw a thing. What presence of mind that girl had.

The ship continued on its way. Next morning I offered myself up to the mercy of the Master, Captain Alec Fraser, who saw no humour in the situation, and offered no mercy at all. 'For Christ's sake,' he said, grabbing his glass of scotch, 'of all the trips to do this to me, when I've got Leon Gotz and Jock MacEwen and God knows what other VIPs on board!' He had the New Zealand Shipping and Seamen's Act open before him (the largest single Act in New Zealand legislation) and proceeded to read the appropriate passages, describing his powers (all-embracing) and my rights (nil).

I was put to work in the galley, helping the cook, and there I was next day, peeling spuds, when all the VIPs came through on a conducted tour of the ship, including Noel Holmes of the *Auckland Star*, who described meeting 'the two sensations of the trip' — the cook and the stowaway. Amongst the passengers, sharing a cabin with Neil McKegg, was Ron Boyd, the CITC auditor, a small, quiet, unassuming man who wouldn't even say boo to a mynah bird, and no relation to Bob Boyd. But Gotz had seen the name R. Boyd on the passenger list and assumed it was Bob. He passed the comment to McKegg, 'Hmph, of course Boyd knows all about this', and poor little Ron suffered the indignity of being thought to be an accessory to the crime.

Alec Fraser was determined to protect the dignity of his command and when the ship arrived in Rarotonga he told the police he wanted to press charges, but he found that there is no law in the Cook Islands against stowing away. Then he insisted on taking me back to Auckland, to face charges there. He did allow me to go ashore in Rarotonga while the ship took the ministerial party around the Southern Group, peddling the idea of self-government (much to the bewilderment of the people), and this gave me time to get the plans and specifications approved for the new ship, and get what amounted to a letter of intent that we would be granted a licence. I now needed to get back to Auckland and get the new company 'Silk & Boyd Ltd' registered (there was still no Companies Act in the Cook Islands) and find a bank willing to lend it some money, so I thought it was rather nice of Captain Fraser to offer me a free passage back to Auckland, especially as the ship was, as always, fully booked.

In Auckland the police came on board and formally arrested me, warning me that anything I said might be taken down and used in evidence against me. I was whisked up to the Magistrates Court where Neil McKegg explained to the judge that I was only here for the good of the people, although he didn't use those exact words. His Honour fined me ten pounds and recommended to the prosecuting lawyer that he find me a passage to Rarotonga on the next sailing. It didn't seem such a bad price to pay for a round trip to Rarotonga. While waiting for the *Moana Roa* to sail I was able to complete all the company business and send off the contract to Cheoylee for building the ship, they having the better price of the two shipyards.

With the lagoon closed, there wasn't much point in keeping the store going in Manihiki, but nor was there much point in both of us running the *Siren*. What we needed was money to meet the progressive payments on the new ship being built in Hong Kong. Bob decided he had best go back to New Zealand to earn some money while I should stay on and keep the *Siren* going until the new ship was ready, at which time the *Siren* would be sold.

It was a busy year for the *Siren*. There was always cargo offering for the outer islands, with full loads back: oranges from Aitutaki and Mauke, oranges and pineapples from Atiu, pineapples and tomatoes from Mangaia. Things were going so well it seemed that nothing could go wrong — but something did.

We had almost finished loading a full cargo of tomatoes at Mangaia when the RA, Jim Little, came out and asked us if we could take a patient to Rarotonga. The patient, a woman with a complicated pregnancy, was loaded on board. We put her on a mattress on deck and rigged up an

Loaded to the gunwales ...

awning. Her husband came along to look after her. Everything seemed to be under control as we left the island in the late evening.

The weather was fine and calm and we were to be in for a slow trip, depending solely on the Lister. Next morning we found that the patient was suffering from a severe haemorrhage; there didn't seem much we could do. Her condition went downhill during the day and by 1800 hours her breathing was very shallow and her pulse indiscernible. I radioed ahead for an ambulance to meet us at the harbour at 1900. As we approached the island it grew very dark, with heavy cloud cover spreading from the south and west. The sea was flat calm and there was practically no break on the reef. The glare of shore lights and lights from fishermen on the reef made it almost impossible to see. There were no leading lights into the harbour at this time, but local fishermen had rigged up a lead light of sorts, in the form of a milk-powder tin over a street light. The tin had a slot cut in the side, and the idea was that when you could see the light shining out through the slot you knew you were off the passage. I had never used this before, and ships never went in at night, but the condition of the patient warranted a certain risk — I figured if she wasn't dead already she soon would be — so when I could see the light shining through the slot in the milk-powder tin, I headed in. I didn't know that the arc of light was wider than the passage.

We struck fairly gently and I tried to slam her into full astern, but the impact had been sufficient to dislodge some cases of tomatoes stacked around the engine and it was a little while before I realised these cases had knocked the gear-lever into ahead again. Whether this made the difference we shall never know, but she wouldn't come off.

I called the radio station and asked them to organise a Union Company launch for us. Meanwhile we launched our own small boat and with one man in the boat, two of us tried to lower the patient on the mattress into it. Even in a calm sea there is always the odd swell, and one of these hit us at the critical moment, sweeping the deck from stern to stem. We snatched the patient back on board. She was still breathing. Meanwhile the boat got swept away over the reef with our man in it.

Quite a crowd had gathered at the harbour along with the ambulance. They couldn't see what was going on, but Brian White realised we must be in trouble and commandeered a canoe and came out to investigate. We sent him back for a bigger boat, in which we eventually got the patient ashore. Meanwhile both Union Company launches arrived and we ran out a couple of kedge anchors and made fast to them. There was no point in trying to pull *Siren* off because the water was over the engine by this time. I gathered up the radio gear and my sextant and we went ashore.

At daylight we started unloading the tomatoes, floating the cases ashore. There was lots of voluntary labour to assist. Then we packed the hold with empty drums and tried to pull her off with the launches, but they didn't have enough power. The *Apanui* was the only mobile ship in port, but Dick wanted to check with his insurance company that he was covered for such a salvage operation, by which time it was too late. The planking on one side had burst open and the ballast was dropping out. The keel was torn off and the rudder and stern-post were broken. Andy Thomson did a survey on behalf of Lloyd's agent and we declared her a Total Constructive Loss.

The woman survived, although she lost the baby. The tomatoes were dried and repacked, but eventually condemned for export. Also in the cargo were five tins of cine film, *The Ten Commandments* in Technicolor. Joe Browne, the theatre proprietor, was in a sweat over that lot, for although the film was insured for ten thousand pounds, it was not covered for shipping to the outer islands. Divers recovered the tins, and the film was all taken off the reels and draped over the seats in the Victory Theatre on Sunday. After being wiped dry, it was re-reeled and shipped back to Auckland, the distributor none the wiser. In Mangaia another 1000 cases of tomatoes were left to rot. It was July 1963.

The loss of the *Siren* was a bit of a blow emotionally and (more particularly) financially. Although the insurance company sent their cheque, it was less than half what the vessel could have earned in the remaining period while waiting for the *Tagua* to be completed. A financial crisis loomed, so I thought I had better follow Bob's example and get to New Zealand to earn some money.

Meanwhile the other two licence holders were pressing on with replacement ships. Donalds had purchased an old coaster in Holland, the *Start Point*, and were spending money putting accommodation on her. Dick Brown had found a ship in the Caribbean and she was already on her way. 'It looks like you're going to be last on the scene, Don,' said Ollie Dare.

'Never mind,' I said, 'ours is going to be new, so we'll be here the longest.' A prophetic statement.

Dick had his ship, the *Bodmer*, delivered out to Tahiti, and sent a crew over on the *Taveuni*, under Captain Peter Scott, to pick her up. *Taveuni* was in a sorry state by this time, so much so that in Tahiti the French authorities were reluctant to let her sail. They finally agreed on condition that the *Bodmer* keep her company. The French had just been tidying up their own local shipping, which had been in an even worse state than the Cooks'.

Everybody wanted to come back on the new ship with Peter Scott, so Lorin Smith (of the yacht *Tahiti*), who had gone as mate, was left with a handful of doubtful characters and no engineer to bring the *Taveuni* back. Being an engineer himself, Smithy didn't mind that so much, but he told the crew, 'When I'm asleep keep an eye on the engine, and if anything happens, give me a call.'

The two ships set off in company, heading for Rarotonga. The first night out Smithy lay down for a sleep, knowing the boys would call him if anything happened. They didn't need to call him, for he woke up with a jolt when the two ships collided. The *Taveuni* started to leak worse than ever, but everything was under control. Peter Scott, captain on the *Bodmer*, said, 'I'd better go on ahead. Give me a call on the radio if you need us.'

Smithy lay down to sleep again, knowing the boys would call him if anything else happened. They called him. 'Something wrong with engine, Captain!' Smithy went below, and sure enough there was something wrong with the engine. Although it was still running, a broken con-rod was poking in and out the side of the crankcase. Smithy arrived just in time to see the whole lot burst into flames — not such good news when the cargo was a full load of fuel.

It took an hour for the *Bodmer* to get back to them and paddle across with some fire extinguishers. They managed to put the fire out but the engine-room was completely gutted. They took the *Taveuni* in tow, but between the two ships they didn't have much to tow with. After three days they had used all their mooring lines and winch runners and any piece of rope that happened to be lying around, and they hadn't even got as far as Mauke. Word went out for assistance, and although there was a Union Company ship in the area, they weren't all that keen, as the *Waitemata* hadn't been paid for going to the assistance of the *Mahurangi* yet. Fortunately, the *Moana Roa* was in port with Tony Thomson as master, and he went and completed the job.

The *Taveuni* lay in Avarua Harbour for a long time after that and nothing was done towards fixing her engine; she was hardly worth it. Eventually her lines parted and she went aground and sank. There was no insurance.

CHAPTER FIVE

SHIPBUILDING IN HONGKONG

That year (1963) the Silks took paid passage on the *Moana Roa* to Auckland, a voyage that was comparatively uneventful, although young Gary gave us some anxious moments. One night we left him asleep in his bunk (and Karen asleep in her cot) while we watched a movie in the saloon. Part-way through the movie I slipped back to the cabin to check on the kids; Gary's bunk was empty. A quick search of the likely adjacent areas revealed no trace. I raised the alarm; the movie was stopped, and an announcement made over the Tannoy. Everyone was asked to look for a missing two-year-old boy. The following ten minutes seemed like ten hours as we dreaded the worst until he was found, happily chatting away to the engineers.

Neil Mortimer always said, 'Selling is the highest-paid profession'. Arriving in Auckland on a wet, windy winter's day, I looked around to see what I could sell that would keep me out of the cold. *Encyclopedia Britannica* was training reps, so after a week of brainwashing I was on the road selling 'Great Books of the Western World'. It was a soft-selling technique and a great product. Interviews with clients were by appointment, so there wasn't any knocking on doors. To my surprise, I became one of their top salesmen, and Neil was right about the pay! It seemed so easy, and the money rolled in — until I went down with the mumps and lost my voice.

We had been getting concerned about the lack of progress reports from Cheoylee and we got the impression that perhaps now they had the contract and the deposit they might not be worrying about getting on with the job. We thought I should go to Hong Kong and keep an eye on things. Finding myself a room in a Chinese doss-house, I tried to pretend I was Robert Mitchum in *The World of Suzie Wong*, but unfortunately Suzie herself was missing. Most of my neighbours were young Filipino entertainers, and a real happy bunch they were. They had a variety of musical instruments amongst them and the place was always filled with laughter and music when they weren't out working.

At the Cheoylee Shipyard work was proceeding, but there had been delays in the arrival of machinery from the UK and the job was running about a month behind. It was good to be able to sit down with Mr Mak day by day. Discussing the many small details resulted in getting things done just the way I wanted. A bracket here, a pad-eye there, a scupper somewhere else; I had only to make known my wants to Mr Mak, or directly to the workers in sign language, and the things would be done.

Lloyd's surveyor was also most helpful, not only in ensuring the vessel was built to Lloyd's Class +100A1, the highest standard possible, but with many suggestions such as by making small alterations and additions here and there at little expense we could save money in maintenance and operating costs in future. All these things required additional funds and I cabled Bob to send more money. Bob became quite used to such cables over subsequent years.

The shipyard was as fascinating as ever and I never tired of admiring the skill and speed of the shipwrights, working away with fairly primitive hand tools. (Often the tools themselves would be handmade.) The *Tagua* was built of steel, but it was the wooden boats I was most interested in. Later on there was woodwork on the *Tagua* too, when they came to interior work. Curves, angles and bevels would be cut by eye with seldom any reference to plans or drawings. Cabin furnishings were made in the joinery shop and were always a perfect fit on the first try. And everywhere was the unforgettable smell of freshly worked teak. Cheoylee had their own sawmill, and their own teak forest in Burma.

Mr Mak, like many of the shipyard workers and indeed half the population of Hong Kong, was a refugee from China. He never talked about his reasons for escaping from China, but simply said there was no way he could ever go back, even to visit his relations. Although the flood of refugees had by this time slowed to a mere trickle of the former torrent, the Bamboo Curtain was still very much in place. Even so, Hong Kong could hardly have survived without a certain amount of trade with the mainland. I doubt if the American tourists in the Hilton realised they owed their bacon-and-egg breakfast to the daily goods train that came down from Canton with fresh produce and livestock. I became fascinated with the idea of somehow visiting China.

The opportunity came when I learned through an organisation called the New China News Agency that China was holding an international trade fair in Canton, and that representatives from different nations could apply for a visa to attend. (Americans needn't bother to apply.) I introduced myself as representing business interests of the Cook Islands, leaving my address as care of Cheoylee Shipyard, which I thought was more appropriate than care of the doss-house. It came as some surprise when I was asked to collect my visa. The visa was not merely a stamp in my passport, but a complete miniature passport in itself, which was then cleverly affixed to my real passport in such a manner that when removed later on, there was no evidence that I had ever been to China, a precaution that was to prove handy when a few years later I applied for a visa to enter the United States, a visa which incidentally was much more difficult to obtain than the one for China.

Along with a dozen or so representatives from other countries, I boarded the train to the border at Lo Wu, where we were given a little lecture about what we could do and where we could go. Basically, we would walk across the bridge over the border and board the train for Canton, where we would be met and escorted to our hotel. We would be allowed to leave the hotel only with the guides provided, and then only to visit the trade fair. We would return in four days' time. No photographs were to be taken outside the trade fair hall, and all films were to be handed in for processing before we left.

Gathering our bags, we walked across the bridge. Because the Cold War was at its height, this trip was something of an adventure. The train we boarded was similar to the one we had just travelled on, a relic of the Hong Kong–Canton railway built by the British and still maintained in reasonable condition. The stations along the way were all well kept, nicely painted and surrounded by flower gardens. The countryside was not so different to that of the New Territories, with fairly intensive cultivation and little habitation outside the walled villages. An obvious contrast was the apparent lack of any motorised transport.

Canton itself was really only interesting because it was such a dull contrast to the glamour and glitter of Hong Kong. The trade fair was an eye opener, not so much for what it had to offer, but for the way it demonstrated how far China was behind the industrialised nations. The fair was a two-way thing in that it was an opportunity to sell, as much as it was to buy. The Hong Kong representative for Gardner engines was in our party; he consulted with the corporation concerned and got a tentative order for six engines, subject to delivery times. Although it was only for six engines, he was ecstatic, for it was a foot in the door of a market of 900 million people. He rushed off a cable to England asking for confirmation of delivery, and was devastated by the reply; the Chinese would have to take their turn like everyone else at the end of the queue, which was two years long. Which reminded me how lucky we were to have scored a Gardner engine for the *Tagua*, only because Cheoylee had one on hand from a cancelled ship-order.

Our hotel was a block-shaped building a couple of miles from the trade hall. It had apparently been closed since the last tourists passed through prior to the lowering of the Bamboo Curtain. Certainly the wing we were in smelled musty and mildewy like a disused attic. The staff were as drab as their uniforms, totally unsmiling and almost afraid of us it seemed. Communication with them was practically nil. Communication with the outside world was practically nil also, apart from a cyclostyled newsletter delivered to our room each morning, detailing in brief the latest world events as seen through the eyes of a Communist reporter. Indeed the news was so slanted and biased the author could have had a counterpart writing for the *Reader's Digest*.

Back at the border on the way home we had the film removed from our cameras, which seemed a bit illogical, for why let us take our cameras in anyway? Fortunately I had removed the film from my camera already, not that I had much of interest on it, but I did have one shot I thought the kids at home might enjoy, and that was of a gang of women in black pyjamas using wheelbarrows to pour asphalt on the road.

Progress at Cheoylee was quite satisfactory, with the necessary components now having arrived from the UK. The contract for building the ship didn't include the supply of items such as bedding, linen, crockery, galley equipment, deck stores such as paint, brushes, scrapers, buckets, spare rope, slings and cargo nets, or engine-room stores like oils and grease, cleaning materials and spare parts. I therefore had a big shopping list to complete before sailing time, and meanwhile I took time to case the joint, as the Americans say.

My exploring trips on foot around the backstreets were fascinating and rewarding. There was hardly any conceivable thing that couldn't be found, and usually at bargain prices. I could even have bought a completely rebuilt Gardner engine off the footpath. Of particular interest were the shipbreaking yards, I could have filled the ship with enough nautical bric-a-brac to satisfy every barkeeper in the South Pacific. One interesting find in a dusty loft was several cases of 240V electric-light bulbs all stamped 'N.Z. Govt'. I bought a year's supply for a song, and wondered how they got there, and how I would explain their presence on the *Tagua* if anyone asked. The answer came one day when, standing on the Star Ferry wharf, the old New Zealand Government vessel *Maui Pomare* sailed past, still with the same name, still the same colour, and you'd have thought she was just arriving off Avarua, except for about 500 Chinese passengers crowding the decks. The ship had been sold by New Zealand, presumably for scrap, when she was replaced by the *Moana Roa*, but probably the only parts to get to the scrapyard were the spares. She looked in good shape, and Captain Bolton would have been proud of her.

With an eye on expenses, I advertised in the paper for a crew willing to work their way, the attraction being a once-in-a-lifetime chance to visit some of the remote South Sea islands. Wages would be one shilling per month. Quite a mixed bunch showed up, but only one, an unemployed German seaman named Ulrich, had any experience worth talking about. I signed him on as ship's carpenter, and he turned out to be a handy little guy. There was a Canadian real-estate agent from Montreal on a round-the-world air tour who knew nothing about ships but attracted my sympathy when he said they had to be better than aeroplanes.

A young Englishman, Michael Swift, asked to join. He was tall and clean shaven, simply dressed and well spoken. I took a liking to him straight away, and during the two weeks left prior to sailing he was of great assistance procuring supplies, running errands and being a general dogsbody. He knew his way around as he had been in Hong Kong for some time and was living on a Chinese junk.

A most unexpected and unusual applicant was a delightful old English lady doctor, Dr Pringle, who thought it would be an awfully nice lark to go on such a trip, and since she wouldn't be able to do much work she wanted to pay her way. I explained that it was a very small ship without many creature comforts, but she wasn't to be deterred. I took her down to the yard and showed her the ship, thinking one look would scare her off, but she thought it was so cute, and very romantic, and such a nice pretty blue colour. So I said she could come — it wouldn't do any harm to have a doctor on board, especially one who wanted to pay. But it turned out that Dr Pringle was a Very Important Person back in the UK, and soon word was around the hierarchy in Hong Kong about her proposed escapade. Suddenly I had a call from a Marine Department official who was very concerned that should anything happen to Dr Pringle, there would be questions asked in the House. The last thing I wanted was the Marine Department breathing down my neck, so reluctantly I told her she couldn't come.

'Isn't that like officialdom?' she said. 'Even at my age one isn't allowed to have any fun.' But she took it in good part and donated a full medical kit to the ship.

After that the Marine Department started taking an unusual amount of interest in the ship. It turned out that a previous ship built by Cheoylee had disappeared with all hands on her delivery voyage to the South Pacific, and they had also lost an RAF Shackleton while searching for her. It seemed prudent to employ a fully certificated captain for the voyage, for although I knew I was capable of delivering the ship myself, I still didn't have sufficient papers to convince the paper-clip manipulators in the Marine Department of the fact. The man who seemed to fit the bill, and who had followed our adventures with keen interest, was Captain Warwick Dunsford of Auckland. An Extra Master in Sail and Steam, Warwick not only had impeccable qualifications but could bombast his way past any bureaucratic barrier we were likely to encounter, better than anybody we knew. (We hadn't met Harry Julian yet.)

Our engineer was Les Livingstone, ex the *Dobiri*, a dour Australian who always saw the worst in any situation or, if things were going perfectly, would tell you it couldn't last. Les never missed listening to the world news on Radio Australia every day, only because world news is almost all bad. He neither drank nor smoked, but had the greatest command of swearwords outside Australia. After keeping the *Dobiri* afloat for years, I didn't think he was going to have much of a challenge with the *Tagua*. Les, too, was short on paper qualifications, so I ran an advertisement in the press for an engineer, and a week later looked the Marine Department Shipping Officer square in the eye as I told him there had been no replies.

One of my most useful acquisitions was a Mini Minor station wagon. When it came time to commission the ship, I was able to buy all the gear that I had already lined up in my meanderings around some of the more sleazy areas, and that little Mini carried some impressive loads, in it and on it — and got lots of parking tickets too. Before sailing I just drove it down to the yard and loaded it on board, parking tickets and all. I'll bet the police wondered where on earth that Mini disappeared to.

The Mini Minor that carried some incredible loads in Hong Kong. Before sailing I just loaded it on board, parking tickets and all.

The delivery date was approaching, and Bob joined me, followed a few days later by Warwick Dunsford. Harbour trials were carried out and the ship performed to the satisfaction of all concerned, actually exceeding the eight knots specified. At last came the handing-over ceremony and the final payment. Mr Lim, the owner of the yard, whom I had met only once previously, joined us as we gathered in Mr Mak's little office. I pointed out that under the terms of the contract we were entitled to an adjustment of price for late delivery. Well, it was like farting in church. Mr Lim changed from most pleasant to most furious when Mr Mak interpreted what I had said. He let off a barrage in Chinese and immediately left the room. Mr Mak was very embarrassed and had obviously lost face. He explained that the delay was due to the late delivery of machinery from the UK, and a clause in the contract allowed for this, but what had made Mr Lim so angry was the fact that they had gone out of their way to accommodate my every wish, they had put a lot of work and material into the ship in excess of that called for, and Mr Lim had a reputation for giving a good deal.

We asked for time to think about it, and agreed to meet after lunch. Over lunch we met with a lawyer friend of Warwick, and explained the problem. The lawyer said he was unable to act for us as he happened to be Cheoylee's lawyer, but as Warwick's friend, he gave us some advice. He had the previous year acted for Cheoylee in a dispute over slipway repairs to a floating restaurant known as the *Hong Kong Lady*. The case took months to come to court, during which time the *Hong Kong Lady* remained welded to the rails at Cheoylee Shipyard. He advised us not to tangle with Mr Lim.

Back at Mr Mak's office we explained that it was all a misunderstanding, that of course they were right, and we apologised for any inconvenience. After that it took only minutes to sign papers, hand over the cheque and break out the champagne, with lemonade on the side for Les. For years after, just about every time I looked at the magnificent teak-laid decks, the mahogany woodwork and the solid teak doors with their genuine brass ship-style locks, I would think of that silly bickering argument over a few pounds and feel thoroughly ashamed of myself. For what we paid for the ship we had the deal of the decade, a deal that our contemporaries were very envious of when they saw the ship.

The delay had put us into the typhoon season, and just to let us know, one developed in the South China Sea and gave Hong Kong a bit of a brush, dropping a foot of rain as it went by. The ferries stopped running, bamboo scaffolding came tumbling down off buildings, and whole slum areas slid down off the hillsides, but otherwise the town kept going as usual. Driving in torrential rain, I was let down by my faithful little Mini. With its athwartships engine it had a habit of cutting out when heavy rain drove through the front grill on to the distributor. It did just that one night as we were turning into Chatham Road in heavy traffic. With one accord Bob and I jumped out to push her to the side of the street. A tremendous gust of wind caught us with both doors open and she took off like a Hobie Cat, sailing straight into the Mee Sik Pharmacy, which fortunately had its typhoon shutters up. Later, in Rarotonga, I cured this problem by lashing a coconut shell over the distributor, a trick that intrigued the mechanics at Seabrook Fowlds in Auckland when I took the car in for servicing one time. They thought I should patent it, as all Minis had the same problem.

Everything was squared away. With all stores loaded, fuel and water aboard, crew all present, I made one last run to the hotel to clear out the last of my papers, then all I had to do was load the Mini on board, complete with all its parking tickets, and we'd be off. I was just entering my room when a girl came out of the room next door, a young blonde

European, not bad looking. She had to be the only European girl in the whole place. We said hello, and blow me down if she didn't have a Kiwi accent. She was stranded in Hong Kong with visa problems (and money problems too, I thought to myself, if she was staying in this place). She asked what I was doing in Hong Kong. I said been building a ship; 'In fact, I'm leaving for Rarotonga. Do you want to come?'

She said, 'When?'

I said, 'Now.' So she came. I arrived back at the shipyard and introduced her to Bob and Warwick and said she was coming with us. Bob just about swallowed his tonsils while Warwick just stood there in disbelief. They refused to believe that I hadn't had her stashed away for the last three months. I just let them believe what they wanted to. She turned out to be a really nice person and an asset to the ship and I'm sure the boys kept themselves spruced up more than they would have done otherwise.

The first leg of our voyage took us across the South China Sea, thence down through the many islands in the Philippines to the southern port of Zamboanga. The crew soon settled down to a steady routine of two hours on and four off, which gave plenty of time for sleep and relaxation. We started to notice that Michael seemed to require an unusual amount of sleep and relaxation. He took little interest in any activities we tried to organise and invariably headed for his bunk at the end of his watch. At the picturesque and unusual city of Zamboanga he took one brief stroll ashore and hastened back to his cabin, which he shared with one of his fellow countrymen, a long-haired Cockney lad who had jumped ship in some Eastern port.

When it came time to leave Zamboanga, a burly officious Customs officer brought our clearance certificate, then asked for cigarettes. We had already had a plague of these pests on arrival, demanding cigarettes and whisky as if it was their God-given right, so Dunsford said he couldn't have any — we had only enough for ourselves for the voyage. The official then became rather nasty and started dredging up a list of imagined infractions we may have committed, including, he said, failure to put up our flag in the morning; he himself had had to tell one of our crew to put it up. Whereupon Dunsford drew himself up to his full six feet two and put on the sort of plausible display of bombastic bullshit for which he was renowned. 'You!' he roared, '*you* gave an order on *my* ship! I'll report you to Manila!' But it didn't work. The official dropped his hand to his gun and said that the Mayor of Manila was his brother and

Latitude sight on board *Tagua*

demanded the clearance back. Dunsford gave it to him. And some cigarettes. We finally got away. Perhaps we were lucky; the next time I had a clearance certificate taken off me it took nine months to get it back.

Down through the Sulu Sea, past Mindanao and through the Celebes, through the Molucca Sea and along the coast of Halmahera with myriads of exotic-looking islands covered with dense tropical growth to the water's edge. As we slid past deep bays with dugout canoes pulled up on white sandy beaches in front of the thatched huts of native villages, naked children would run down to the water's edge to wave to us. This is the stuff people pay millions to see, we thought, as we gazed in wonder at the everchanging scene before us. Here we were enjoying it for free — except Michael, who would be flat on his back in his bunk, gazing into space.

We crossed the Line and began the long downhill run home. At 1100 hours one morning at latitude 00 degrees, King Neptune and his fair Lady Mop and retinue appeared on the fo'c's'le-head and hailed the bridge, wanting to know what ship was entering his domain. He was answered by no less than the President of the company who replied 'The good ship *Tagua*, Your Majesty' (at which some remark like 'Good ship be damned' was heard) and welcomed his august personage on board. His Aquatic Majesty wanted to know who on board had not previously entered his Domain, and was informed there was one poor miserable Canadian Wretch. 'Bring him forth,' bellowed the King, so a small search ensued and the Wretch was brought forth to pay homage.

Before dealing with the foul landlubber, King Neptune read a proclamation, wherein the owners of the said vessel were fined large sums of beer and cigarettes for starving the crew in bad weather. The landlubber was then forced to kneel before His Majesty and beg permission to enter Neptune's Kingdom and offer his filthy body for cleansing. Before the cleansing ceremony he had to sing to King Neptune's Equator Bird, carried in a cage by one of his flunkeys. It bore a striking resemblance to a potato, with matchsticks for legs. The landlubber was then well lathered with shaving soap of a special preparation, the ingredients known to only a few, and shaved by Neptune's barber with a razor a foot long. Several buckets of firewater were needed to remove the remains of the lather and these were applied with some gusto by all King Neptune's several assistants, and a more bloodthirsty-looking lot were never seen.

That evening when we adjourned to the saloon for supper, who should already be seated in his chair at the head of the table but the Captain, dressed in white shirt, black tie and peaked cap. But no, on closer inspection it proved to be not the Captain at all, for the face consisted of a roll of toilet paper, the hair was rope yarn (very realistic), with two toilet brushes for arms. It was never learned who perpetrated this hoax, but there was a certain Canadian Wretch with a very smug look on his face.

We cruised for days along the northern coast of New Guinea, dodging logs and debris, even complete floating islands with trees growing on them, disgorged by huge rivers in full flood. Mountains towered in the background and there were some spectacular displays of lightning at night. Michael remained unimpressed, just spending most of his off-duty hours meditating or reading odd books on philosophy. Between these books and a perusal of his passport, plus talking to him, I tried to put together some of his background.

He had been an art student in England and had for a wager hitchhiked to India with only ten pounds in his pocket. From here on the story gets a bit fuzzy, but he spent some time living in a monastery in India, studying under a Hindu teacher. He said that he was in search of the meaning of life, and that what we were living was all a great sham, and that nothing was what it seemed. He was working on some religious philosophy which he tried to explain to me but the more he tried the more confused I got. He said there were no problems in life, the only problems were in man's mind. I said he should try life as a country carrier in New Zealand and then tell me there are no problems in life.

I suggested he just get on with living the present and enjoying it. 'People spend half their lives worrying about the future,' I said. 'They wait, dreading what's going to happen next, and go from one wait to the next, and lose their ability to enjoy the present. Come on, let's have a beer and to hell with the future.' But he retired to his cabin, presumably to worry over what I had just said. As time went on he became even more morose and withdrawn. Refusing most of his meals, he lost weight and assumed a gaunt look, heightened by the growth of a stubbly beard.

The last 1500 miles to Suva were a hard slog to windward against the trades and it was with some relief we slipped into the calm waters of Suva Harbour. Most of the crew wanted to carry on to Rarotonga, but we would be stuck with trying to get them out of there to any onward destination, so they had to stick by the agreement, which was to pay off in Suva. The only one we kept on was Ulrich, and we made out he was a professional cook. He was actually the worst cook we ever had. We all parted good friends, and never expected to see each other again, but Michael was to show up in some odd places over the next few years.

It wasn't any trouble finding enough Cook Islanders in Fiji who wanted to get back home. Dick Brown's *Bodmer* was on the slipway having some major work done to the hull. It seems they must have had some short-sighted surveyors in the Caribbean because for a ship that was supposed to be 100A1 at Lloyd's she was in a sad state. She had been there for some time and looked like being there a while yet. Some of the crew were anxious to get home, and indeed the ship needed to reduce her payroll. And a great joy it was finding Joe Balewai, the ex-bosun from the *Dobiri*, on the wharf, looking for any excuse to get to Rarotonga. With Joe on board to lead a bucket brigade, and Les and I to fix the pumps, we would be unsinkable.

Undoubtedly the biggest joy of all was being reunited with my family. Olly and the kids had flown from Auckland to join us for the final 1200-mile leg to Rarotonga. And maybe to check out the young Kiwi blonde?

Tagua in front of A.B. Donald's store

One thing we were all going to keep a check on was Gary Silk. At three years he could be expected to be a bit more responsible than he had been when he disappeared on the *Moana Roa*, but to his mother's horror one day he climbed out through the cabin porthole and up on to the boat deck. She was not amused, and neither was he when she had finished tanning his bottom.

The 6000-mile voyage ended with our landfall at Rarotonga on 22 July 1964, and we felt we had done a pretty good job, arriving with the first brand-new ship to enter the Cook Islands trade for over 40 years. But we got no accolades. On the contrary, our reception was somewhat of a contrast to what we had experienced on *Patsy Jean*. Not this time was the Collector of Customs going to jot our names down on the back of his packet of Greys and say, 'Call by the office on Monday'. No, this was a whole new ball game, led by a brand-new Collector, named Chapman, recently seconded from some remote Customs House in New Zealand, where they must have heaved a sigh of relief to be rid of him. With a cigarette hanging from his lips, his expansive stomach hanging over his shorts, and his socks at half-mast, he marched on board and demanded to see our papers. His face displayed increasing disappointment as he found everything in order, until he came to the stores list; I had carefully declared our few remaining bottles of rum, not wanting to run foul of the law at this stage of our career. This was his moment of triumph! This was equivalent to the traffic cop catching me unloading beer on the vicar's lawn.

Rushing out on deck, scarcely able to conceal his glee, he called to his boss on the wharf, 'Hey, Tim, they've got liquor on board!' Tim, who as the previous Clerk of Public Works had been so helpful when we were scrounging material to rebuild the *Siren*, called back, 'Confiscate the lot! Silk's been here before. He knows the rules.' Apparently it was okay to be a destitute yachtie, but to come back with a brand-new ship to try to contribute something to the economy — well, it just wasn't on, we were obviously trying to get above ourselves, and needed to be told so.

So we lost our precious few bottles of rum. Not that it was such a big deal. What they did was quite legal; only the Government could import liquor. It was just the principle that rankled, plus Dick Chapman's manner, which we were to become endlessly frustrated with over the years to follow. He was the epitome of the public servant bully, using the power of his position to make life a misery for all those below him, including the public, while being subservient to all those above. A measure of his unpopularity was demonstrated one day when, during what should have been a few quiet drinks after work at Cook's Corner, Dick, loud and abusive as ever, received a well-aimed punch in the face from a junior public servant. The result was a broken pair of glasses and a bloodied nose, with the poor bloke (by now almost a national hero) in court on a charge of assault. A sympathetic judge discharged him without conviction, although he did extract a promise that the glasses would be paid for by the accused.

The officionados hadn't done with us yet. Next came the Health Department officers, whose attitude was that as we had just arrived from the plague-infected Far East, we must be carrying all sorts of dreadful diseases not even heard of in the Cook Islands. The ship would have to be fumigated with deadly cyanide gas for 24 hours, and, as this was highly dangerous to people ashore, the ship would have to be moored in the middle of the harbour while it was done. As a concession, the crew would be allowed ashore during the process.

This fumigating of our ship had dire consequences for the famous brigantine *Yankee* anchored offshore. In the early hours of the following morning she dragged her anchor and stranded on the reef. *Tagua* was the only ship in port and we could easily have towed her clear, but by the time we rounded up the Health boys to clear the ship of gas, the poor old *Yankee* had been thrown right up on to the reef and became a total loss for the owners, and a goldmine for Bud Sperber, an American who spent three years soliciting money to salvage her. On the other hand, the way she was being operated by the present owners, she would have found a reef before long anyway, as did her captain, Derek Lumbers.

Much progress had been made on Avatiu Harbour in our absence. A lot of dredging had taken place and there was now a sheet-piling wharf to tie up to. Bob knocked up a lean-to office and, with telephone and power laid on, he was in business as general manager of Silk & Boyd Ltd.

A.B. Donald's new ship, the *Akatere*, was already well established, mainly supplying goods to their outer islands branches and bringing back copra from the Northern Group. It had always been Donalds' policy to serve their own stores and only carry cargo for others if space permitted. It was this policy that had been instrumental in the decision of CITC to take a share in Silk & Boyd Ltd, and it was a policy that had

Wreck of the *Yankee*

caused a lot of bad feeling in the past when A.B. Donald had had a monopoly of inter-island shipping. Willie Watson, a rival trader, got around it by breaking down cargo for his outer islands customers into parcels and posting them, the ship having by law to carry any mail offering. Willie asked his customers to return the stamps, and then did a tidy business on the side selling Cook Islands stamps to philatelists.

Akatere was a little larger than *Tagua* and, although 17 years old, was in pretty good condition, but with a single mast amidships and very small hatches, she was a cow of a thing to work cargo. The mast was built in tabernacles so that it could be folded down for going under bridges, a handy trait on the canals of Holland, and would be handy in the Cook Islands too, if they ever got around to linking the islands with bridges! Her biggest disadvantage was that she was underpowered for the open waters of the Cook Islands, and would sometimes take a week or even ten days to beat her way back from Pukapuka in a decent trade-wind blow. Another problem was the lack of space for cabin passengers. Being built as a cargo vessel, she was never intended to carry passengers. To try to overcome this they had ripped out all the crew accommodation aft and turned it into one big saloon, with a table down the middle and four bunks on either side. A shower and toilet opened directly off it. The arrangement had operational cost advantages for the owners, in that very little food was consumed by the passengers, for those who weren't already sick before mealtime were soon put off by the smell of the head and by the sounds of those being sick around them.

What with the shortcomings of the *Akatere*, and with the *Bodmer* spending much time away in Suva and Auckland for repairs, we were pretty happy with our *Tagua*. She ran like clockwork, the eight-cylinder Gardner never missing a beat, and even Les had to admit it would probably go like that forever. We would be in and out of port with a full load while the others were still getting their hatches open. We seemed to create history by advertising a schedule and keeping to it.

Christmas came and, having money in hand, we decided to give each of the crew a bonus. The problem was what to do about Fijian Joe? Any money we gave Joe would straight away find its way into the nearest bush-beer school. However, Bob had another of his brilliant ideas; we

Akatere and *Tagua* in Avatiu Harbour

would give Joe a bicycle. The crew were called together and the bonuses passed out, but none for Joe. Then Bob pretended to have suddenly remembered something, and the bicycle was brought out of hiding and suitable words of presentation made. Joe appeared to be quite overcome, judging by the odd tear escaping, but it turned out the tears were because he didn't know how to ride it!

The following year we took the ship to Auckland for her first annual survey and dry-docking. We loaded copra in Penrhyn, and also a family as passengers, none of whom had ever been outside the Cook Islands before, and only the father had been off Penrhyn. It took four days from Penrhyn to Rarotonga, and another ten days to Auckland. We made our landfall early in the morning and, after following the coastline for an hour or so, Tangaroa said to me, 'Hey, this New Zealand's a big island eh?'

'Yes,' I said, 'but what you see is only Great Barrier Island. Wait until you see the North Island!'

If the city of Auckland was an eye-opener to a family from Penrhyn, the waterfront was an education for our crew. I explained about unions, and that we wouldn't be allowed to work our own cargo, or even use our own derrick. The ship was lying at Marsden Wharf, the tide was in and the deck was about level with the wharf. The wharfies, vast in number, all assembled on the wharf, but no work began. After some time I made inquiries as to when was the usual starting time. The answer was that nobody would be starting until we provided a gang plank. So there was quite a delay while we got our agent to hire a gang plank from somewhere. The gang plank all rigged, with a safety net underneath, the wharfies then stepped over the bulwarks and started work.

Work proceeded between smokos and meals, with half the men working and the other half resting in turns, until when, about halfway through the job, the carcass of a centipede was discovered, long since expired. This resulted in an immediate stoppage, everybody ashore, no more work for the day, as the ship would have to be fumigated. My crew thought all this was a hell of a joke.

'It's no joke,' I said. 'When you think what it costs to discharge this copra, remember it is the grower in the islands who is ultimately paying, and remember too that the cost of loading cargo for the islands is all passed on to the consumer in the islands. And all those many highly paid crews on the New Zealand ships that carry the cargo to the islands contribute to very high freight rates, all of which is added to the cost of your corned beef and cabin bread.'

'Then why don't we run our own ships to New Zealand, Boss?'

'Because the unions won't allow it. This one trip is being done with special permission from the unions just so we can do our survey. That's why we had to give you all 'membership cards' before we left Raro. For God's sake don't let on that we don't have a seamen's union — they'll stop again.'

Yes, it was an education all right. The situation didn't seem to be much better than it had been in 1951 when the then government under Prime Minister Sid Holland, realising the country had had a gutsful of wharf stoppages, de-registered the wharfies and brought in the troops. The coalminers went out in sympathy and the railways ground to a halt. We country carriers were given an open licence to run wherever we wished, and for once remote districts like Hokianga enjoyed a direct trucking service with Auckland. Everybody had a ball, except the Auckland trams, which had some difficulty avoiding the sudden large number of trucks that invaded the city, the drivers of which were more accustomed to dodging cows than trams.

One day I was driving a truck and trailer down Symonds Street when I had to swing out to avoid a car that suddenly double-parked in front of me. A tram had made the unfortunate decision to overtake me and, when I pulled out, my trailer hooked in behind the driver's compartment, demolishing the compartment, scattering glass all over Symonds Street, and jamming the electric controls into full astern, causing the tram to suddenly start trundling back uphill. The driver was unhurt, and bravely rushed towards the other end of the tram so as to operate the controls from there, but the passengers, less bravely, panicked into the aisle and blocked his path. Nothing if not quick thinking, he then bailed out and began to sprint up the street, hoping to board the tram from the back, which had now become the front. But the tram was gathering way, for its load was lightening as passengers abandoned ship with the utmost alacrity, until it reached a junction in the overhead lines, whereupon the pole jumped off. Now without power, it began free-wheeling down the street, with the back becoming the front again, and the driver was able to jump on and apply the emergency brakes. It was shortly after this little event that the city council decided to scrap its trams, which was a pity, as they could be a great source of entertainment on occasion.

Who should come wandering along Marsden Wharf one day with a sugarbag over his shoulder but Michael Swift. Wearing long hair and a full beard, he was if anything thinner than when I had last seen him in Fiji. My crew decided I did indeed have some strange friends and irreverently dubbed him Jesus Christ.

Michael said he had been living in a tent near Ninety Mile Beach. When I asked him what he was doing for a living he said, 'Oh, nothing really. The Maoris are very good and often give me fish, and I can get pipis and toheroas any time.' We talked of various things. He seemed to have difficulty keeping track of the conversation, as if his compass had a deviation or something, and I gathered he was still searching for the answer to his philosophy. Eventually he got round to the real purpose of his visit to the ship.

'I say, Don, this might sound a bit silly, but do you know of any island in your part of the Pacific where I could live on my own?'

Coming from Michael this didn't sound silly at all.

'There is only one place I know of,' I said. 'That is an island called Suwarrow about 500 miles north of Rarotonga. It abounds in fish and birdlife and has been lived on in the past. It was a coast-watching station during the war and there are still one or two buildings standing. There is a water tank, still serviceable as far as I know.'

Michael immediately wanted to know how to get there. 'That's quite a problem,' I replied, thinking of his philosophy that there were no problems in life. 'Ships don't usually go there — it's off the beaten track — unless there are divers there for shell, but that's only every four or five years. Used to be an old bloke named Tom Neale lived there. Last time he went he chartered a yacht from Rarotonga. Another yacht picked him up a few years later after he dislocated his back. Another problem is the Government would probably ask you for a bond of a hundred pounds to enter the Cook Islands. Then of course they might not let you go to Suwarrow. How are you holding for funds?'

'Just about nil,' he admitted. 'However, I really want to get to this place — Suwarrow is it? It sounds like just what I want.'

'Do you really have any idea what it would be like living there? Although Tom Neale lived there on his own, he knew what he was about. He'd lived in the islands most of his life. Can you climb a coconut tree? And there are no pipis, and no toheroas, and no Maoris to give you fish! Better forget it!'

'Well, thanks anyway, Don,' he said, hefting the sugarbag over his shoulder with that far-away look in his eyes again. 'I'll be getting along now.' We shook hands, and once again I thought it would be for the last time.

Later that year I was yarning with a bloke off a yacht just come in from Tahiti. 'What do you know about Suwarrow?' he asked.

'Not much,' I said. 'Why, you thinking of calling there?'

'Not me, but there was this yacht *Highlight* in Bora Bora which was going to call there and drop off this crazy Englishman.' I knew the *Highlight*, a New Zealand trimaran which had called at Rarotonga for repairs after hitting a whale. Two brothers, John and David Glennie, owned it.

'The Englishman's name wouldn't be Michael Swift would it?'

'Well, I don't recall hearing his name, but he was a tall, thin fellow, with long hair and a beard.'

'That's Michael,' I said. 'But the Glennies should have got permission. The Government won't be too pleased if they hear about it. It's not the sort of thing I'd do myself. Too risky.'

'Perhaps the risk was worth it. The skipper told me he was getting a hundred pounds for it. Maybe the Government will never hear about it.'

'You haven't heard of the coconut wireless,' I said.

Other yachts on the way through from Tahiti that year confirmed the story. Rumour had it that Michael was building a canoe, that he was taking 10,000 cigarette-lighters, that he was looking for a Tahitian woman to take with him, and so on. Then in a bar in Apia a couple of yachties were heard to tell of how good it was to be able to afford a few beers again. This crazy Englishman had paid them a hundred pounds to be dropped off in Suwarrow.

You could say things moved Swiftly. In less time than it takes to kick one of Aggie Grey's cats out of the kitchen, the Glennies found themselves invited to an audience with the New Zealand High Commissioner, who suggested diplomatically that if they deposited the sum of a hundred pounds towards the cost of getting Swift picked up again, the Cook Islands Government would not press any charges under its Immigration Act.

Most of Michael's hundred pounds had by now gone to support the poor and needy barkeepers of Apia, but David Glennie was a refrigeration engineer and was able to find work, and the hundred quid was eventually paid. The Glennies sailed on to further adventures, and the last I heard of John Glennie he had survived a month at sea living on an upturned trimaran, drifting off the coast of New Zealand.

In early February the following year, 1966, a hurricane swept through the Cook Islands and did quite a bit of damage in the Northern Group.

The *Tagua* was loaded with emergency supplies and the Government asked us to divert to Suwarrow during the voyage to pick up this illegal immigrant named Michael Swift. The Government would pay us a hundred pounds if we brought him back.

Our first call was Palmerston Island. Apart from losing a few hectares of the main island, and the radio station being relocated a few hundred metres inland, there wasn't too much damage. Nevertheless, the islanders were, as usual, glad to receive hurricane-relief supplies. After embarking several large turtles as deck passengers, we continued the voyage and raised the tiny motus on the southern side of Suwarrow at noon on the second day. We made our way round to the pass on the eastern side, immediately south of Anchorage Island, which is the largest motu, and the one on which Tom Neale lived. Dropping anchor in ten fathoms of clear blue water, I scanned the beach for signs of life. Coconut trees fought for position, the outside ones leaning over the water — vegetable giraffes, Robert Louis Stevenson called them. Underneath was dense foliage, right down to the beach. A canoe was pulled up under the trees, but otherwise there was no sign of life. I had the crew launch a boat and we rowed ashore.

An overgrown path led inland from the beach, and as we walked up it, rats moved lethargically out of our way. Tom had told me of the occasional plagues of rats, and I had heard about them on Raoul Island where Tom Bell used to catch up to 200 in a single night, but I never imagined anything like this! They were everywhere, and quite unafraid of us. Tom had told me a lot of other things too, about Suwarrow, but I had really only got to know him as a result of Michael's interest in the island. In fact, I had a bit of a guilt-feeling about being responsible in a way for Michael being on 'Tom's' island, for that was the way Tom looked at it. He was distressed at the fact of Michael being there, while he, Tom, was living frustrated in Rarotonga, unable to get permission to go back. After he told me of his first year on Suwarrow, when mere survival was a full-time occupation, I really worried about how an Englishman, who had never before been on a tropical island, would make out. I worried about it now, as we walked up the track, and came to Tom's shack, much in need of repair, and the leaking water tanks also. But at last there was a sign of life ; a shirt and a pair of shorts hung on a line, and there were ashes in an outside fireplace.

'Ahoy!' I called. No answer. We reached the veranda. 'Hey, Michael!' Not a sound. I peered in through the doorway of the only room. The lower half of a man's body was visible on a makeshift bed. I glanced over my shoulder for moral support, but my companions were suddenly showing great interest in the chicken-run on the far side of the garden. I was thinking of our deal with Government; a hundred quid if we brought Michael back from Suwarrow. Did that mean dead or alive?

I gave another croaky call. 'Michael?' The feet leapt to life, and Michael appeared, stark naked. 'Hullo Don! I thought I heard voices. I was sleeping.' He shook my hand and reached for a pair of tattered shorts. He looked in fairly good condition, but we learned that he was a bit disillusioned with living alone on a coral atoll. The rats had been a problem, chewing his hair while he slept, and nibbling at the callouses on his feet. I asked him how he liked the island. 'Oh, the island's all right,' he replied in an offhand way, which I thought was a bit poor, as it had to be one of the prettiest places in the South Pacific. 'Yes, the island's all right,' he repeated. 'It's me, I'm the problem.' Which seemed to be a strange statement, coming from a man who believed there were no problems in life.

'Look,' he said suddenly. 'Can I come back with you? Of course I don't have any money, and can't offer you much. I would like to come back though. It's just that my teeth are giving a bit of trouble.' I didn't think to mention that Government were paying us to take him back anyway, dead or alive.

'We don't have any spare bunks,' I said, 'but we'll fit you in somewhere, just for old times' sake. We're sailing in an hour's time.'

We gave him a hand to gather a few things, and carried his canoe up from the beach and left it on the veranda. By sunset we were steaming out the passage, bound for Pukapuka. During the voyage we managed to give him a haircut and he trimmed his beard. He chatted freely with the passengers about his sojourn on the island. He still hadn't learned how to climb a coconut tree and his fishing expeditions had left much to be desired. The sharks had really been a problem, for a shark would often take his hook when he was fishing from his canoe, or take a fish he had already caught and then get caught itself. Either way, he would then be stuck with the shark, which he couldn't just cut loose, for he had only a limited amount of tackle. Trying to get it into his canoe to take it ashore was a bigger problem, for the canoe had very little freeboard and on one occasion it overturned, landing him in the water with a very agitated shark. Probably neither the shark nor Michael saw the humour in the situation, but in Michael's case he got such a fright that when he finally got ashore, with the canoe, he gave up fishing for three days until his nerves settled down a bit and hunger drove him out on the lagoon again.

Back in Rarotonga not too much was said by officialdom. The Government had enough problems trying to sort out its new status of 'Internal Self Government in Free Association With New Zealand' to worry too much about Michael. They paid us our hundred pounds and took his word that he would take the first available passage to New Zealand. Meanwhile he stayed at the Silks' place, where he made himself useful doing odd jobs around the house including painting the whole outside of the building. In the evenings the children would sit for an hour at a time, Karen on his knee, the others clustered round, while he told the most improbable children's stories, all fabricated as he went along. During my next trip at sea I wrote a story about him and sent it off to the *Sunday News* in the UK. That brought in another hundred pounds ...

One day in 1966 our old friend Tig Loe drifted in. We hadn't seen him since our trip to the Tuamotus on *Patsy Jean*. At the same time Olly's mother was visiting from New Zealand. We persuaded Tig to run the *Tagua* and Grandma to look after the kids for a while, so Olly and I could go to Canada and see what we had been missing all these years.

During a brief stopover at Honolulu we were whisked away by Bev Hale, now Mrs Brian White, to see *Patsy Jean* for what was to be the last time. She looked quite tiny and insignificant among the magnificent yachts in the Ala Wai boat harbour, and we were quite happy to climb back on board our Pan Am 707, which sure went to windward a hell of a lot better than *Patsy Jean* ever did. We landed on Vancouver Island on a clear, crisp morning, seven years to the day since sailing out of Auckland harbour on *Patsy Jean*. Canada proved to be all we had expected and we began a love affair that grew with subsequent visits.

We bought warm clothes and camping gear, and a station wagon for $380, less than £NZ130. That old car took us thousands and thousands of kilometres through British Columbia, Alberta, the Yukon, Northwest Territories and Alaska. Perhaps the highlight of the visit, and an experience that had later implications, was meeting up with a couple of characters in Dawson City who operated a tug and barge on the Yukon and Porcupine rivers, servicing the remote Arctic village of Old Crow.

This was real wilderness country, with hundreds of kilometres between villages. The tug, named of all things *Brainstorm*, pushed two barges, carrying much the same sort of cargo as found on ships servicing outlying Pacific islands, although the return trip was different in that the principal cargo was muskrat skins rather than copra and pearl shell. Another difference was the depth of water, sometimes only 60 centimetres, instead of 2000 fathoms, and the hours of daylight, 24 instead of 12. The 2500-kilometre round trip to Old Crow took us three weeks.

Later, we were to see much larger tugs and barges on the McKenzie River, carrying hundreds of tonnes down to Tuktoyaktuk on the Arctic Ocean, where cargo was transferred to ships for supplying the Distant Early-Warning stations along the Arctic coast. Even these tugs and barges were minuscule affairs compared to the ocean-going monsters to be seen operating out of Vancouver Harbour; tugs of several thousand horsepower towing barges of 10,000 tonnes, even two at a time. This was a common means of transportation all along the West Coast of North America, right up to the Gulf of Alaska and out to Hawaii. The two main advantages over conventional ships were simplicity of loading and discharging the barges, and the economical manning-scale of the tugs, which had a crew of only six or eight. I thought surely the same system would work in our part of the world, except where there is a need to carry passengers, which ruled out the idea within the Cook Islands, and between the Cook Islands and New Zealand. Two years later I had second thoughts about this.

CHAPTER SIX

THE HERMIT OF SUWARROW

Tom Neale had been back in Rarotonga for some years. Now that I had been to 'his' island, I realised how much he loved it, and how upset he was at the idea of someone else being there instead of himself. Since we had our own government it wasn't the Resident Commissioner who stopped Tom going back, it was the Premier and his Government. I agreed with Tom that the Government's attitude was unreasonable and between us we started to hatch a plan. Meanwhile he was writing a book about the years he had spent there.

During the writing of his book he had done a lot of research into the history of the place, and an interesting history it was, considering it was little more than a few tiny motus scattered around the edge of a rather large lagoon. Stories I had heard from old Tere Kainuku in Aitutaki about buried treasure in Suwarrow were probably based on fact, although stories that Kainuku knew how to find it were more likely a figment of his imagination. Be that as it may, early Spanish coins and bits and pieces had been found there. However, the real wealth lay in its pearl shell. About the turn of the century, Lever Bros. had planted gold-lip shell there from Torres Straits. This was done at the time they had a small team there cutting copra. Ships calling for copra would sometimes bring soil as ballast, and this would account in some measure for the success of Tom's garden, for the soil was much better than the pure sand and coral you expect to find on an atoll. At the same time it also explained the presence of weeds found nowhere else in the Cook Islands, and perhaps the termites as well.

In later years Manihiki black-lip shell was introduced, and what was there now was a cross between the two, a large shell of high quality. The lagoon hadn't been worked for years, and Tom reckoned there must be

Tom Neale, the hermit of Suwarrow

plenty there now. Maybe Tom had a reason for saying that. In any case, Bob and I had had a taste of pearl shell, and it wasn't long before we were talking to Tekake Williams, the champion diver of Manihiki, who at that time held the world record for the deepest free dive and longest duration under water. We suggested taking a team to Suwarrow for three months. We would get the diving licence and provide the transport, Tekake would find the men and do the diving, and Tom would be caretaker on behalf of Government, just to make sure no undersize shell was harvested.

We put the idea to Premier Albert Henry, who gave his okay. He made two stipulations — one, that we had to be sure to get the men out before the hurricane season, and two, Tom had to come with them. Tom gave a written undertaking to the effect that he would come out with the divers, if he was able. Tom asked about the cost of his fare, and we said that would be on the house, but he could put something towards any cargo he took. I knew Tom had been collecting stuff for years in preparation for the day he might return, and sure enough, when we came to load, there was a mountain of gear: timber, roofing iron, fuel, boats (2), rope, wire, crates of chickens, cats — you name it, if it was going to be useful on a desert island, Tom had it. 'A lot of stuff for three months, Tom!' I said. Tom slapped a roll of money on the table.

'I don't know how much the freight is, but there's a hundred quid, and that's all I've got!' It looked as though a hundred pounds was becoming the established figure for anything to do with Suwarrow.

We arrived at Suwarrow on 1 July 1967, and it didn't take long to get Tom's gear ashore. He had it all figured out. First, bundles of timber were dropped into the water. These were lashed together to form a raft, on to which went everything else. At high tide we used the boats to tow the raft across the shallows to the beach. I had reckoned on taking two days, but it was done in one, so we spent another day helping him get all the stuff up the track to his house. By the time we sailed we had our freezer full of fish and crayfish and the rigging festooned with live coconut crabs, each carefully slung out of reach of its neighbour, for they would tear each other to pieces if they got a chance.

Leaving Tom and the diving gang in Suwarrow, we hastened back to Rarotonga, where we loaded a full cargo of Raro juice, and sailed for Auckland for our annual dry-docking and survey — but this was to be a dry-docking with a difference....

Coconut crabs

The previous year while we were on dry-dock the yard manager, Graham Wilde, was chatting away one day, asking how business was going, and I said, 'Pretty good, but the trouble is this bloody Bob Boyd. The way he books cargo, you'd think the ship had elastic sides! We should have built her six metres longer. Do you think you could lengthen her if we asked you to?' Graham supposed it would be possible, although such a job had never been tackled in New Zealand. before. He got a bit of a surprise later that year when I called him from Rarotonga and said we wanted it done. He said to just measure the midships section and they would fabricate the piece and have it ready for us when we arrived.

The more we thought about this measuring business, the more sure we were that we had the potential for the cock-up of the century. There was no saying how accurately the ship had been built to plan; I had seen Cheoylee's men doing a lot of work by eye. Imagine if, after cutting the ship in half, it was found the new midship section didn't fit. I called Graham, and said, '*You* come and measure the ship, then *you* go back and build the new piece!'

Operation Stretch: cutting complete, the *Tagua* slides back down the slip to make way for the new section, overseen by Don Silk (left) and Bob Boyd. The new six-metre hull section was then welded into position.

We had rendezvoused with him in Papeete and the measurements were taken. Now, when we got to Auckland, there was the new midship section waiting to be inserted. And there, too, were some of Graham's men out with their tape measures as soon as the ship was hauled out, just checking to make sure! The ship was slipped on two adjacent cradles and cut in half, then the after-portion was rolled back to allow the new piece to be fitted in. And it did fit, perfectly, thank goodness, for the job attracted a lot of attention and we had our share of TV cameras and press reporters on hand as the two halves were separated. When asked what it felt like to see one's ship cut in half, I replied that I had complete confidence in the ability of A. & G. Price to put it all back together. What I didn't add was that I was dead scared of some union dispute halfway through the job, then where would we be? Might as well be welded to Cheoylee's slipway.

As it was, we had five trade unions involved, four of which held stop-work meetings during the job, but none resulted in serious delays. All in all, things went smoothly. The whole job was completed in ten days, including the installation of a new hydraulic crane to accommodate the increased length of the hatch. The result was a better-looking ship, six metres longer, with 60 per cent more cargo capacity, 100 per cent more deck-passenger space, more sea kindly, and half a knot faster on the same fuel consumption.

Bob suggested we lengthen the ship every year — soon we would have an ocean greyhound capable of carrying a year's supplies for the outer islands on one voyage.

The other media attraction on board, although much too shy and quiet to be good media material, was our bosun, Teehu Makimare, who had come back from London after receiving the Royal Humane Society's highest award, the Stanhope Gold Medal for the most outstanding act of bravery for the year.

Caught in a storm in a disabled pearling cutter on a voyage between Rakahanga and Manihiki, the crew of seven had lost all hope of survival until Teehu took over the leadership, and by sheer guts and determination drove the rest of them to attempt a survival downwind voyage to Pukapuka. They survived the storm, but missed Pukapuka, and got capsized in another storm, by which time they were in poor physical shape and scarcely able to help themselves. With the boat upside down and seas breaking over it, Teehu repeatedly dived to cut away the mast and rigging, enabling them to eventually right the boat and bail it out.

Two of his companions drowned in the process. Now they were without food and water, totally dependent on catching rainwater and eating the odd flying fish or squid that landed on board. One man died during the ensuing drift, which took them to Erromango in the New Hebrides (now Vanuatu), 2000 miles away and 64 days after leaving Rakahanga. Helping to drag his three mates ashore, Teehu then husked nuts with his teeth and kept them alive until they were found by natives and carried on stretchers for two days to reach the nearest village, where one of the survivors died. The other three were taken by yacht to Port Vila and, after a spell in hospital, were repatriated to Rarotonga, eventually rejoining their 'widows' in Manihiki.

It was time to go back and uplift our diving team. In the meantime Dick Brown had got wind of our Suwarrow activities and had sent his own team from Manihiki, complete with diving machine. This didn't worry our guys too much, as by the time the others arrived, they had already cleaned out the shallow beds and the easy pickings. Actually the amount of shell was disappointing, and the sharks had been a problem, which surprised me as I had been spearfishing with Tekake and seen him treat sharks with complete ignore, except for the black papera, for which everbody has great respect. It became obvious that the beds had been poached, something that probably wouldn't have happened had there been a resident caretaker on the island.

Just before arriving I swore the crew to secrecy about the ship now being longer. 'Let's first see if anyone notices, then if they do, let's tell them it's a figment of their imagination.' The crew caught on.

Tekake came out as soon as we dropped anchor. I noticed him casting his eyes back and forth over the length of the ship as his boat got closer, but he didn't say anything. It was almost impossible to see the joins unless they were pointed out. Later, when we opened the hatch, I saw him puzzling again. 'Don, somehow the ship looks bigger.'

'Oh, that's strange,' I said. 'It's probably the new crane.' By and by somebody started laughing, and the secret was out.

'You had me worried,' Tekake said. 'I thought perhaps my eyes were playing up.' We tried the same trick on Tom, but that old sea dog picked it straight away.

We soon had the bags of pearl shell loaded, the freezers full of fish, the rigging full of coconut crabs, and the team all aboard. 'Waiting for you, Tom,' I said with a straight face.

'Can't come,' he said, with an equally straight face. 'I'm the Government caretaker. Got to see Dick's divers don't take any undersize shell.'

'OK, see you in Raro when the *Bodmer* brings the other divers back.' Tom gave a grin. 'Like hell,' he said.

Back in the Southern Group the pineapple season was just coming on and it was going to be a record year. The *Tagua* with her increased capacity was like having an extra ship on the job. The hydraulic folding-jib crane proved to be super-efficient compared to the old swinging derrick, and we were able to load and discharge in less time than previously, despite carrying 60 per cent more cargo. With her extra length, *Tagua* was better able to handle the short trade-wind swells, and we found we could comfortably make three round trips a week to Mangaia. The only bottleneck in the whole operation was the lighterage operation at that island, where the problem was to find enough labour to man the old wooden lighters propelled by oars, for just about every able-bodied man was a planter.

The solution seemed to be to replace the wooden boats, which were village-owned, with one or two steel self-propelled barges, but none of the villages could come up with the necessary finance, and there was no way they would join forces in such a venture. In desperation we had a suitable barge built in Suva and sold it to one of the boat companies on what amounted to a hire-purchase agreement, although such a term didn't exist in the Cook Islands at the time. To assist in launching and recovering the barge, we designed it with wheels on the bottom, and it proved such an outstanding success that there was soon demand for a second one. This, too, we eventually had built, and it was just as successful as the first, although we had a bit of a tragedy delivering it.

It was towed to Mangaia by our vessel *Manuvai* (whose acquisition I deal with in my next chapter). On arrival at Mangaia there was wild celebration by its owners (a rival village that had been still struggling along with an old wooden lighter), who leapt on board, yelling and yahooing, so that there was total confusion as the ship neared the reef, the barge still in tow. Before the owners got the engine started, the tow-line was round the ship's propellor. With an on-shore wind, it was going to be only a short time before the ship hit the reef. The engineer, Jimmy Woonton, grabbed a knife from the galley and leapt overboard to cut the rope free, while the Mangaians on the barge continued their bedlam, probably not understanding what was going on. The captain, Bruce Carnahan (on his first trip), was quite unable to restore any kind of order, and the barge was allowed to drift under the stern of the ship just as Jimmy came up for air and threw his arm over the rudder to take a rest. The barge hit the rudder and Jimmy was left with his arm hanging by a bit of skin. That soon sobered up the Mangaians, who quickly got him ashore to the hospital where the doctor completed the amputation.

The ship arrived back in Rarotonga next morning, with Jimmy on board. A crowd was on the wharf, including Jimmy's family and an ambulance to take him to the hospital. Jimmy came ashore unaided and not requiring an ambulance, but when his wife saw him with only one arm, she screamed and fainted, so they put her on a stretcher in the back of the ambulance, while Jimmy rode in front with the driver.

Apart from this dreadful mishap, things were going well. Les predicted they wouldn't last — and this time he was right.

Rarotonga hadn't had a decent hurricane for 20 years. If anyone had asked Les, he would have said we were due for one — and he would have been right again. When the meteorological office reported a deep depression northwest of Palmerston, people shrugged it off — it was just another deep depression northwest of Palmerston. When it developed into a full-blown hurricane, people hoped it would veer away, as these storms usually did. When it blasted through Palmerston and headed straight for Rarotonga, the island started to batten down for the onslaught. The hurricane control office was set up in the communication centre above the post office, and the broadcast station, Radio Cook Islands, went on the air 24 hours a day, instead of the usual four, broadcasting the latest reports as they came through from the met. office. People in low-lying areas were encouraged to move to higher ground or take shelter in the hurricane centres established in each village, usually a school or church building. Radio broadcasts told people to stock up on food and water, torch batteries and kerosene lamps. Everyone was told what to do.

The *Tagua* and the *Akatere* were both in port. Archie Pickering and I were at the met office, and we agreed it looked like a direct hit for Rarotonga, or at best a near miss. Either way, we would have to put to sea, which was nothing unusual, for the harbour offers little protection from the north in strong winds. In a hurricane it is a death trap for any ship caught in port. We put out a call over the radio for our crews, which as expected turned up to a man. Hatch tarpaulins were carefully secured, wedges driven home, locking bars in place, cargo nets stretched over the lot. Ventilators were fitted with their wooden plugs and canvas covers, watertight doors tightly closed. We were as ready as we could be.

'Well, Les,' I said, 'this is where we find out how good A. & G. Price's welding is!'

'Yeah, I can't wait to get back to tell my kids about it,' he replied.

The harbour was still relatively calm, for the wind was from the northeast, howling in on the Matavera side, while the huge swells generated by the storm centre were beating in on the Black Rock area. Once we got clear of the land we felt the full force of both.

Archie and I had independently figured that the hurricane's most likely path would take it south of Rarotonga, and, unknown to each other, we both headed north to get sea room. In these days of radar and global positioning systems the technique is to hug the lee of the island to get what little shelter you can, but we didn't run to such gadgetry then. Sea room was the thing; no use hugging the lee of the island when visibility is down to zero and you know the reef is half a mile offshore. Perhaps it was just as well we hadn't compared notes because we had enough to think about without the worry of another ship close by. The *Akatere* had left port first and straight away disappeared into driving rain. We lost sight of the land less than half a mile out.

There wasn't much to be done except keep her plugging slowly into it. We weren't in a hurry to go anywhere for, although the further we could put ourselves from the hurricane centre the better, the difference between three knots and five wasn't going to make much difference in the end. I had the cook make a huge pot of stew, enough for three days if need be, and everyone was to help themselves when and if they could. There wouldn't be any table settings this trip. I also urged them to get some sleep if they could, for we would need all our energy and faculties later, but of course we weren't yet tired and the thought of what we were in for kept sleep very much at bay.

The seas got steeper and higher as the strength of the wind continued to increase. Not only did the wind get stronger, but it seemed to be holding steady in the northeast, instead of backing to the north as I would have expected it to do as the centre of the hurricane headed towards the south of us. Perhaps it wasn't going to pass south of Rarotonga after all.

By late afternoon it was blowing a whole gale. The crests of the waves were toppling forward and forming large patches of broken water with dense streaks of foam so that the whole surface of the sea was taking on a white appearance, like the surf on the reef after a long ocean swell has crashed on shore, except that these weren't isolated patches waiting for the next wave, these were everywhere at once, as if we were amongst the reefs. There was intermittent rain, but it didn't make much difference, for wind-blown spray affected visibility even worse. Day turned into night, and that didn't make much difference either as far as visibility went. We had all our decklights and floodlights on, something we never do at sea, for a helmsman can't see beyond the range of lights. In this case there was nothing to be seen beyond the range of lights anyway.

Steering became heavier. *Tagua* never had any expensive hydraulic steering gear, only rods and chains connected directly to the rudder quadrant, so that the helmsman felt every shock and jar from the force of the waves on the rudder transmitted right back to the spokes of the wheel. Wheel watches were reduced from two hours to one hour, and then to half an hour. By midnight we had two men on the wheel together, and it was taking all their strength to turn it as the ship staggered up the face of each succeeding wave, threatening to fall off to one side or the other, so that we had to apply increasing power from the engine, for to broach would be disastrous. Finally she would reach the crest and there would be a sensation of feeling her poise for a moment, like a high diver taking a breath, gathering herself for a desperate leap.

We had direct control of the engine from the wheelhouse, so that as she breasted the wave we could immediately cut the revolutions as the stern flew clear of the water and the screw raced madly in the air. This was the moment, too, to apply some helm one way or the other as required while the rudder was clear of the water and easy to turn, for she would be off a bit to one side or the other, and we needed to tackle the next wave square on if we were not to be thrown aside like so much flotsam. It wasn't as much a roller-coaster motion as a see-saw action, for the sudden pitch as she took the plunge down the other side was enough to throw you off your feet if you weren't hanging on to something. Although revolutions were cut right back, it didn't prevent the headlong plunge into the abyss of the next trough, like taking a header into the void — and like hitting a rock wall at the bottom.

Through the smother of wind-blown spray the face of the approaching wave could be seen in the glare of the lights and it was awesome and frightening to watch her bury the whole fo'c's'le head into a solid wall of water, and even more frightening still to see the top of the wave come curling over like a breaker on Bondi Beach, smothering the whole ship right back to the bridge in a welter of foam. She would take these dives as if she never meant to come up again. For a while you had to wonder how she ever would, but she always did, rising to the next one while a great wall of water came rushing back over the hatch, like the bursting of a dam.

When the ship was designed, the only access to the accommodation was through a watertight door opening off the main deck. I was now very grateful that I had had Cheoylee build an emergency access hatch above the mess-room, for this was the only way we could now get below. Even that was fraught with difficulty, for it meant negotiating the open boat deck from the wheel-house door to the access hatch, only a few metres to be sure, but in that fierce wind-driven spray, with the extravagant motion of the ship, it was not that easy. The moment you left the protection of the wheelhouse you were breathing in gasps, eyes forced shut, feeling your way along from one solid handhold to another. Always two went together, not so much for moral support but to wrestle with the access door.

The night wore on. The wind continued to back to the west, although it wasn't easy to tell as the compass was almost useless because of the violence of the motion. The barometer not only continued to fall, but fell more and more rapidly. Readings were taken at the top of the swell, for there was a marked difference as the ship rose and fell. We had calibrated it before leaving port, and it was now lower than the predicted pressure at the centre. Not only was the hurricane deepening, but it was also obvious the centre was going to pass very close. The ship was still handling the seas, but it was taking the full 200 horsepower of the Gardner engine to keep any sort of course up the face of the waves. In fact it was becoming nearly impossible to stop her falling off one way or the other. The only alternative was to turn and run before it, but the very idea of turning the ship round in those conditions was horrifying. At some point during the turn, she would be broadside on to the approaching seas and that situation didn't bear thinking about, but we would have to do it, for we couldn't continue on much longer. I thought I would just give it a few more minutes and watch my chance for a bit of a lull before making the final decision.

The decision was made for me. We were climbing this never-ending wall of water, the ship's head falling off to starboard, the engine on full power and two men unable to turn the wheel. The ship fell headlong on her side. Everything disappeared, even the power of thinking. We were all thrown bodily across the wheel-house, whether or not we had hold of anything. My whole life flashed before my eyes, I really thought this was it. To say that we hadn't already been scared shitless would be a lie, but strangely enough, in what I thought was the final crisis I had no feeling of fear at all, only a sense of sadness that the Angel and the kids would have to box on without me.

The ship righted herself momentarily before the next onslaught. The engine was already on full ahead, and the rudder must have been knocked hard over, for by the time we sorted out the mass of humanity piled against the starboard door, she was already well through the 180-degree turn. The next wave caught her on the port quarter and for a moment I thought we would be thrown on our beam ends again, but she went down the face of it like a surfboard. The wave broke on either side of us with a roar like an express train which could even be heard over the roar of the wind.

Wind? What wind? It was like somebody had turned off the jet engine. It wasn't so much the sudden absence of the screaming wind that was so eerie, but the realisation that it was the vibration of the air that had stopped. The quietude was startlingly tense and almost felt unsafe in itself. And it was light, not real daylight yet, but you could see. No longer was the air full of spume. We opened the wheelhouse doors and with the sudden entry of fresh air I realised what an unpleasant smell we had been experiencing; it wasn't just human sweat, it was the smell of stark, naked fear. I had last smelt it on myself cooped up in a cattle pen with an enraged bull for company.

The scene outside was uncanny. The seas were still mountainous, and the surface of the water still white, but you could actually see stars in a clear sky. We still had our hands full trying to control the ship, but the waves soon lost their pattern. We were in the eye of the hurricane, and the sea was unlike any I had seen before. The nearest thing like it would be the millrace outside a lagoon passage, with waves and overfalls running in all directions at once, and no wind to lend any sort of sense to the scene.

I knew we still had the other side of the storm to weather, but day was breaking and things looked much less worse. Miraculously we didn't have any broken bones among us, although some spectacular bruises showed up later. Stew and coffee were the order of the day and we had only an hour before we were into it again. We turned the ship into it once more, for running before it was just too scary and only to be done as a last resort. This time it didn't seem so bad, and being daylight was a big help. After about three hours it started to ease, and 24 hours later we were back in port. What a shambles! The whole northern coast was strewn with coral boulders right up to and across the main road. In Avarua Harbour the Union Steamship Company's wharf was completely demolished, while in Avatiu Bob's office was reduced to kitset form and scattered far and wide. At home the sea had been all around and through the house. What had been a lawn was now a rock garden, and what had been an orchid house was now barely useable as a hen-house. However, what made it almost all worthwhile was the way the neighbours from the inland side of the road, the Pukapuka people from Pue village, rallied round and came in force to clean up the mess. And so it went on around the island, with every able-bodied man, woman and child, and every piece of mechanical equipment, be it Government-owned or private, fully engaged in getting things back to some sense of order, without waiting to see who, if anybody, was going to pay.

Akatere came back looking a mess. She too had been thrown on her beam ends. Seas had smashed in the wheel-house windows and flooded down into the galley and saloon. Archie said he thought they were a goner, but the storm suddenly eased. We estimated our positions weren't far apart at the time.

It was to be 20 years before we were to see another hurricane like that, and then they became all too common. Yet when the call goes out for crews to join a ship to take her out into a hurricane, the boys are always there, a fact I have never seen commented on by the media. On many occasions crews and waterfront helpers have battled a whole night fighting to save ships in the harbour, and never a word of acknowledgement. Perhaps it's just as well, for they would only be embarrassed.

After the hurricane there were trips to be made to all the Southern Group islands with relief supplies, for they had all taken a hammering. The Government was concerned about Dick Brown's divers on Suwarrow, having memories of the devastation of 1942. The *Bodmer* was away on one of her extended refit voyages, so we were asked to make a call at Suwarrow on the way north and return the divers to Manihiki — and be sure to bring Tom Neale. I said he might refuse to come — what do I do? The authorities therefore sent the Hon. Apenera Short, Deputy

Premier and Minister of Police, to do the trip and check on hurricane damage in the north.

At Suwarrow they had had massive seas but these hadn't gone right across the island as feared. We found the divers in pretty good shape, except for poor Bob Marsters, who had died of the bends. I tried to conduct some sort of inquiry but when it came to pinpointing how long he had been down and at what depth, no one had much idea — they didn't even have a watch with them.

Everyone was keen to leave and it didn't take long to load the shell and all their gear. Apenera asked Tom how long he would be, as we were just about ready.

'Oh, but Mr Short, I couldn't possibly get ready! It would take me too long to pack up my things. Then there's my chickens, and my cats. No, no, I couldn't possibly make it for this trip.'

Apenera asked me how much it would cost to hold the ship. I said I would really have to call Bob on that one. He decided he had better call Albert Henry. So we went back on board and tried to raise ZKR Rarotonga, but there seemed to be peculiar atmospheric conditions that prevented the transmission of radio waves, and we had to sail, leaving Tom behind. It was New Year's Day 1968. I told Tom we would come back and pick him up, which we did — in March 1977. He waved farewell with his pareu from the beach as we sailed out the passage.

We were never short of passengers on the *Tagua*. The Government usually took most of the cabin berths; there were always Government people travelling, some on transfer from one island to another, such as doctors, teachers and radio-operators, while others would be on a mission such as building overseers, while still others like co-operative officers and the copra extension officer would just keep going round and round. Then there were the missionaries: the Mormons in pairs with their bicycles, the pastors of the Cook Islands Christian Church on transfer with their complete families and worldly possessions, often a Catholic priest visiting the other priests who never got transferred anywhere, and very occasionally a Seventh Day Adventist pastor and his family. Then, with self-government in 1965, there were Honourable Members travelling home to their constituencies between hectic sessions of legislation, or perhaps even the Premier, on his way to rustle up votes or quell any dissension.

Deck passengers: a tere party preparing to go ashore

Bath-time for the passengers on *Tagua*

There were some interesting conversations around the saloon table on occasions, and nobody better skilled at stirring up a debate than the Hon. Julian Dashwood, Minister of Police and the member for Mauke. He was better known as Rakau, which in Maori has a generic meaning of 'wood', but also a range of connotations including 'stick', which could in this case apply equally well, for he was as thin as one, and always complained about our hard wooden chairs because he didn't have enough built-in upholstery on his backside. Then, with Dashwood's reputation, there is the possibility that the phallic connotations of the term were what led to the nickname. Perhaps Albert Henry had a sense of humour when he made Rakau the first Minister of Police, for he was a bigger reprobate than Albert himself. (Or so we thought at the time. After being knighted by Her Majesty the Queen when she came to open the airport, Sir Albert got up to more skulduggery than Rakau had ever dreamed of, finally losing his Prime Ministership and his knighthood as well.)

Rakau's linguistic artistry and stinging wit would always get things moving, and he loved baiting the clergy, especially the young Mormon missionaries straight down from the States. An avowed atheist, he was

Under cover — deck passengers

very knowledgeable on a wide range of religions, all of which, he claimed, offered eternal life in some form or other. 'What nonsense! Who wants eternal life? How utterly and positively boring! Not for me.'

Rakau was pontificating to us one night on the necessity to have scrupulous honesty in politics, right from the start, maintaining that the first politician found to be straying towards the slightest suspicion of graft and corruption should be unmercifully crucified, so it was somewhat ironic when he was the first one caught soliciting bribes, and was himself unmercifully crucified. When he was returning home after having accepted the guilty verdict I reminded him of the need for scrupulous honesty in politics.

'That's quite correct,' he said, 'and they did the right thing, throwing me to the wolves, but I still wish I had got away with it. And I would have, but for that bloody Dawson. Fancy going through a man's waste-paper basket when he's not looking. The man's got no principles!'

Rakau had had a room at the old Otera, the government hotel in Rarotonga, which doubled as his accommodation and office. For some reason he couldn't get on with Albie Dawson, the manager. (There was some talk that Rakau had caught Albie out over not depositing the full amount of hotel revenue at the post office.) One day, while Rakau was busy attending a cabinet meeting or other affairs of state, Albie's wife, Jessie, went through his waste-paper basket. Rakau was putting together a deal for contracting out the printing and marketing of Cook Islands stamps. Notes from the waste-paper basket, pieced together by Jessie, allegedly indicated how this was going to work, with a percentage for Albert and a percentage for Rakau. Jessie became known as Jigsaw Jess, and people who didn't know better thought the nickname stemmed from her ability to help Judge Morgan — a resident of the hotel for 26 years — with his 2000-piece jigsaws.

I thought myself that it was a pity it had happened, for Rakau was good value in that first cabinet. Apart from Albert, few of his colleagues knew what this self-government business was all about, whereas Rakau revelled in sparring with the Wellington bureaucrats and could beat them at their own game when it came to diplomatic obfuscation.

There was some benefit in Rakau's departure from the Otera. He had bought Allen McQeen's old Ford 8 when Allen left the island, and to give it a bit of protection from the sea breeze he used to park it round the side of the hotel between the two wings of the building. Then, while he was still on good terms with Albie, he had the whole area roofed over, making a magnificent carport, big enough for ten Ford 8s. This later became the first venue for Rotary Club meetings, and eventually was transformed into what is now known as the Banana Court, a bar renowned throughout the Pacific for its local colour. Rakau would have approved.

Like a few other people I know, Julian Dashwood had chanced to call at Rarotonga on his way somewhere else. In this case he was a passenger on the way to Tahiti, having shot through and left his wife in Sydney with half the proceeds from the sale of his only possession, an ancient Buick. Stepping ashore in Rarotonga, he met an old friend on the wharf, Carfax-Foster, who invited him out to his 'plantation' at Titikaveka. Dashwood had been putting on an act of travelling as an ex-British-Army captain 'stiff upper lip and all, old chap' — a gentleman of means. He was just the sort of partner Carfax-Foster was looking for, and he encouraged Dashwood to stay on, not realising the man was flat broke. The visitor needed no encouragement, for he assumed Carfax-Foster was in funds, owning a plantation and all, whereas in fact Carfax-Foster was flat broke too. By the time each realised he was being hoodwinked by the other, the ship had long since sailed.

Over the next 30 years Rakau eked out a living of sorts in the Cook Islands. The going was tough at times, he told me, but he never considered leaving. Two things kept him going financially; one was writing (not very rewarding) and the other was dealing in sea shells, which started as a hobby and became sufficiently lucrative for him to be able to build a very fine house in Mauke, where as a store manager he had been doubly fortunate, for he met and married a lifelong partner whose family land included one of the choicest building sites on the island. Now their own family included two girls and a boy, one of the girls graduating as a schoolteacher in New Zealand. In fact I had met the children before I met Rakau, travelling to and from high school. The older girl was named Burma, and when I asked her one time how she came by such an unusual name, she explained that she was born during the Burma Campaign in World War II.

'Lucky you weren't born during the North African Campaign', I remarked, 'or the Battle of the Bulge.' I thought at the time her old man must be a bit odd, giving a girl a name like that. She thought so too, but then he thought she was a bit different when she came back from New Zealand and went ashore in Mauke in a pair of flame-coloured tights.

Although there was no air service most of those years, the RNZAF would usually put on a Hastings aircraft at the end of January to take the 'scholarshippers' to New Zealand, bringing them back again for Christmas. We always tried to schedule a trip to the outer islands to coincide with these flights, and it was an education to see how much the kids had matured in a year or two away, especially the girls, who no longer seemed able to cope with sleeping on deck under an awning.

In those colonial days any papaa who criticised the system stood a good chance of being labelled a Communist, and Rakau, who loved to needle petty authority, helped things along by always having a framed picture of Lenin on the wall of his sitting room. When Leon Gotz visited Mauke with his entourage on board the *Moana Roa*, trying to sell the idea of internal self-government (I was in Rarotonga resting between my spud-peeling voyages), Rakau, acting the reserved country squire, instead of attending the official ceremony, let it be known that he would be 'at home' if the Minister cared to visit.

The official party arrived at the imposing mansion, set in its well manicured lawns, and the squire welcomed his guests aboard, serving champagne as they admired the heavy columns supporting the front porch and trod the parquet flooring in the immense living room. Rakau expounded his theory that the Cook Islands would be better off being a part of Great Britain, rather than having any 'free association with New Zealand' (Gotz's favourite phrase), but Gotz seemed more interested in the crossed polo sticks on the wall and the wooden saddle-horse complete with saddle, not an everyday sight on a remote South Seas island. Gotz was passing on when he pulled up short in front of the portrait of Lenin.

'The party seemed to be in a hurry to leave from then on,' chuckled Rakau. 'Anyway, it wasn't really champagne, only cider, and do you know, I don't believe anyone twigged it.'

Although I never had the privilege of having Sir Leon as a passenger, I did have his successor, Phil Amos, who took the Manurewa seat from him and in turn became Minister of Maori and Island Affairs under the new Labour Government. As it happened, Phil had been a neighbour at Opononi when he was a school-teacher, and had taken much interest in the building of *Patsy Jean*. The Amoses had a particular interest in the Cook Islands, as they had adopted a Cook Islands girl from a very early age, and when Phil got his portfolio he lost no time heading for the Cooks to see how New Zealand could best help this new self-governing nation.

One place we needed help was on the island of Atiu, which the previous administration had decided should be the new pineapple-growing centre for the Cook Islands, if not the South Pacific. The climate and soil were ideal, and the people very industrious. As in Mangaia, the fruit had to be shipped to Rarotonga for processing at Island Foods' factory. We had the pineapples, we had the ships, and we had the factory. The problem was getting the pineapples from the shore to the ship. The landing was about the worst in the whole group.

With the existing system, pineapples were packed in cases, loaded on a trailer and backed down a one-way track to sea level through a cleft in the makatea cliffs. Here they were manhandled case by case into wooden lighters. The lighters, rowed by eight men plus one on a steering oar, negotiated their way to the open ocean, a hundred metres away, through a tiny gut in the reef, thence out to the waiting ship which, if weather conditions were exceptionally favourable, would be anchored close by, otherwise it would stand offshore. More often than not, there was a surge in the passage, and it would take a dozen men on ropes to hold the lighter in place while the cases were loaded. For a lighter to overturn during the passage out to the ship was a not uncommon occurrence, and I have seen many a VIP swimming for his life at Atiu.

I was almost praying for a bad reef when I took the Minister to Atiu, but for once conditions were perfect. However, knowing me of old, Phil believed every word when I described what things could be like. He asked what should be done. I said, 'Burn the pineapples and pay the people to go to New Zealand. It's got to be cheaper than any other solution.'

'Yes, it probably would be,' he said, 'but it's not the way things are done.' I then explained how I thought a practical harbour and lightering facility could be built, providing expense was not a problem.

'See that cleft where the road comes down? There is another like it just a couple of hundred metres further on. You make a road down that one, too, and join them together with a road along the base of the cliff. Traffic can then come down one way and up the other; no more backing trailers. Then you build a solid concrete breakwater along the outer edge of the reef, to enclose the whole area between the cliff and the sea. Then you blast and dredge a harbour within this area, and last of all you open one end of it to let the sea in, not too big an opening, just enough to get lighters in and out. And for lighters you need motorised steel barges like the ones we built for Mangaia, and a small truck-mounted crane for loading them, so the fruit can be packed in decent-sized bins to cut down the handling.' While telling him all this I was sketching the whole thing out on the back of a chart, which he took away with him. He knew that a country carrier from Opononi would know what he was talking about.

I never got my chart back, but we got our harbour on Atiu. Only God and the New Zealand Army knew what it cost.

CHAPTER SEVEN

FLEET OPERATORS

'Dick Brown's dead!' The news stunned the country. The funeral that followed was the biggest funeral in memory, and it was like the passing of an era. Certainly shipping in the Cook Islands was going to lose some of its glamour and excitement. It would be hard to find another Islands shipowner who had survived the loss of so many vessels in a relatively short space of time. There were people who said Dick made his money out of insurance claims, having lost so many ships, but in fact he was paid on only one claim, the *Rannah*, and it is unlikely she was insured above her market value. He certainly didn't die a wealthy shipowner.

The *Bodmer* was mortgaged to the topmasts with Island Foods Ltd. The family wanted nothing to do with it, or any other ship for that matter. Island Foods asked us if we would take it over for the price of the mortgage, payment to be made out of fruit cargoes. No fruit, no pay; it sounded like a Lloyd's Open Salvage Form. It was a big decision to make. The ship had given nothing but trouble, and if it cost us as much as it had cost Dick, it could drag us under. On the other hand, it was a chance to double our fleet without immediate investment, and if we could keep the old girl going, we could make a buck or two. In the end greed won.

We talked to Fellie Hendriks, the Jamaican engineer who had come out with the ship. Better known as Slim, Fellie was as black as they come; even at the end of the day, when he would go ashore shiny-clean and dressed to kill, he would still be as black as the *Bodmer*'s engine-oil. Whether it was his colour, or his ready smile and charming manner, the girls found him irresistible. He also had a winning way with engines, and was ingenious at improvising repairs; nevertheless, the *Bodmer* occasionally got him down.

The main engine was an eight-cylinder two-stroke Widdop, one of only three ever built before the manufacturer went out of business. Spares were unobtainable. Slim explained that the main cause of breakdowns was the scavenge-pump drive system; the drive chain, if it got too slack, would jump the sprockets and break. The loose ends would flail around and jam the drive-crankshaft, and that would break too, and sometimes the casing as well. Then you would wait three months for new parts to be made in England.

We worked out a rigid schedule for adjusting the drive chain, and we installed a standby scavenge-pump driven by its own small diesel auxiliary. As an additional precaution we adjusted the governor, reducing the horsepower of the engine, so that although the ship went a little slower, she had more chance of getting there. During the two and a half years we had her, she made 90 voyages and never had a breakdown. The standby scavenge-pump was never used.

That same year, our partners, CITC, were negotiating to buy out the firm of A.B. Donald Ltd. The problem was what to do with the *Akatere*. CITC didn't want to operate in competition with us, and A.B. Donald didn't want to sell the rest of the business without getting rid of the ship as well. Donalds' general manager, Sam Bennett, came from New Zealand to sort things out, and called us into his office for a 'very confidential' meeting. The meeting was so confidential that, once we were ensconced in the tiny room, Sam tried to shut the door, something that hadn't been tried since the turn of the century probably. The hinges were rusted solid, and Sam had to give it a good shove with his shoulder to move it, whereupon it fell to the floor with a crash, which attracted the attention of everyone in the store, and by the time the sun was over the yard-arm the whole island knew there was something 'very confidential' going on between Silk & Boyd and A.B.Donald.

We bought the ship, so in one year we increased the fleet by 300 per cent. It made a lot of sense to have the three ships under one management. Rationalisation brought economies in operation plus a more regular service. Calls were now more evenly spaced, and in the fruit season there was greater flexibility for handling peaks in production. If properly scheduled, the ships were not fully utilised within the group, and we had the capacity for more work. Government was importing large amounts of fertiliser from Germany, trans-shipped through New Zealand at great cost. By getting it trans-shipped through Tahiti and picking it up in our own ships for discharge directly at the outer islands, we saved government money and put some of the freight content into the local economy — and made a bit for Silk & Boyd as an afterthought. During 1970 and 1971 calls at Papeete were made almost monthly, and it became convenient to do our dry-dockings there instead of in Auckland or Suva.

I found myself spending more time ashore, more in the nature of a fleet superintendent — which sounded pretty imposing — and relieving master. Things were running as smooth as Silk. As Les would say, it couldn't last …

We had a semi-retired Norwegian captain on the *Tagua* known as The Pelican-headed Peanut. Although he was a sober, reliable type and a capable ship-handler, he got caught off-guard for just a few moments one day when they were loading pineapples at Mangaia. Like Atiu, the island is very steep-to, and you have to anchor within spitting distance of the reef. Thus you are totally dependent on the wind to hold the ship off, and constant vigilance is required. The captain realised too late that there was a change of wind and that the ship was swinging in towards the reef. He threw the controls into full ahead and made a grab for the wheel, just as the rudder struck the reef; the wheel kicked and a spoke punctured his abdomen. He survived, but the ship didn't. In moments she was hard and fast, and by the time we got there with the *Bodmer* the following day she was high and dry. We very nearly got her off, but the *Bodmer* just didn't have enough grunt. The *Holmburn* diverted to Mangaia on her way from New Zealand but by that time the *Tagua* was badly holed and beyond salvage. She lay on the reef with her stern overhanging

Mangaia Harbour

the boat passage, and the cost of removing the wreck far exceeded the value of the ship. It was Christmas 1970, and we had lost a third of our fleet. The Pelican-headed Peanut went back to Norway.

The needless loss of the *Tagua* was a sad blow. Although the smallest of the fleet, she carried in total more cargo and passengers than either of the others, and her running costs were far less. The Government was sympathetic, and urged us to find an immediate replacement. Currency restrictions were waived and financial assistance was offered in the form of freight payments in advance. Urgency was the key word. Northern Europe seemed to have lots of small ships for sale, and so did Japan, where prices were cheaper. We decided I should go and look for a ship of 250 tonnes deadweight and not more than ten years old.

I flew to Tokyo and with the help of Jardine Matheson located a handy little coaster in good condition. However, she would need alterations to meet the requirements of the Cook Islands trade, and here I found a major problem. Although there were shipyards ready to start building a super-tanker tomorrow, nobody was interested in making alterations to a small coaster, or, if they could be talked into it, the cost exceeded the value of the ship. After wasting some weeks and much money, I headed for Europe.

The flight across the frozen wastelands of Siberia in a Russian Ilyushin seemed never-ending. I hadn't overcome my allergy to flying and it didn't help when we made a sudden change of course and an unscheduled, unannounced landing in what seemed the middle of nowhere. Armed guards came on board and checked our passports against a manifest but made no comment. It got freezing cold over the next couple of hours. Finally they left and we took off into the darkness. At altitude it got light again, and we saw a remarkable sight — an immense vapour trail from an ascending rocket. Two weeks later the Russians announced the launching of the biggest ever spacecraft with three astronauts on board. (They all died on re-entry.)

Denmark had the best choice of ships in Europe, but it was difficult to find one small enough that wasn't too old. The trend over recent years was towards larger coasters, so little ships of the size we needed were no longer being built. To meet our criterion of not more than ten years old, it was necessary to think in terms of 400 tonnes rather than 250.

In the quaint little seaport of Marstal lay the coaster *Mik*. As with the Angel, it was love at first sight, although, unlike the Angel, I thought she looked too big. By now I had spent 18 years with the Angel and never regretted it. I was to spend the next 18 years with the *Mik* and not regret that either.

Inspection started with the captain's liquor cabinet in the warm confines of his saloon. After a few shots of akvavit with Carlsberg chasers we got down to the business in hand. The wheel-house was a dream, with gadgetry like radar, auto-pilot, echo-sounder, radio direction-finder and engine alarms, never before seen on ships in the Cook Islands. Cargo gear was simple and efficient with two 3-tonne derricks and diesel-driven winches. The hatch was 19 metres long, compared to the *Tagua*'s ten metres (and only five metres before we lengthened her). The only problem was the cost — well over our budget.

The ship sailed for Poland and the following day I had concluded a deal with the owners. I cabled Bob so he could start worrying about how to find more money.

Mik arrived back from Poland and, after dry-docking, the Sale Agreement was concluded. Then began an extremely busy time, for there was much to do before sailing for the Cook Islands. There were two shipyards in Marstal, the larger of which was called the Marstal Staalskibsvaerft og Maskinfabrik (Steel Shipyard and Machine Shop). I tried to get my tongue around the Danish language, but it seemed to be more of a throat complaint than a language.

I met the manager, Joergen Schmidt, a heavy, thickset man with a good sense of humour. On board I explained some of the jobs I needed done:

1. Strip out the fo'c's'le, insulate and install accommodation for seven men, including heads and bathroom facilities, plus additional heads and showers for 70 deck passengers.

2. Strip out the accommodation aft and install new accommodation for captain, engineer and 20 cabin passengers.

3. Fit hydraulic slewing winches to both derricks.

4. Clean out the forepeak tank and install the necessary plumbing for it to be used as a fuel tank.

5. Electrically test all generators, motors and circuits.

6. Remove the existing name and weld the new name, *Manuvai*, on both sides and on the stern, along with the new port of registry.

'Mr Silk, why don't we just build you a new ship?'

We split the work between Marstal's two yards, Schmidt doing mostly the steel and engineering work, and the Marstal Traeskibsvaerft (Wooden Shipyard) doing the accommodation. There was friendly rivalry between the yard gangs, and a competitive spirit to see who was going to get their part done first. There didn't appear to be any union demarcations; a chippy seemed free to pick up a welding torch or run a bit of wiring if he wanted to. Other small firms were employed, including the town's electrician, and the upholsterer, who made all the mattress covers and canvas awnings. We seemed to have the whole town working for us, and merchants and professional people were all taking an interest in this ship which was going off to the South Seas. At the bank the manager himself would always come to attend to me and at the post office I could never pass by without sharing an akvavit or two with the postmaster. Everybody seemed so friendly, it was like being back home. At the stationery shop I introduced myself to the proprietor and he said, 'This is my name here,' pointing to the invoice he had just written out. It said 'Wilhelms Boghandel'.

'Pleased to meet you, Mr Boghandel,' I said holding out my hand.

'No, no,' he said, 'my name is "Wilhelms". "Boghandel" means "Bookshop".'

There were other matters to attend to, like finding a crew and cargo, plus arranging insurance and the registration as a British Ship, and de-registration as a Danish one. I announced that I would be away for a few days. 'Aha!' they said, 'going up to Copenhagen to see a few live shows, I suppose.' I didn't have much time to spend on live shows, only enough to broaden my cultural background. I thought it would be a fair while before we saw anything like it in the Cook Islands — live or otherwise.

With the help of the shipbroker, John Cahnbley, and the British Consul, Mr Ridpath, the considerable paper work was completed and a Provisional Certificate of British Registry for the Port of Suva was issued. I now had ship's papers, and bought a briefcase to carry them in. Catching the North Sea ferry to England, I arrived in Harwich where a black Pakistani immigration official glanced at my arrival card. 'President of the Cook Islands?' he asked.

'Well, no,' I said. 'There's a full-stop after the "P". It means Permanent Resident of the Cook Islands.'

'Welcome to my country,' he said.

In London I donned my suit and, briefcase in hand, headed for the City. I felt a bit naked without a bowler and brolly, walking down

Leadenhall Street, right past Cunard House, where in bygone days I would call for mail, and perhaps a small 'sub', or advance, on my salary of seven pounds a month.

At 142 The Minories I called in at Bradley British Overseas Ltd, a subsidiary of Jardine Matheson, and explained that I was associated with their client company, Cook Islands Trading Company, and got treated like royalty. 'Do come in. We are always happy to see anyone from the Islands.'

I explained my mission. I needed insurance, cargo, a crew and an office. 'Well, just make yourself at home. You can use Mr Catlin's office — he's travelling. Help yourself to the telex machine. If you need to make long-distance calls we have IDD. What? Never heard of it?' I explained that in the Cook Islands we just turned a handle and asked for a number.

'It's nearly lunch time. We'll go for a pint before you get started.'

At the impressive offices of Jardine Matheson I received equal attention and hospitality; the magic of 'the Islands' was working wonders. Insurance for the voyage was soon put in hand. They took me around the corner to Lloyd's and gave me a conducted tour of that historic institution. In the Loss Register was written, in exquisite copper-plate, brief details of the loss of the *Tagua*: 'Stranded on the reef at Mangaia, 21 55,S, 157 58,W. 14th Dec 1970. Total Constructive Loss,' it said. And hanging there was the famous Lutine Bell, which is still rung on the news of a major loss. I doubt if they rang it for the *Tagua*.

At New Zealand House in the Haymarket they had been advised by the Cook Islands Government of my impending arrival. I was starting to feel quite important. The wheels of commerce were in motion to try to secure a cargo. They allowed me to pin a notice on their bulletin board to the effect that young Kiwis wanting to get home could apply to work their way on the *Manuvai* to Rarotonga.

Back in Marstal I found work proceeding apace, but there was still much to do. Besides the work in the shipyards there were a thousand and one things to attend to. For the long voyage ahead and subsequent operations in a remote area, much thought had to be given to spare parts for the main engine and all the machinery and electrical equipment on board. We had to carry lifesaving equipment for 100 people, rather than her previous complement of five. These people had to have sufficient fresh water for a three-week voyage; some of them had to be fed, all had to have shelter. Storage was required for food, including frozen food,

Tagua on the reef at Mangaia

and galley equipment and bedding was needed for 20 cabin passengers and nine crew. For the voyage we needed a variety of lube oils and greases, plus sufficient LP gas for cooking, as well as paint, paintbrushes and scrapers. There were charts and pilot books to be found for the intended route, and Light Lists and the Admiralty Lists of Radio Signals.

Replies to my advertisement for crew started coming in. One applicant wrote, 'I want to come to the Cook Islands. My mother is an Atiuan, and my father was a missionary.' Another wrote, 'My total sea-going experience has been crewing on my friend's yacht around the Hauraki Gulf.' I made him the first mate. Yet another letter said, 'I am only a girl, but I can cook.' That solved another problem.

I could only interview them by phone, but I reckoned that any young Kiwi who had enough initiative to get to London and work for a year or two couldn't be all that bad. Three blokes and two girls joined the ship and they turned out to be a great bunch, willing workers and good company. The mate and the cook found each other to be very good company, and got married when they reached New Zealand. The Provisional Certificate of Marriage I gave them was good only for the duration of the voyage. (These certificates were to became a popular feature of Silk & Boyd cruises.)

But I still had no engineer. Bob was trying to send Slim but, with no planes and a dearth of passenger ships, it was difficult getting him out of Rarotonga. It looked as though Slim would have to catch up with us on the way. The previous captain, Hans Filipson, had been helping me in various ways and now he offered to come as engineer for the first part of the voyage. This worked out well and he was able to give me a good grounding in running the engine-room.

It was a month since the *Mik* had arrived in Marstal. I cabled Bob: 'Sailing tomorrow ETA Rarotonga August 30th.' The latter date was a wild guestimate, but it was to prove surprisingly accurate.

Our first port was Copenhagen, where we loaded a consignment of Tuborg beer for the Cook Islands Liquor Store. The brewery kindly donated 20 cartons for the crew, not realising there were only seven of us on board. From Copenhagen we went down to Kiel, through the canal, and on to Bremen in Germany, where a load of fertiliser for the Cook Islands Agriculture Department was ready for us. Hans flew back to Denmark and Slim arrived the following day.

Traffic in the North Sea and the English Channel is heavy and we would pass more ships in an hour than we would see in the Cook Islands in a year. There wasn't much sleep for me until we cleared Ushant on the northwest tip of France, and had the whole Atlantic Ocean before us. I told the lads, 'Wake me when you see Panama.'

It was now midsummer and the Atlantic didn't have many thrills to offer. It was a contrast to a crossing I had made from Falmouth to New

The author

York in the old *Port Chalmers* in the severe winter of 1947-8, when we encountered gales the whole way. Our steering gear broke down and we steered by the engines, until one engine broke down and we wallowed in the trough of gigantic seas. Our cargo of motorcars broke loose, and another ship foundered not far from us. Quite an experience for a lad off the farm.

This crossing was to be a dream. The further south we sailed, the warmer it got and all hands soon had their shirts off working on deck in the sun. In the evening we would have a happy hour in the wheel-house and work on the Tuborg, helped along with the 11 bottles of akvavit we found in the captain's bonded locker. I was determined not to arrive in Rarotonga with any for Customs to seize.

In Cristobal we berthed at the oil dock for bunkers. Anchored not far away was a 15-metre ketch with rather pleasing lines. The name *Jonathan Swift* rang a bell and sure enough we soon had a visit from two old friends, Tig Loe and Bo Bergh. They were delivering the yacht to the Pacific after doing a couple of years chartering in the Caribbean. Bo was an old hand in the Caribbean and had spent years in various maritime adventures, some of them quite legal.

We had to wait our turn to go through the canal, so we repaired to the yacht club and made serious inroads into their stocks of beer. Back on board I introduced Tig to akvavit (Bo being a Swede needed no introduction), and left them in the mess-room while I met the pilot in the wheel-house.

By this time the crew had become pretty handy on board, but nobody had yet learned to steer the ship as we had always been on auto-pilot. I wasn't looking forward to steering all the way through the canal by myself, especially after a skinful of beer at the yacht club, so while Tig and Bo were enjoying their akvavit, we quietly cast off, and by the time they came up to see what was happening we were heading towards Gatun locks. I introduced them to the pilot as the two quartermasters who would be doing the steering through the Canal, and slunk away for a nap. It was as well I had some help, for the pilot was an unfriendly type, not about to take a turn at the wheel himself; he preferred to sit in a corner giving the orders. He may have thought we were just a bunch of piss-heads.

After clearing Miraflores lock in the early hours of the morning I explained to the pilot that Tig and Bo would go ashore in the pilot launch with him. 'Like hell,' he said, 'only the pilot goes ashore in the pilot launch.' That was what *he* thought. As he climbed over the rail into the pilot launch, Tig and Bo leapt across in unison right behind him, as if they had rehearsed it a thousand times. I slammed the engine control into full ahead and away we went down the the channel and out into the wide Pacific. We never heard from Tig or Bo for years. For a while we asked every yacht passing through if they knew of Tig or Bo, or the *Jonathan Swift*, but they seemed to have vanished off the earth. Then one day Bo blew in, skippering a yacht for some lady, and brought me up to date …

When they got ashore in Balboa on the pilot launch, the authorities gave them a hard time, and they got thrown in the cooler until they could establish their identities — but that was only the start of the story. After transiting the canal they spent some time in the Perlas Archipelago in the Gulf of Panama, and there they were blown ashore and dismasted. They got the boat off and made their way back to Balboa, but they were denied entry to the Canal Zone, even for repairs. They got the boat up a creek in the Republic of Panama, miles from anywhere, and did the repairs, including building a new mast. Bo said it was heavy going without any proper facilities, and not a pub for miles.

By this time they had had enough of the *Jonathan Swift* and decided to sail her up to the States and sell her, which they did. 'But it took a while,' said Bo. 'Hell of a trip actually, getting past all those bars up the coast of Central America and Mexico.' I assumed he was talking about sandbars.

From Panama our course took a dog-leg southwest to the Galapagos Islands to pick up the Humboldt Current and the South Equatorial Current. The Humboldt Current sweeps up the coast of South America, bringing cold water and even penguins from the Antarctic, before swinging west across the Pacific as the South Equatorial Current.

Crossing the Equator at Isabella Island, the crew were glad to don warm jerseys while they gazed at sea elephants basking on the barren rocky shore. We anchored for a few hours in Tagus Cove and added *Manuvai* to the hundreds of yacht names painted on the surrounding cliffs. A couple of the boys were about to go swimming but were deterred by the sight of a pair of huge manta rays resting in the shade of the ship. The water was freezing cold for swimming anyway. Mindful of the experience of Captain Derek Lumbers of the brigantine *Yankee* who lost an American tourist without trace on nearby Floreana Island in 1964, I warned the crew not to stray too far inland. The dry landscape with tangled thickets of wiry bushes didn't encourage nature walks as it turned out.

The *Manuvai*

The currents helped us on our way, adding 20 miles to each day's run. Soon the weather was warm again, and the sea really blue. Flying fish skimmed the surface and were eagerly gathered from the deck each morning. Skirting north of the Tuamotus, we passed close by the phosphate island of Makatea, now worked out, where 12 years ago, in 1959, we met our first Cook Islanders and had decided to call at Rarotonga. It seemed an age ago.

A brief call at Papeete for bunkers, then on our way again. It looked as though we would meet our guestimated ETA of 30 August, but two days out of Raro we received a message, 'PLEASE DIVERT TO ATIU PICK UP SICK PATIENT REGARDS HEALTH'. It was only a small diversion, but as we had to wait for daylight to load the patient, it delayed us a day, and we didn't arrive in Rarotonga until 1 September 1971.

'You're late,' called Bob as he caught our first line.

There was a nice welcoming committee on the wharf, with speeches and dancing girls, the latter much appreciated. Customs didn't want to know about liquor or anything else. Everybody said what a nice ship she was, and over the next 18 years she carried more cargo and more people than any other ship in the history of the Cook Islands. She made thousands of landfalls, all but one of them successful.

CHAPTER EIGHT

GOING INTERNATIONAL

There was great excitement when in 1968 New Zealand announced that it would build an international airport on Rarotonga, something that had been mooted for years. There was much speculation on what changes would come about with the advent of a direct jet-service to New Zealand, and it was mind-boggling to think that Auckland would be only four hours away. The monopoly on passenger travel would move from the *Moana Roa* to Air New Zealand, and thinking about that, what would become of the *Moana Roa*? Without the need to carry passengers, the run could be serviced by a conventional vessel — or a tug and barge. Canadian impressions flooded in on me.

If the *Moana Roa* with her crew of 40 could be replaced by a tug crewed by six or eight men, towing an unmanned barge, the savings would be enormous. Even supposing the tug was New Zealand-manned, it should still require less than a dozen crew. In addition, stevedoring costs and port-time could be slashed. Lighterage could be eliminated at Rarotonga, for a barge could be berthed in Avatiu Harbour and discharged in a day. I only wished I had spent as much time on ocean-going tugs as I had on the *Brainstorm* on the Yukon River. Bob thought I should make another trip to Canada and get the full story. I said I supposed I would have to.

At the offices of Island Tug and Barge in Vancouver I explained what we had in mind and asked if I could pick their brains. They not only allowed me to pick their brains, they gave me all the help I could possibly wish for, as if it were their own project, and even found me a berth on one of their tugs for a trip down to the States towing a barge loaded with 4000 tons of crushed limestone. The tug's crew of six operated the unloading machinery on the barge and the 4000 tonnes was discharged in six hours.

The most spectacular operation was one of their new self-dumping log barges, which by flooding ballast tanks discharged her deck cargo of 10,000 tonnes in 45 minutes, but of most interest to me was their barge *Island Express*. This 2000-tonne barge was doing a weekly run out of Vancouver, calling at ten ports around Vancouver Island delivering general cargo and back-loading newsprint. The barge was like a floating warehouse and was loaded by forklifts in one day. It seemed tailor-made for the Auckland-Rarotonga service. The tug had a crew of six.

Island Tug and Barge introduced me to the naval architect who did most of their work, and using information I was able to give him, he designed a tug specifically for the job. I was able to take preliminary drawings back to Rarotonga with me. It was to be 37 metres long and have 2600 horsepower.

I arrived back in Rarotonga bursting with contagious enthusiasm. Bob was immediately infected, and so was Neil McKegg as soon as his cautious solicitor's mind was convinced the idea was indeed practicable. Albert Henry was quite ecstatic at the possibility of a Cook Islands-owned-and-operated shipping service running to New Zealand and promised his full support. There was a lot of preparation and research to be done, but by September 1968 we were able to present Wellington with a draft proposal to put a tug and barge service into operation by the time the new airport opened in late 1970 or early 1971. We needed the blessing of the New Zealand Government to smooth over union and regulatory problems, but, more important, their assurance that they would withdraw the *Moana Roa*. Since the *Moana Roa* was losing millions, we assumed this to be a foregone conclusion. We should have known better.

An inter-departmental committee was set up to study our proposal. Meanwhile there was a lot more research to be done on our part, collating figures on import and export tonnages, seasonal variations, predictions for future years, not to mention operating and maintenance costs for the proposed vessels. Quotations were sought from shipyards around the world for building the vessels, and financial accommodation had to be arranged.

All this was heavy going, working from Rarotonga, which was without the benefit of telex or even airmail. International phone calls could be made only by going to the communications centre and waiting your turn, hoping radio reception would be favourable. What we needed was one of us to live in Auckland, but there weren't any volunteers. Besides, we were both pretty busy, for during this period we were acquiring the *Bodmer* and the *Akatere* and negotiating with shipyards for an early replacement of one of them. The idea of a New Zealand partner for the tug and barge venture came to mind, and Harry Julian's name was mentioned as having a reputation around the waterfront in Auckland for getting things done. Also, he seemed be to one of the few people in New Zealand who had any experience with tugs and barges.

We sent word to Harry; was he interested in some sort of joint venture? Next thing, Harry arrived in Rarotonga, having pulled strings and got a ride on an Air Force Hercules. He was very good at that sort of thing. Harry proved a real live-wire and go-getter, perhaps just the sort of partner we laidback beachcombers needed. We immediately formed a company, Cook Islands Shipping Co. Ltd, with Silk & Boyd Ltd and Harry Julian holding equal shares. We appointed Harry general manager, as he would be doing most of the work and making the day-to-day decisions. (It wasn't long before Harry was making all the decisions.)

It was now two years since my trip to Vancouver. Negotiations with the inter-departmental committee in Wellington were frustrating to say the least. Shipbuilding costs around the world were escalating alarmingly, and yards were now incorporating escalation clauses into contracts. It would take the best part of a year, if not longer, to get the tug and barge on stream, and Harry suggested we start off chartering a small vessel to share in the large volumes of cargo being generated by the airport construction and related activities.

Dredging was proceeding in Avatiu Harbour and, although it was never anticipated that it would ever accommodate ships the size of the *Moana Roa*, by October 1970 depths of 3.5 metres had been reached. Atholl Rusden's refrigerated vessel *Thallo* was available, able to carry 500 tonnes deadweight on a draft of 3.5 metres, and, although she was a bit small for the trade, the indications were that she would be a commercially viable proposition if manned by an Island crew. She already had a Fijian crew with New Zealand officers and there were rumblings from the unions in New Zealand, but as there weren't any New Zealand-manned vessels available, they closed their eyes and we took the ship on a year's charter. She would be the first 'big' ship to berth in Avatiu Harbour, and there was nobody more keen to see it happen than Albert Henry, who had been advised by experts, including Alec Fraser, captain of the *Moana Roa*, that nobody in his right mind would take a big ship through that narrow passage into Avatiu Harbour. I asked the harbour engineer, Win Ryan, would he have 3.5 metres by the time the ship arrived. 'Yes, of course,' he said. 'Albert says there has to be!'

Thallo, the first 'big ship' in Avatiu Harbour

The day before the *Thallo* arrived Bob and I paddled around and took soundings. It looked pretty doubtful, but a reception had already been arranged, and the harbour engineer had said there was sufficient water. We had to give it a go.

I went out to pilot the vessel in. Captain John Sutherland asked, 'Is there enough water?' 'Certainly,' I replied. 'Bob and I took soundings yesterday, and the harbour engineer confirmed it just today!' So we steamed very slowly in through the passage. The wharf was gaily decorated. There were rows of chairs for dignitaries. Dancing girls were in attendance. The Boy's Brigade struck up *When the Saints Come Marching In* (always a favourite at the opening of Parliament). We were about nine metres from the wharf when John said, 'We don't seem to be moving.'

'Give her a bit more power,' I said.

'I think we're aground.'

'Then you must be drawing more than 3.5 metres,' I replied.

'Bullshit!'

So there we sat, about nine metres from the wharf. Albert Henry had been unable to attend, and left things in charge of the Deputy Premier, Apenera Short. The harbour engineer had taken to the hills. The Boy's

Brigade Band had gone right through their repertoire, and the crowd was getting restless. Apenera called out from the wharf, 'I say, Don, when is the ship going to come alongside?'

'When there's enough bloody water!' I replied. I could have swallowed my tongue when I realised the language I had used addressing the Deputy Premier in front of the crowd, but it seemed to go unnoticed.

We got the Union Company lighters to come around and we offloaded deck cargo until the ship was light enough to get alongside. There weren't any wharf sheds as yet, but we had knocked up a bit of a lean-to, thatched with kikau, or coconut fronds. We had no forklifts or modern gear but we did have plenty of willing manpower. We got the job done and turned the ship around in a couple of days. Everyone was impressed. Avatiu was now a deep-sea port!

We had a successful year with the *Thallo*. By the second voyage there really was enough water in the harbour. She was always full leaving Auckland, and often full with fruit and canned juice on the voyage south. Although too small, she actually made money for us, which sort of proved something. But the threat of union intervention was always there.

At this time Matt Thompson of Car Haulaways was trying to establish a tug and barge service on the New Zealand coast, mainly for transporting vehicles between the North and South Islands. The few trips he made proved that the cost savings could be enormous, but the unions were not about to allow that sort of thing, and soon had him closed down. The message to us was loud and clear: we were at their mercy. Investing a million dollars in a tug and barge began to look a bit dicey.

The *Thallo*'s charter ran out and we looked for something bigger, beause now we had an alleged four metres of water in the harbour. We found the *Lorena*, or Harry did — we were hardly consulted these days. We had been operating the *Thallo* with a Fijian crew, but now the unions said we had to have a New Zealand crew. We appealed to both governments: here was a ship belonging to a Cook Islands company, carrying cargo for the Cook Islands — what the hell did it have to do with those bastards? But the governments, although sympathetic, were afraid of rocking any boats. Without a New Zealand crew, the wharfies wouldn't load the ship. It was, in effect, government by union.

Trying to operate a ship with a New Zealand crew was like pushing sewage uphill with a broomstick. The *Lorena* was doomed from voyage one. They had completed loading in Auckland and were ready to sail when the union rep informed the captain they needed television sets on board. For Rarotonga? At Rarotonga the ship was ready to sail and the crew had failed to report on board. Bob went looking and found them in the Banana Court. They said they weren't sailing until tomorrow. Bob said the ship had to sail before dark and if they didn't come right away the captain would sail without them. 'Let him try!' they said. Bob reported to the captain, who said, 'I don't need them. I'll sail without them.'

Bob pleaded with him to wait outside the harbour, fearing repercussions in Auckland. He then saw the Chief of Police, Tangata Nekeare, who sent a sergeant along to the Banana Court to tell them that if they didn't join the launch which would be waiting for them in half an hour, they would spend the following month in jail waiting for the ship to come back. They had seen the ship sail, and the union delegate was already on the phone to Auckland. They joined the launch, but that was the last voyage that that particular captain made with the Cook Islands Shipping Company.

Bob and I had had a gutsful. We didn't need this kind of nonsense. It wasn't our scene. We gave our shares to Harry, who then sold them to the Cook Islands Government. She was a good ship for the job, and made over 60 voyages. Properly manned, she could have made money, but she wasn't, and didn't.

There had never been any system of crew training in the Cook Islands. Sailors just came up through the hawse pipe. Some stayed a few trips; a few made it their career, but there was no way they could ever hope to get beyond a job of non-qualified mate. No amount of experience would qualify them for acceptance into the New Zealand Seamen's Union, which was a closed shop. The same applied to engineers; no matter how brilliantly you applied yourself, there just wasn't any machinery in place whereby you could sit any kind of certificate that entitled you to call yourself an engineer, as far as the authorities were concerned.

There were all kinds of educational scholarships available for Cook Islands students to study overseas, not only in New Zealand, but also at the University of the South Pacific in Suva and Avele College in Apia. There was nothing available in the maritime field, although Fiji had a School of Maritime Studies where Fijians could train to become deck officers and engineers. We inquired if it might be possible to sponsor a

Cook Islands trainee in their engineering section, and after some correspondence and a lot of help from Ken Mills, a great friend of Cook
Islanders living in Suva, we got Lance Simiona accepted into the school.
The son of an Aitutaki trader, Lance disappointed his father by leaving
home instead of carrying on the family business (which continued very
well without him). Large and jovial, and a ball of energy, he had a
natural bent for anything mechanical. The Millses accepted Lance into
their home as a boarder for a nominal fee, and they assured us he wasn't
much trouble, apart from chopping down their favourite breadfruit tree
with the best of intentions. Lance completed his three-year course with
flying colours and got his chief's ticket, something to be proud of. It
made us feel good too, and Lance became a dedicated employee for
years after.

With this encouragement we got two more students enrolled over a
period of three years as trainee deck officers, and for these the New
Zealand Government picked up the tab for the expenses, other than
wages. Paranapa Ben gained his Certificate of Competency as Master,
Pacific Islands, enabling him to command ships anywhere in the Pacific,
including in and out of Australia and New Zealand. The next step was
to get our own Port of Registry in the Cook Islands, enabling us to fly
our own flag, but this was to be a long way down the track. Many
people believed this was the only stumbling block preventing us running
Cook Islands-manned vessels to New Zealand. We weren't so sure.

The superiority of the *Manuvai* over the other two ships was immediately
obvious. Larger and faster, with more modern equipment, it was clear
that with another ship like her, we could easily handle the trade with
only two ships. The *Akatere* and *Bodmer* were old and tired and uneco-
nomic by comparison. They had to go. It would be easier to sell them
once they had done their annual survey.

The Cook Islands wished to send a strong contingent to the South
Pacific Games in Tahiti in 1972, since it was close to home and wouldn't
cost much to get there. All three ships sailed for Tahiti in February with
a capacity load of passengers, and while the games were in progress we
put both *Akatere* and *Bodmer* on the French naval floating dock. A Lloyd's
surveyor flew from New Zealand and the surveys were completed, in
spite of the appalling heat, torrential rain, and everyone having the spirit
of the games at heart, and other spirits down their throats. A buyer flew

in and bought the *Bodmer* subject to delivery to Apia, and another buyer wanted *Akatere* delivered to Suva. Although both ships sold, the expense of their surveys was probably wasted, for they were never maintained in Class afterwards. The *Bodmer* eventually sank alongside the Starkist Dock in Pago Pago, and the *Akatere* foundered in Suva Harbour.

Being Tahiti, life here also had its lighter moments. We had engaged an additional engineer to assist with the survey work. Dick was a Yorkshireman, in the South Seas for the first time. Like many Englishmen, he arrived with preconceived ideas of free love and so on, and was just itching to contribute to this intriguing way of life. His chance came when, heading back towards the ship on his rent-a-bike late one night, he stalled at the traffic lights outside the 'Whisky-a-Gogo', just as the patrons were pouring out at closing time. By chance he happened to exchange glances with a gorgeous creature on the footpath, and in less time than it took to kick-start the Lambretta, he had a pillion passenger aboard and, with arms encircling his hips, he roared off towards the docks.

Once on board ship, Dick lost no time in carrying out a loadline survey and, finding little offering up for'ard, began concentrating on the area of double bottoms, checking on ballast and discharge lines as you would expect of a good engineer. It was a bit dark in the cabin and much of his work was being done by feel, so it was with total shock that he suddenly found himself with a fistful of gonads, and realised he had a fafafine on his hands, or rather, in his bed. Well, it wasn't in his bed for long; Dick went berserk, and it was a miracle there wasn't murder done. He was never the same again, and returned to Yorkshire a broken man. As if we didn't have enough problems, our cook went mad on the way home, finding a demon in his watch. The demon instructed him to jump overboard, and he had to be forcibly restrained from doing so. He later died in a mental hospital in New Zealand.

We took everybody home after the Games, and sent the *Bodmer* off round the Northern Group on her final trip. She arrived back with a full load of copra and after tying up in port the crew whistled ashore for the weekend. That same evening the *Holmburn* arrived from New Zealand with a full load of cement for the airport. She went aground broadside across the harbour while trying to turn around. *Akatere* was also in port. Then out of nowhere appeared Hurricane Agatha.

With the *Holmburn* aground and blocking the entrance, there was no chance of the *Akatere* or *Bodmer* getting out, and if this hurricane developed into a major one there was a good chance of losing all three ships, plus blocking the harbour for an extended period.

We anchored the *Akatere* in the middle of the harbour, with lines out either side and astern. Archie and his crew stayed on board all night, keeping the propeller turning ahead to take the weight off the anchor cables. There wasn't room to anchor the *Bodmer* as well, so we tied her to the wharf on the eastern side with all the lines we could find.

As the sea rose with the northerly wind and the drop in barometric pressure, so did the level of water in the harbour, and the *Holmburn* was able to complete her turning manoeuvre and put to sea, although it was really touch and go and she only succeeded due to good luck and the superb seamanship of her captain.

By this time it was pitch dark and we were fighting to hold the *Bodmer* to the wharf with 40 lines out. There was no hope that we could let all lines go simultaneously and get her under way before she bore down on the *Akatere* with the probable destruction of both ships. So we hung on and battled all night, joining lines as quickly as they parted, in between running for our lives as waves surged across the wharf.

Shortly before dawn the wind switched to the west and the harbour soon quietened. At daylight we surveyed the scene; there were 47 lines holding the *Bodmer* to the wharf. We seemed to have used every piece of rope in Rarotonga. Five days later she was on her way to her new owners in Apia, and two days after that I was on my way to Europe to find a replacement.

We had been keeping in touch with shipbrokers in Europe and had the market pretty well sussed out before I left. There was a ship for sale in Holland somewhat similar to *Manuvai,* so I headed straight for Rotterdam, where Rudy Dee ran a brokerage and chartering business under the name of Supervision Shipping and Chartering. Almost all his business seemed to be done on the telephone or by telex, and he seldom saw his clients. Super-tankers and bulk carriers were bought, sold or fixed on charter without his leaving his office. I was bemused that he could find time for me and my itty bitty coaster, but I was treated with the utmost deference and the deal with the ship was concluded with the minimum of formalities. It seemed that even in this day and age a man's word was as good as his bond, at least in shipbroking circles in Europe. (I was to learn it was different in Australia, when involved in the purchase of the very same ship some years later.)

The *Trio* was the last of three sister-ships, the others having been already sold; in fact it looked as though the whole Dutch coastal fleet was being disposed of, and I lost no time making up my mind on her. She was still trading, and while waiting for delivery and inspection on dry-dock I went across to London and, again with the help of Bradley British Overseas Ltd, I soon had my office in the City and started to get a crew together and look for some cargo.

My father, now a widower, had come to England for a holiday and was looking forward to joining me for the trip back to Rarotonga. One day I suggested we visit some of the old battlefields in France. Dad's regiment had been the élite New Zealand Rifle Brigade and their last fight had been to liberate the town of Le Quesnoy in northern France. This ancient town was (and still is) surrounded by walls and moats which presented a formidable obstacle to the attacking party, but after intense fire and bombardment by trench mortars, and with the help of a scaling ladder, the New Zealanders were over the wall before the Germans knew what was happening.

Dad missed all the fun, for he stopped a bullet in the face as they approached the town through the woods at daylight and spent the rest of the war in hospital. It was fortunate it didn't kill him, or we would both have missed an interesting day 54 years later.

Arriving at Le Quesnoy, I parked our rental car and we headed for the town hall where in my broken French I explained that this was my father, an old soldier from the World War I. I didn't have to say any more. The whole staff gathered around, and we were soon ushered into the office of the Mayor, where a large New Zealand flag decorated one wall, while on another was a painting of the scaling of the ramparts.

The Mayor was most effusive and couldn't do enough for us. He had his staff prepare the mayoral limousine, and personally took us on a tour of the town. Several of the streets had New Zealand names, including 'Rue de Nouvelle-Zélande' and 'Avenue d'honneur des Neo-Zélandais'. We were taken to see where the actual scaling took place, and there, let into the wall, was a large plaque showing a replica of the painting in the Mayor's office, with the words 'In honour of the gallant men of New Zealand through whose valour the town of Le Quesnoy was restored to France 4th November 1918'. I asked the Mayor why there were a lot of withered wreaths and flowers around. 'Don't you realise,' he said, 'last Tuesday was Anzac Day. Every Anzac Day the children are marched down here and told the story of the liberation.'

By the time we had visited the war cemetery, where there were about 50 New Zealand graves, it was eight o'clock and the Mayor then took us to the nearest estaminet where we were introduced all round and had much refreshment pressed upon us. A hotel was arranged for us to stay at, and at some late hour we were delivered to it — or so I believe.

We returned to Rotterdam in time to take delivery of the ship. The formalities of changing ownership, changing the flag and changing the name all went smoothly enough. To choose a name, Bob had sponsored a competition at Tereora College, the prize being a trip to any Southern Group island. (Some wag was heard to remark that the second prize was two trips.) There were over 120 entries, some of them very humorous and original, like Dosibobo, and it was no mean task picking the winner, which was *Manutea*, meaning 'white bird'.

After dry-docking and a few repairs and alterations, we loaded a full cargo of bagged fertiliser for the Republic of Panama and headed out into the North Sea and the English Channel. The weather was kind to us, and remained so for the whole of the Atlantic crossing. It was really great having Dad with me on this trip. We hadn't seen enough of each other over the years, and we had a great time going over the past.

In the depth of the Depression Dad had bought a farm, or rather a 360-acre block of land which he tried to turn into a farm, so that at least he would have something to leave his two sons. Much of the land was in native bush, most of which the loggers had been through years before. Some bush had been felled and burned, and the rest had been cleared but had reverted to gorse and ti-tree. There wasn't a fence on the whole place, and the only building was an old house which had originally been the logging camp. This became the family homestead. The land was situated at the head of the Tauranga Valley, outside Whangaroa Harbour, and we had a great view right down the valley to the sea, and could occasionally see North Cape, 95 kilometres away.

Gradually we built up a herd of dairy cows, built a cowshed, and raised pigs and chickens. The cows were milked by hand and many a time I would fall asleep against a cow in the process of milking her. After milking came the hard part, separating the cream with a hand-turned separator, until the herd reached 16 in number and we bought a milking machine driven by an ancient single-cylinder petrol engine.

My brother Brian was four and a half years older than I was and rode off on horseback to school every day. When I reached five I rode behind him. Our saddle was a chaff sack, and for the first two kilometres we towed a sledge behind us down to the road where it would be left with its can of cream. Matangirau Native School was a bit under five kilometres away, and for the first few years we were the only Pakeha kids; it never occurred to us that we were a racial minority at school. After school we would catch the horse in the horse-paddock and pick up the sledge on the way home with the empty cream can from the previous day, along with the mail and anything else the cream-truck had left. Once home it would be just about milking time again.

We must have had the makings of a good-quality herd, for Brian and I always did well at the school calf competitions. There was also a calf-judging competition where we had to judge the merits of other calves and compare the results with those of the judge. It was all done scientif-ically, with points allocated for different parts of the animal, even down to the number of teats on their little embryo udders.

Depression years slipped behind us and things gradually became more prosperous. The price of bobby calves went up from two shillings to half-a-crown and Dad showed me the difference between these two coins so I could make sure the truck driver didn't short-change me. The big breakthrough into affluence came with the purchase of a car, a 1928 Chev tourer, and now we were able to make fortnightly trips into Kaeo, and once a year to Auckland, the latter being a major adventure. I was given a few shillings to spend and left pretty much to my own devices. The waterfront proved to have an irresistible attraction and for threepence I could buy a return ticket on the ferry to Devonport. I found that if I didn't get off, I could ride back and forth all day on the same ticket. This probably instilled in me a latent propensity for stowing away on ships.

Other acquisitions came with the rise in the price of butterfat. We got the telephone on by running our own line to the nearest neighbour, two kilometres away, and joining the party line, with the permission of the other 12 subscribers already on it. Another big event was the radio. A family friend was coming to spend Christmas with us, and he promised to bring his homemade radio with him. We had prior instructions on how to rig up an aerial and also an earth, which was two golden syrup tins buried in the ground outside the kitchen window. The great day arrived and the equipment was assembled on the kitchen table after the evening meal; our friend donned his earphones amidst much crackling and staticky noises. Suddenly there was a brilliant flash and a cloud of smoke, and there ended our introduction to the world of radio. Later we did get our own receiver, a rather massive affair which ran off a 12-volt battery. The battery had to be carried to the cowshed for charging by the milking-machine engine, and many happy evenings were spent listening to 'Tales of Cappy Ricks' and 'Khyber and Beyond'. It also saved the three-kilometre walk to the nearest neighbour with a radio to listen to the All Blacks playing the Springboks.

Dad always listened to the BBC news before going out in the morning, and one morning he woke me to tell me that we were now at war with Germany. He must have given a lot of thought to this eventuality and was all for rushing off to fight the Germans, but what to do with the farm? Brian was already away at high school and I was only eleven, so my offer to run the farm while he sorted out the Huns wasn't taken all that seriously. A compromise was reached when all returned servicemen were called up to form the National Military Reserve. Uniforms were issued, and later rifles as well, and parades held in Kaeo every Sunday. I became adept at cleaning brass buttons, and a fair shot with a .303.

The entry of Japan suddenly brought the war closer to home. The National Military Reserve was mobilised, Brian had left school and couldn't wait to join the Air Force, and I became Farmer Don, doing high-school lessons by correspondence in my spare time.

Dad had been trying to sell the farm, but it wasn't a seller's market. In the end we had a clearing sale of all the stock and implements, and walked off the land. It was a crying shame after all the work that had gone into it, especially now that it was producing results. But who said wars were fun? Secretly, I thought if I never had to wash mud off a cow's teats again it wouldn't bother me that much.

Apart from Bill Smith, our engineer, all the crew were new to ships, but once we got away from port all hands quickly settled into routine at sea. Our course across the Atlantic took us through the Azores, where we went close by one or two of the islands. Horsemen herded cattle in small fields fenced by stone walls. Picturesque whitewashed houses and churches added to the peaceful look, but I still didn't feel that much urge to go farming. The days got warmer as we headed southwest and good weather enabled us to do quite a bit of carpentry on board, fitting extra bunks in cabins in preparation for carrying passengers in the Cook Islands.

Once through the Panama Canal we turned up the coast, almost as far as the border with Costa Rica. Our destination was the tiny port of Pedrigal, 16 kilometres up the Chiriqui River. The Pilot Book didn't have much good to say about the river, describing it as 'intricate and dangerous and the services of a pilot are absolutely essential; the channel is only available for vessels drawing less than ten feet of water, and then only at high tide'. We waited for high tide, and even then bounced heavily several times before we were over the bar.

The Chiriqui River got narrower and narrower, then we branched off into the Rio Pedrigal, which was even narrower. We reached Pedrigal itself, and it became obvious I had made a dreadful mistake. The width of the turning basin was less than the length of the ship! But the pilot had apparently met with this problem before. Ordering 'full ahead, hard a-starboard', he drove the bow of the ship three metres into the mudbank and let the tide swing the stern round with 30 centimetres to spare on the other bank. Thirty men using the ship's gear and hand trolleys laboured all day in the boiling sun to discharge the cargo. Dad reckoned the Watersiders Union in New Zealand wouldn't have approved.

In Papeete we were cleared by our old friend Gigi Grand, whose incredible memory never forgot a face or a name. He still recalled the *Patsy Jean* and the *Siren*, and always had a soft spot for Cook Islanders. This was the last time I saw him before he died. Was it coincidence that shortly after that Cook Islanders lost their privilege to enter French Polynesia without passports?

We arrived in Rarotonga on 28 July 1972, and that night the Swedish yacht *Tuatua* went on the reef just outside Avarua. Next morning we were able to do our first good turn with the *Manutea* and pulled her off. A pity we hadn't been able to do the same thing to the *Yankee* with the *Tagua* in 1964.

There was some delay finalising the sale of the *Akatere* and we were more than pleased when a large deposit arrived from the buyer in Fiji. We loaded a full shipment of now redundant heavy machinery from the airport job for Suva, where I arrived in October, but the purchaser was still a bit hesitant about the final payment, so I decided to take the ship back to Rarotonga.

The evening before our departure, a bunch of us were yarning in the yacht club when the conversation turned to hurricanes. Everyone had his own story about hurricanes. 'Anyway,' I said as we broke up to leave, 'it's a bit early to be thinking about hurricanes yet.' All were agreed; it was only 21 October 1972.

We sailed the next afternoon. It was blowing a strong southeaster and the poor old *Akatere* plowed along at ever-decreasing knots. At 8pm we could still see the lights of Suva behind us, and at 8am next day Suva Radio reported a major hurricane on its way down from Rotuma. Remembering Archie Pickering's description of riding out the hurricane in the *Akatere* in 1967, and thinking of the maze of reefs and islands of the Lau Group still ahead of us, I decided discretion was the better part of valour and turned back for the shelter of Suva Harbour. With the wind behind us, we made it back in six hours.

Someone High Up had decided by now that hurricanes should have names, and this one was called Hurricane Bebe. It was a whopper, even by Fiji standards. It took three days to work its way down to Suva, with everyone hoping and praying it would veer away. Rotuma experienced winds of 160 mph. Funafuti was devastated. At Lautoka several ships sank in the harbour, with others adrift. Part of the hospital collapsed and had to be abandoned. The Suva harbourmaster recommended we go into the Bay of Islands, which is like a harbour within a harbour, and that's where all the local small craft and yachts take shelter. By the time we got there all the local vessels had already taken shelter, plus about 30 or 40 yachts. We squeezed in, laid out both anchors and awaited the storm, which struck that night.

We kept our engine going all night, to ease the strain on the cables. The wind kept increasing in force and we couldn't see anything beyond the bow of the ship. In the middle of the night a flare went up close by; one of the government ships was adrift and bearing down on us, broadside on and right across our bows. I felt sorry for the captain, as it didn't seem possible he could miss us, and indeed he didn't; he caught both anchor cables square on and the wind held him there, while we watched helpless. There was nothing we could do except coax a few more revs out of our engine and hope our anchors would hold, for there was a reef close behind. Fortunately he managed with a burst of power to clear himself and he disappeared at full speed into the murk. I felt sorry for the poor blighter, for it would be impossible for him to see where he was going and it would be only a matter of minutes before he hit another ship or ran aground. The answer came next morning; there he was, fast aground amongst some trees only three or four ships-lengths away.

No sooner had we got rid of him than another distress flare went up just ahead of us. It was the yacht *Camdella* adrift, heeled right over in the wind, with two people clinging to the rigging. We prepared to throw them a line, but realised it was hopeless to throw anything anywhere in that screaming wind. They were lucky enough to crash right into us and grabbed a line before they bounced off again. It was a young Kiwi couple, John and Dianne Barrowclough, with a two-year-old child, on the last leg of a round-the-world cruise. Terrified, they scrambled aboard and we made the yacht fast astern.

As if that wasn't enough excitement, yet another yacht crashed into us, this time without anyone on board. This yacht was still on a mooring, but the mooring had dragged and was hanging straight down from the stemhead. We didn't need any more yachts hanging off us, so the boys went on board and, finding a couple of anchors, threw them over and let her go.

The wind abated towards dawn and by daylight there were ships aground or sunk all over the bay. The yacht we had set adrift on its own anchors was serenely anchored just astern of us, almost touching the reef which we had been afraid of dragging onto ourselves. That afternoon we sailed again for Rarotonga. Two months later I was back in Suva with the *Akatere* and this time the sale was completed.

While Rarotonga was booming with the airport construction, the outer islands were being drained of their manpower, with a corresponding decline in copra and fruit production, which in turn lowered the buying power of the people of the outer islands, resulting in a drop in outward tonnage as well. In the previous two years we had been operating almost monthly voyages to Papeete, mainly for fertiliser trans-shipments, but the quantity of fertiliser was now reduced to a trickle. There wasn't enough work for the ships. Between the sale of the *Bodmer* in March 1972 and the arrival of the *Manutea* in July the same year, the *Manuvai* and the *Akatere* had been able to cope quite well. We certainly didn't need three ships.

An application for a freight increase remained in limbo for six months before it was declined. Our accountants told us we were losing a thousand dollars a week. Letters to the Premier and the Minister of Shipping went unheeded. The proceeds from the sale of the *Akatere* at the end of the year went to meet unpaid accounts.

Unknown to us, Hugh Williams had been pestering the Government for a licence to bring in another ship. Obviously Hugh didn't know how bad things were, but on the other hand the Government probably felt pretty smug having him waiting in the wings. With the sale of the *Akatere* the Minister presented us with an ultimatum: either we replace the *Akatere* or the Government would grant Williams a licence. We replied that not only would we not replace the *Akatere* (and were financially unable to do so anyway) but, if they granted Williams or anyone else a licence, the *Manuvai* or the *Manutea* would have to go as well. Williams got his licence.

Our financial situation was critical and we advertised the *Manutea* in *Pacific Islands Monthly* as being for sale or charter, with a nice photo of the ship. Much to our surprise, we got an immediate response, and by the time Hughie arrived with his ship *Moana* in April, two months later than promised, the *Manutea* was already on charter as a supply vessel for a copper mine in West Irian. She had spent only nine months in the Cook Islands, and the only profitable voyage she ever made was one to Fiji with heavy machinery from the airport job.

The charter was for a year, and it wasn't any trouble to find a Cook Islands crew, but nobody wanted to go as captain, least of all Don Silk. A delightful old English captain named Allan Clark had been pestering us for a job for some time. He was a bit long in the tooth to stand up to the rigours of the islands trade, but we thought on the run to West Irian there would be little for him to do but take a few sights in between his pink gins.

The first voyage started in Sydney. The ship was loaded, ready to sail, and Nobby was asleep in his cabin. The first mate took charge and got the ship under way. They were well down the harbour when the captain staggered on to the bridge. 'Let's get going!' he ordered. 'Let go forward! Let go aft! Full ahead!'

Going up the coast he became a real banana case. He would call me at home in the middle of the night, completely oblivious of the time difference, in fact completely oblivious of everything by the sound of him. 'Don,' he would plead, 'I don't like this run. I want to come back to the islands. Please do something.'

By the time they reached West Irian the crew had had enough. We received a joint cable from the mate and the chief engineer saying they refused to sail with him on board, and we had to fly him out to Darwin. The mate, who had a Foreign Going Master's ticket (and had come out of retirement for this job) was persuaded to take over, while Paranapa Ben, whom we had been schooling as a future captain, was promoted to acting mate, an experience which stood him in good stead in future years.

The charterers decided to service their copper mine out of Singapore, rather than Sydney. They put generating sets on board and she carried reefer cargo as well as dry goods in specially built containers to suit the size of the ship. At Ammamapere in West Irian the containers were trucked to the mine which was hundreds of metres high up in the mountains. The road was an impressive feat of engineering in itself. The crew thought some of the stevedores in West Irian pretty impressive, too, clad only in penis sheaths. But at least these penis sheaths didn't get caught up in the cargo winch like a guy's lavalava one day in Apia.

The ship performed like clockwork, never missing a day on hire. Compared to working the outer islands it was like a holiday for the crew and they were able to keep the ship looking immaculate. But good things come to an end, and at the end of a year the charterers decided they needed a larger vessel, so we looked elsewhere for work for the *Manutea*. We needed the revenue to subsidise the *Manuvai* in the Cook Islands.

CHAPTER NINE

FORTUNES MADE AND LOST

The *Moana* had been built for the Gilbert and Ellice Islands (now Kiribati and Tuvalu) in 1958, so was only two years older than the *Manuvai*. But she was an example of what the rigours of the Islands trade, coupled with poor maintenance, could do to a vessel. She really showed her age. Although supposed to be in Class, her certificates had expired by the time she arrived, and the ship was in a mess. The two Crossley engines gave nothing but trouble and the filthy engine-room could best be described as the black hole of the Pacific. The smoke from the stack could be seen long before the ship hove over the horizon. Life-saving equipment and fire-fighting appliances were grossly sub-standard. Even the radio didn't meet the local requirements. It was a pity she had been let go, for she was one of very few ships designed and built for the Islands trade.

We were asked to bring back the *Manutea* but by now she was on charter in Papua New Guinea, where there was a fleet of indifferent ships under several different owners. One of them saw the chance to get an edge on his competitors by chartering the *Manutea* and she was kept busy carrying empty bottles from the glass-works in Lae to the brewery in Port Moresby, and beer from the brewery back to Lae. It was a really sweet number and the brewery provided all the paint for the ship to be painted in the brewery colours, while Silk & Boyd laughed all the way to the bank.

It was time to think about another ship. The *Manuvai* was hard-pressed to cope on her own, but we had been reluctant to invest in another ship for the Cook Islands trade until the final fate of the *Moana* was known. Even then, it looked a pretty doubtful venture. The building of airstrips on all the islands of the Southern Group had created work for the *Manuvai* but in the long term had a negative effect with the establishment of an internal air service. Apart from tere parties, sea passengers, which had accounted for 30 per cent of our revenue, all but disappeared. The fresh-fruit production was in serious decline, a situation accelerated by the mass migration to New Zealand once the internationai airport opened. However, what with the success of the *Manutea* in the charter game, coupled with the potential for some trade between Fiji and the Cook Islands, we reckoned we could keep another ship employed, so off I flew again to Europe and headed for the office of Supervision Shipping, the brokers who had sold us the *Manutea*.

'Well, well,' said Rudy Dee, 'I can't offer you much this time.' We went through his files and it was amazing how the Dutch coastal fleet had been decimated in the two years since I was there. From 930 ships on the coastal register in 1972, there were now only 270 left. 'It's regulations that's mainly putting them out of business,' said Rudy, 'that and the competition from containers, ro–ro's and trucks. Then there's the unions with their ever-increasing demands.'

The phone went, and Rudy spoke in Dutch for a while. 'Talking about unions,' he said, 'that was a long-time shipowner friend of mine. He has two 700-tonners running to Ireland. He has just had a con-frontation with the unions, and he's had a belly-full. He rang to tell me to sell them both.'

He dug out the files. The two ships were identical, raised quarter-deckers, pretty ships. I went over the plans and specifications, and although the ships were a little larger and more expensive than we had planned, the price was right. We got into Rudy's Porsche and roared off to where they were lying. They were beauts, with nothing to choose between them.

'Which one?' asked Rudy.

'The *Florida*,' I said. 'I like the name. We won't have to change it.'

The captain, Jack Ridderhoff, introduced himself. It was like shaking hands with a ten-ton vice. Tall and rangy, with greying hair and wonder-fully bright blue eyes that had searched for a thousand landfalls, Jack had a ready wit and a laugh that could be heard from the engine-room to the bridge. Like many European captains, he was equally at home in either place, the engine-room or the bridge. I asked him to come with me as engineer/mate, and suggested he bring his wife, Pimmy. Olly had come with me and was with friends in England, and I guessed that Olly and Pimmy would hit it off together. I wasn't wrong. So within a few

Florida, a wonderfully sea-kindly vessel

hours I had not only bought a ship but had half the crew as well. Since we were not fitting out the ship for passengers, there was little to do compared with previous purchases. I arranged for dry-docking and, with Jack to organise spares and work out fuel and oil requirements, I was able to concentrate on finding the rest of the crew and looking for cargo.

With Rudy's help I fixed a part-cargo of fertiliser from Rotterdam to Panama, topped up with a part cargo of hand-grenades from Bremen to Guatemala. We had a nice load to pay for the delivery voyage.

The English Channel and the Bay of Biscay threw everything at us, but *Florida* proved a wonderfully sea-kindly vessel, and took it all in her stride.

At the port of Santo Tomas de Castilla, on the Atlantic seaboard of Guatemala, the navy came out to escort us in. The first man on board was our agent, whom we had chosen by sticking a pin in the Shipbrokers Register. He explained that it was the custom to present each official in the boarding party with a bottle of spirits and a carton of cigarettes.

Fortunately we had ample stocks of both on board; there were 13 officials in the boarding party.

The official business was quickly dispensed with and the bottles and cartons stashed away in briefcases and satchels. As they all trooped out of the saloon the senior Customs officer requested to have another look at our bonded stores. There was still a generous supply left. He called his assistant to bring a gunny-sack, and they took half what was left. He probably thought he was smart, but back home Chapman would have taken the lot.

Our cargo of fertiliser was consigned to the Panamanian port of Aquadulce. I had been unable to find a chart of this place, or even any reference to it in Lloyd's Atlas. I had asked Rudy Dee, and he said, 'Oh, you just go through the canal and turn right. It's the first creek you come to!' Creek it was, and we had to wait outside for the first spring tide before there was enough water for us to get over the bar, then there was a further wait of several days anchored just inside the mouth of the river, surrounded by mangrove swamps and alligators — and mosquitoes as voracious as the alligators. There wasn't a breath of air, nor a human being in sight. According to the Pilot Book, 'In the rivers of this hot moist region great precautions are necessary to counteract the effect of the climate. Fevers often resembling yellow fever of the West Indies both in suddenness of attack and violence of the symptoms are very prevalent and require similar treatment. During the hot season all the inhabitants, able to do so, migrate to higher lands.' We weren't geared for treating yellow fever of the West Indies, or anywhere else for that matter, but an extra ration of rum seemed to be a reasonable substitute.

We had been trying to find a cargo for the last leg of the voyage, and it was frustrating sitting amongst the mangroves wondering what was happening, so one day I took the boat and outboard and went up to Aquadulce to get access to a telephone. Coming back in the evening the mosquitoes were abroad in full force and I wondered about that yellow fever …

At last we made it up the river to the little port. Not having had any luck with securing further cargo for the voyage, we sailed for Rarotonga, arriving there on 18 February 1975.

Rather than feeling a sense of elation at the prospect of another delivery voyage successfully completed, the closer we got to Rarotonga the more despondent I became. There didn't seem to be any reason for it, but then I began to get fearful headaches and aches and pains. There wasn't any partying to celebrate our arrival, at least not as far as I was concerned; I just slunk quietly off to bed, where I felt worse. Fevers started to come and go, it felt as if every bone in my body was broken. The doctor came, and was at a loss to diagnose the problem. He took a blood sample and came back again. 'It's strange,' he said. 'It looks like dengue fever, but we haven't had dengue in Rarotonga for years.'

I asked him what the incubation period was for dengue. 'Oh, about three weeks.' That year dengue fever reached epidemic proportions in Rarotonga. At least that's what the doctors called it, but I wondered about that yellow fever of the West Indies ...

After a week in Rarotonga, during which I spent most of the time laid up, we continued the voyage, sailing for Suva, where Bob had organised a full load of cargo for Niue and Rarotonga. With the *Manuvai* fully employed in the Cook Islands, and cheques arriving regularly from the *Manutea* in Port Moresby, things were looking pretty rosy. We might have known it couldn't last. It didn't.

In Suva I received a telex from Port Moresby to say that the *Manutea* had been arrested for two hundred thousand Australian dollars for salvage services and we had 12 days to appeal. Details were sketchy, but the chain of events went something like this ...

The ship had gone to Cape Flattery in Queensland for a load of silica sand for the glassworks in Lae. The chief engineer had finished his contract and was to be replaced by Lance Simiona, who had just completed his second year at the Institute of Technology in Suva. Lance had got as far as Sydney and was held up for a visa for Papua New Guinea. In order not to delay the ship while waiting for Lance, our agents had engaged an engineer locally.

At Cape Flattery the ship was loaded by pumps at an offshore anchorage. There didn't seem to be any proper control as to how much sand was loaded; they stopped pumping while she was still afloat, but well below her marks. On the return voyage the scavenge-pump on the main engine broke down through simple lack of lubrication, and the engineer didn't have sufficient knowledge to continue the voyage without it. They called for help, and although they were still under way, accepted a tow from a local vessel in the vicinity, the MV *Maluka*. A Lloyd's Open Form (No Cure No Pay) was agreed to and signed by both captains on arrival at Port Moresby. No big deal so far.

In Port Moresby the Marine Department officials were unimpressed with the overloaded condition of the ship, and even less impressed that she had had to be towed in for a fault which should never have happened in the first place, and could have been rectified by anyone with a knowledge of basic engineering principles. An inquiry was held and it came to light that the engineer had a bogus ticket, had been using it for some time, and furthermore was an illegal immigrant. We had to pay the cost of deporting him to Bolivia.

By the time repairs to the engine had been effected, Lance arrived and with everybody apparently happy, the ship sailed for Lae. But the salvors weren't happy, or pretended not to be. Actually they were busting themselves with joy. Sea Freights Ltd, who owned the *Maluka*, were one of the local operators who were hurting because of the intrusion of the *Manutea* into the local scene, and here was their chance to retaliate. In the Salvage Agreement was a clause to the effect that the ship shouldn't sail without satisfying the salvors re security, and they claimed we had breached this agreement by sailing to Port Moresby without putting up security.

When the ship arrived in Lae she was arrested on a warrant issued by the Court in Port Moresby. The only way for a quick release was to put up the two hundred thousand dollars demanded and argue later. Sea Freights correctly guessed we wouldn't be able to raise that sort of money as the ship was insured for only eighty-four thousand dollars, so that would keep the *Manutea* nicely out of the way for a while. It also closed down the glassworks.

From Suva I caught the first plane to Sydney and with the help of our shipbroker friends there, I met some of the top brass in the field of maritime law, but we had little information to go on. Trying to get hold of anyone in Sea Freights to find out what was wanted was like grabbing handfuls of fog. The company directors were scattered throughout Papua New Guinea and Australia. The manager appeared to have acted on his own initiative without reference to directors or legal advice. We didn't know what had been agreed to outside the Standard Form, as Sea Freights had the only copy and wouldn't let us see it. The Court was closed so we couldn't find out what the writ contained.

In Port Moresby I engaged a solicitor, Barry Love, to act for us. We tried to meet with Sea Freights, but they refused to talk to us. When the Court opened we found that the writ had been issued by the Registrar and not by a judge, and this had obviously been done without full reference to the facts, one of which was that when the ship sailed from Port Moresby, and until the time of her arrest, we had not yet been notified of what security, if any, Sea Freights required. We put our case before the judge, who came down heavily in our favour. The ship was released, the glassworks was back in business, and we were awarded costs. The salvage claim went to arbitration by the Committee of Lloyd's in London, together with our counter-claim for damages against Sea Freights for the wrongful arrest of the vessel. Lloyd's had great difficulty in getting information out of Papua New Guinea and it was over two years before they finally made their award. We had to pay Sea Freights twelve thousand pounds for the salvage, less two thousand eight hundred pounds, being the sum awarded us for our counter-claim. Each of the parties had to contribute three thousand pounds towards the cost of the arbitration.

Later that year the *Manutea's* charter ran out and she started a new one with Bismark Shipping of Rabaul. Bismark were so pleased with the ship they eventually bought her.

About this time our partners, CITC, with whom we still enjoyed an excellent relationship, decided that our operations were becoming a little outside their sphere of interest, and by mutual agreement we purchased their shares in Silk & Boyd Ltd. We were still grateful for their help at the time we needed it.

On the way back from the Port Moresby fiasco I arrived in Auckland in time to meet up with the *Florida*, loading explosives at Kauri Point for Tarawa. The cargo consisted of old bombs and shells to be used for blasting reef passages, and were something our lads were quite accustomed to carrying around the Cooks, swinging them over the side in cargo nets along with everything else, but the way these Auckland wharfies handled them was quite an education. No cargo nets here with the bombs rattling against each other, but each one individually handled like it was about to go off any minute. It was very time-consuming, but then the wharfies were getting paid by the hour, not by the bomb.

The Bishop in Rarotonga had asked if we could load a tractor which he had been trying to get shipped from Auckland for some time, and Bob had told him if he could get it delivered to the the ship we would drop it off next time in Rarotonga. Getting a tractor driven down to the munitions wharf at Kauri Point must have been a project on its own, but it was nothing compared to getting the wharfies to load it on the ship. Their reasons for not wanting to load it were many and varied, but in short we would have to take it back to one of the commercial wharves over in the city and call for a fresh gang of wharfies the following day. It looked as though the cost would exceed the value of the tractor, on which we weren't even getting freight anyway.

At the end of the day I said forget the tractor, and while the crew were closing the hatches the wharfies got into their hired launch and went off home. We rigged a derrick, threw the tractor on deck, and the ship sailed for Tarawa. But we were a bit too quick. The wharfies were just getting off their launch on the city side when they saw the *Florida* sailing down the harbour with the tractor sitting on deck. They were not amused. We had deprived them of work. It contravened some Act. They worked out what it would have cost us for them to load it and in the end we had to pay.

The next trip of the *Florida* to Auckland was on charter to Brown and Doherty Ltd, who had secured the contract to build the new Rarotongan Hotel. The reputation of the Auckland wharfies being what it was, we decided it was worth the extra distance to go round to Onehunga, where they were a bit more reasonable and they needed the work, for the port wasn't busy. We got on well with them, and Dave Brown or Bill Doherty was always in attendance with suitable incentives to encourage them to get the job done quickly and save charter costs, while Bob or I was always there to see that the ship was stowed carefully, even if it took a little longer and ran up the charter revenue. One way or another the Onehunga wharfies did all right.

On the first trip the sight of all the cargo assembled on the wharf was quite awesome. It looked mountainous beside the ship. Although the numbers had been carefully calculated, nobody believed it was going to be physically possible to fit it all on board. Every cranny of space was used. At last the hatches were closed, and there still looked to be enough on the wharf for a good start to a second load.

Bundles of timber were broken down and stowed along the side decks, right to the top of the bulwarks and level with the hatch. Then came two heavy trucks, a bulldozer, a traxcavator, and a trench-digger. All were slung on board and lashed down. Only two pick-ups remained; the only space left was on the boat deck, so that's where they went. With enough fuel and water for the voyage, the ship sailed right on her marks.

In Rarotonga, the first question people asked was how we were going to get the bulldozer and the trucks ashore, as obviously the ship couldn't lift them, and Rarotonga didn't have a crane big enough. However, we had thought about this, and it was one reason why the side decks were filled to the top of the bulwarks with timber. At the right stage of the tide, with the ship level with the wharf, the *Florida* became the first 'ro-ro' ship in Rarotonga.

Several trips were made to Auckland, in between spot charters around the South Pacific. She was an economical vessel to operate between New Zealand and Rarotonga, or any other island for that matter, but not with a New Zealand crew, and the New Zealand unions were still adamant on this issue. These charter voyages were condoned, but not a regular liner service. While they paid lip service to helping their brown brothers in the Pacific, this didn't extend to depriving themselves of any jobs. This attitude was not only frustrating but was used against us in a battle between two other shipping companies.

In 1976 a few entrepreneurial wharfies in Onehunga formed themselves into a shipping company to run to Fiji and they wanted to charter the *Florida*. We had already done a trip or two to Fiji for Tom McNicholl of Reef Shipping and he had an option on another one. The ship was on its way to New Zealand when his option expired, so she diverted to Onehunga to load cargo for the wharfie outfit, who quickly put money up front to secure the ship. Now Tom was a pretty tricky customer to tangle with; he made Hugh Williams and Dick Brown look like amateurs. He had the ship arrested on arrival for breach of contract. Our lawyers were confident the Court would not uphold the charge, and Tom probably knew it too, but as we couldn't get the case heard before the Easter recess, we settled out of court. But Tom hadn't finished yet. Using his considerable influence, he got the Seamen's Union to picket the ship, on the grounds that we were 'cross trading' on a traditional run. The wharfies refused to cross the picket line, even though some of them owned the company which had chartered the ship, and had cargo ready on the wharf to load. To get out of the impasse, we had to agree to sail without the cargo, never to return.

Jack Ridderhoff needed to get back to Holland to join his family (and collect his pension). Command went to Captain Rob Rae, a pretty switched-on youngish Kiwi with plenty of small-ship experience. Still, it was hard to get enough work to keep the *Florida* going, especially now that we were virtually denied access to New Zealand. We were on the point of putting her up for sale when just in time a charter came to light. A group of businessmen in Sydney formed a company to ship pozzalan from Vanuatu to Townsville. Pozzalan, or pozzuolana, is a type of volcanic rock containing silica, alumina and lime, and is used in the manufacture of cement. Small-scale trials had already been done, and if successful on a larger scale, there would be work for the *Florida* for an unlimited future. It could be the answer to a maiden's prayer.

They were running in towards the Australian coast with their first load on the night of 9 April 1976. Rob was anxious to make landfall as soon as possible after daylight. They had only one isolated danger to pass, a little patch named Myrmidon Reef on the outskirts of the Great Barrier Reef, 70 miles outside Townsville.

All the information on the chart and in the Pilot Book indicated that he might expect a north-flowing current of 0.5 to 0.7 knots as he closed the coast, so he set course to pass about five miles north of the reef. He got a good star fix in the evening, and was confident of his position. Local fishermen said later that the current sometimes sets south closer inshore, and this is apparently what happened, for at four o'clock in the morning, running before a heavy following sea and loaded to her marks, she hit Myrmidon reef at full speed. Later, calculations indicated she had experienced a southerly set of about 1.8 knots. There was no hope of getting her off.

Getting the crew off was drama enough. They spent all day on board with the ship taking an ever-increasing list to port. At high tide seas broke right across the hatch. There were two Australian warships in the vicinity, and one of them, HMAS *Bayonet*, reached the scene the following night. She lay-to on the opposite (lee) side of the reef, which was about a quarter of a mile in diameter. Launching a liferaft, the crew drifted right across the reef and were picked up on the other side, clutching what personal possessions they could hold. I arrived a couple of days later, having hitched a ride from Rarotonga on a RAAF Hercules that happened to be passing through, and I went out to the wreck with an insurance assessor and a Lloyd's surveyor. All agreed she was a Total Constructive Loss.

Back in Rarotonga I presented Bob with the ship's barometer for a souvenir. 'Bit bloody expensive' was all the thanks I got.

CHAPTER TEN

THE ARMED MERCHANTMAN

After the departure of the *Manutea* for West Irian in April 1973 the *Manuvai* had been on her own apart from the fairly brief visit of the *Moana* and other fly-by-night operations which were forever coming and going, usually operating without a licence, in ignorance of safety requirements, condoned by successive governments, and all without exception losing money. Now there was a new broom in the form of a new Minister of Shipping, George Ellis. Born in Manihiki, the great-grandson of an English mariner who had settled and married there in the 1860s, George was well educated, having a BCom. from Victoria University in New Zealand, and an MBA from the University of Hawaii.

George was like a breath of fresh air after his predecessor, Vincent Ingram, with whom we couldn't agree on a full-stop. He was anxious to see us get another ship, and promised stricter control of the Shipping Licensing Act. Our figures showed that there was now insufficient freight in the group to support even two ships. With the exception of pineapples from Mangaia and Atiu, the outer islands were producing nothing, so not only was there no inward cargo, but the people out there had little purchasing power. There had been no Government building projects in the outer islands for years, and any future plans were up in the air. The biggest disincentive to shipowners was the ineffectual Price Tribunal, which, with Dick Chapman at the helm, could never get around to hearing an application, and if it did, professed not to understand it (and probably didn't). With galloping imported inflation, the situation was ludicrous, with the shipping company having to prove actual losses (by this time historical) before getting (if they were lucky) an increase in rates sufficient to break even, providing costs hadn't increased again meanwhile, which of course they had. We had been surviving on existing

The islanders devised ingenious ways of getting cargo ashore

rates only because of our external operations, which now no longer existed. 'Frankly, George, we've about had enough.'

But George was persistent, and kept at us, and kept at his Government to entice us into another ship by offering a subsidy. The Government was in a bit of a bind, largely due to the pineapple industry in Mangaia and Atiu. Thousands of dollars were being poured into propping up what was inherently an uneco–nomic industry, supplying pineapples to the Island Foods Ltd cannery in Rarotonga. Price subsidies were paid to growers in addition to what was paid by Island Foods. When Mangaia had been the only pineapple producer, one ship operating three trips a week was able to uplift the crop in the peak of the season without loss of fruit (except when weather conditions prohibited loading). With the industry now spread over two islands, it was practically impossible to avoid losses with only one ship trying to do the lot, losses which were economically and politically costly. On the other hand, the shipowners saw no future in having a second ship just to move a few part-loads of pineapples at unrealistic freight rates for a very short season. So, no subsidy, no ship.

How to effect a subsidy was the conundrum. When we were trying to establish the tug and barge service from New Zealand, Bob had come up with the idea of loading the freight rate from New Zealand in order to subsidise the rate to the outer islands. Since the volume of cargo from New Zealand was about ten times the volume of inter-island cargo, a five per cent surcharge on the former could justify a 50 per cent reduction on the latter. Now Bob had another surge of voltage to the brain cells and proposed that a subsidy could be instituted by the Government paying for the fuel. Fuel costs were the most unpredictable factor of all, and a fuel subsidy was perhaps the fairest means of subsidising a service; the more voyages we made, the more the subsidy, and on the other hand, if we didn't go anywhere, we got nothing. It was also an incentive to make regular calls at the uneconomical ports like Mitiaro, Nassau and Palmerston, although we had always included them anyhow. If there had to be a subsidy, this was the way to do it. But as a public relations exercise, we were to learn that the very word 'subsidy' stank to high heaven. In the mind of the public, 'subsidy' meant we were getting paid to do something that we were already getting paid for by way of freights and fares. As far as we as shipowners were concerned, it made no difference whether the user paid the total cost of shipping, or whether part of the cost was paid by the Government. At that time, fuel represented about 15 per cent of total costs; we would have been better off with a 15 per cent increase in freights and fares.

The Government had had two separate surveys done by United Nations experts on how to solve the country's internal shipping problems. Each expert in turn spent countless hours in our office going through our records (with our co-operation, for nobody else had reliable records) and each came to the conclusion that with such a scattering of islands with very small populations, there was no cheap solution. Also there was insufficient work for a second ship, but one ship alone would always be hard pressed to provide a service of acceptable frequency. What was needed in effect was one-and-a-half ships.

Even with a subsidy, there was still room for only one-and-a-half ships within the group, so we had to find sufficient work outside the group to occupy one ship for half the time. We thought a regular run to Samoa might be worthwhile. Fuel was cheap in Pago Pago, timber was cheap in Apia, while goods such as flour were cheaper and of better quality in countries other than New Zealand and could now be trans-shipped through Apia or Pago Pago. (Trans-shipping through Auckland was horrendously expensive.) The range of goods that could be purchased outside of New Zealand was, however, limited in many cases by high protective tariffs. Protective to New Zealand of course. Foreign exchange was no longer a problem (although it has taken years to try to remove the bureaucratic hassle of import licensing).

There were some long-standing trading partnerships between merchants in the Cook Islands and merchants in New Zealand, but it was always the New Zealand merchants who dictated the price of both our imports and exports, and too often shipped us inferior-quality goods at top-quality prices, compared to what was offered the home market. (And they are still doing it.) The Cook Islands owed them no allegiance. In the end it was the lack of alternative shipping connections that was the principal barrier to trading with other countries.

We told George we would give it a go. A subsidy agreement was drawn and after a difficult time George managed to get it approved by Cabinet. (His thanks was to lose his seat at the next election.) Finance was arranged and next thing I found myself in Scandinavia in the middle of winter, looking for another ship.

There were by now only a few of the little 400-ton coasters to be found in Europe. *Fiducia* was a sister-ship to *Manutea*, built in Holland for the same owners but since sold to Sweden. I found her lying in the little port of Karlsham and she seemed to be in reasonable condition, although it was a bit difficult to judge the state of her decks under 15 centimetres of snow.

Purchase was subject to the usual dry-docking inspection and the seller had made arrangements for a floating dock just down the coast. We had to crunch our way through ice to get to it, and as it raised us it also raised the floating ice surrounding us. It was miserably cold walking around under the ship on two inches of solid ice with the temperature at minus 12 degrees, and it didn't take me long to complete my inspection. We were just back in the water when Lance arrived. Bundled up like an Eskimo, he had flown from Rarotonga, stopping only long enough in London to buy some warm clothes. He quickly familiarised himself with the engine-room on the short voyage back to the ship's home port of Karlsham.

The Cook Islands Government had offered to help with delivery expenses by ordering a year's supply of liquor for the Bond Store, to be loaded in Antwerp. Before loading any cargo, there were certain alterations that had to be done to the hatch in order to build crew accommodation on deck, as the existing accommodation would be turned into passenger cabins. It was far too cold to be doing deck work in Sweden (and also hideously expensive), so I called my old friends in Denmark, the Marstal Staalskibsvaerft og Maskinfabrik, to see if they could do the job on the hatch. Jorgen Schmidt was only too pleased to accommodate us, but could fit us in for one week only, starting the following Monday, only five days away, and there was a lot to do before we could sail from Karlsham.

Meanwhile there was paperwork to be done. Before we could get the Provisional Certificate of Registry as a British ship, we had to produce the Deletion Certificate from the Swedish Registry. The Swedes weren't about to give us one of these until we could prove the ship was registered somewhere else. While this nonsense was proceeding (or more accurately not proceeding) I was frantically trying to organise a crew.

Jack Ridderhoff, formerly of the *Florida*, had agreed to help deliver the ship as far as Spain, where I planned to do further work on the accommodation, but he phoned to say he was unable to come for another week. Annette, a girl in London who had been engaged as cook for the voyage, likewise couldn't join before Marstal. The previous owner, Captain Matts Mattson, who had been most helpful, said he would come as far as Marstal, so with Lance that made three of us. Then Customs wouldn't give me a clearance because we didn't have our British papers and wouldn't allow us to sail with Swedish ones. We were running out of time; it was already Friday afternoon and it was going to take 48 hours to reach Marstal. I proposed to Matts that we go without a clearance, but he wasn't having any part of that. After all, he had to live here, and the Navy gunboat berthed next to us wasn't lending much encouragement to such a venture.

I said to Lance, 'It looks like you and me, my friend.'

'But won't we get into trouble at the other end?'

'Don't worry, the Danes have liberated ideas on the treatment of criminals. They have some of the most comfortable jails in the world.'

'Then let's go!'

Matts went over the charts with me. 'Here is the three-mile limit' he said. 'Head straight for that, then they can't touch you.' After wishing us luck, he disappeared from the scene.

At dusk we slipped our lines and took off. We hadn't even reached the three-mile limit when our eyes went all funny and we couldn't see a thing beyond the ship. It turned out there was nothing wrong with our eyes. We had run into a pea-soup fog, which lasted until we tied up in Marstal.

It was my first experience of navigating in fog. Not that I was worried; I was simply petrified, but at least we had good radar, and we had a good auto-pilot, and I had a good engineer who was also my assistant watch-keeper and helmsman and made cups of tea between lightning visits to the engine-room — and never lost his sense of humour. What a character! Worth two of almost anyone I knew.

Knowing where we were wasn't a problem as we were always within radar range of a coastline. The biggest and most frightening problem was the amount of traffic around us. Coming around the southern end of Sweden, we had all the traffic coming down from the Skaggerak and Kattegat into the Baltic, plus other ships coming up from the Kiel Canal heading for ports in the Gulf of Bothnia, It seemed that everyone was heading home for the weekend or had just cleared port before the weekend and was heading out. At one stage I counted 24 ships on the radar screen on a three-mile range. There would be congestion in the centre of the screen, which was where we were, and you could see ships merging on each other, and they would stop for a while, then gradually move ahead one by one as we all sorted ourselves out. I would stay glued to the screen giving Lance helm orders until we got a clear space, when I would say, 'You've got five minutes to get a cup of tea!' Lance thought it was a bit different from the Cook Islands.

It was a long trip down to Marstal, but somehow the adrenalin kept us going. Jorgen Schmidt came out with the pilot, and we were able to relax at last for the last few miles up the tortuous channel to the harbour. The Customs Officer came on board and the first piece of paper he wanted was the clearance from our last port. I explained that we had a bit of a problem, and why. He then asked for a crew list, which I gave him. It said: Don Silk, Captain; Lance Simiona, Chief Engineer.

'No, no,' he said, 'I want a list of everyone on board.'

'I'm sorry,' I said, 'we don't have anyone else on board.'

A suspicious look came into his eyes and I sensed trouble in the offing. It looked like we might have a chance to try one of those comfortable jails I had been telling Lance about. But Jorgen and the pilot came to my rescue, and said that Captain Silk was actually a well-respected shipowner from the South Seas, personally known to both of them, a man of integrity who had previously done business with many firms in Marstal, and so on — I wish I could have recorded it all. The Customs man shrugged his shoulders and said, 'Well, if you haven't got a clearance, you can't give it to me, can you?'

I readily agreed that that was indeed the case. Perhaps Customs officers weren't all bad after all. Jorgen was all for having a party, but we declined and slept like the dead for 12 hours.

We spent the rest of the week in Marstal, and it was uncanny the number of people who remembered the time I had sailed off with the *Manuvai*. Lance was popular, and Jorgen insisted on taking us home so his wife and teenage daughters could see a real Polynesian. Mother wasn't so impressed and took the daughters off somewhere, so we drank Jorgen's liquor cabinet dry and went off to a pub, where according to Lance I fell over a table-full of Danes who simply picked me up and propped me in a corner, then proceeded to ply me with more akvavit and beer.

We got the deck work done and the ship duly registered. Jack Ridderhoff and Annette arrived so we had enough crew to get the ship to Antwerp, where the liquor for Rarotonga awaited us, but we didn't have enough fuel, or any money to buy any. I needed some cargo, and managed to find a load of talc, in bags on pallets, from Oslo to Antwerp. So off to Oslo we went and loaded the talc (for making talcum powder) and purchased fuel.

To get all the cargo in we had to load the pallets three high. They didn't look all that tightly stowed but then it was only two or three days to Antwerp. We were making good time across the North Sea, running before a rising northeasterly gale. The seas were curling over both gunwales, for she was quite deeply laden. Suddenly the ship took a sharp turn to port — the auto-pilot had apparently failed — and a big sea caught her broadside on. She rolled well over to starboard, and although we quickly got her back on course, she never recovered from the roll, but lay over at about 40 degrees with the seas sweeping right across the hatch.

We got the way off her and hove to, head to wind. Lance sounded the bilges and reported all dry. Obviously the cargo had shifted, but there was little we could do about it. The only access to the hold was through the hatch, and with seas breaking right across, there was no way we could open it. I really thought we were going to lose the ship, and there was little chance of successfully launching a liferaft in such conditions.

Jack with his local knowledge predicted the gale would be shortlived and if only we could ride it out for a few hours we would be okay, so we wedged ourselves in the wheel-house and waited. Annette would have been the classic example of a person scared stiff. She literally could not move, but at least she wasn't screaming. She reckoned later on that we were all a bit pale around the gills. She could have been right.

Jack was right about the storm. After about five hours the seas settled a bit and the forward corner of the hatch on the port (high) side was clear of the water. Leaving Jack at the wheel and Annette still petrified, Lance and I made our way forward and pulled off a couple of hatch boards. Sure enough the cargo had shifted, with all the pallets jammed down into the starboard side and a big empty gap along the port side. We started heaving bags like demons and although the temperature was below zero we were soon in a lather of sweat. Only our hands remained frozen from the cold bags. Gloves were useless because the talc was so slippery.

As we worked we could feel the ship coming more upright, until, still a long way from an even keel, she started taking seas over the fo'c's'le head and down the part-open hatch, whereupon we scrambled out and closed the hatch boards as quickly as we could — but not quickly enough to avoid a thorough drenching from near-freezing water. We had come out of the hold in a lather of sweat and within minutes we were reduced to a shivering, gibbering mess with just enough strength to stagger into the shower and turn the hot tap. The ship still had a ten-degree list, but that didn't worry us and with the weather quickly abating we were soon on our way.

The cargo looked a mess when we opened the hatches in Antwerp, with loose bags strewn all over the place as if they had just been carelessly thrown on board. I was expecting the consignee to come along with a massive claim, especially as some seawater had entered the hold while we were straightening the ship, but everything seemed to be accepted as normal. Perhaps bags of talc always slide around like that. Anyway, I decided it wouldn't bother me too much if I never saw the stuff again.

Our cargo of liquor was ready for us. What a sight — a million dollars' worth of booze! We wouldn't want to call at Guatemala with this lot. There was also a young couple to join us as crew and everything was falling nicely into place except for two additional liferafts, which were still being manufactured by RFD in Godalming, Surrey. They were to be ready in only two more days and RFD suggested we call at Dover or somewhere to pick them up, as it would save time and expense.

I wasn't too keen on calling at a British port. Our Provisional Certificate of Registry was good only until the first British port, then we would be faced with the paper war of full registration as a British vessel, and I could see this costing very much time and expense. However, I reasoned that if we were to call at one of the more out of the way places it was likely that the 'Provisional' part of our certificate might be overlooked.

I phoned an agent in the port of Shoreham, not far from Brighton, and explained that we wished to make a brief call to pick up some liferafts, and that it was my wish to attract as little attention as possible in the process.

'I understand perfectly, Captain. Leave it to us!'

There was a further small complication. Jack had agreed to come as far as Vigo, in Spain, where we had booked a shipyard to make the additional alterations, but he needed first to slip back to Holland and pick up his pension before the authorities knew he had left the country.

'I'll fly across and join you in England,' he said.

This was okay by me except that having arrived in Antwerp with a chief officer, the Belgians might question my sailing without one. 'No trouble,' says Jack. 'We don't tell them. I'll nip ashore as we go out through the locks, then in England I'll be back on board before they know I'm not there!'

We arrived off Shoreham on Sunday afternoon, and waited for the tide and the pilot; it was dark by the time we got into the harbour. The pilot explained that further in, the harbour branched into two parts. 'On the eastern side you enter through locks and remain afloat in a Customs-controlled area. On the western arm you sit on the mud when the tide goes out. It's a little out of town.' I said that the western side would suit us fine.

A Customs man came on board, checked our clearance from the last port, and asked to see the Ship's Register. The 'provisional' part wasn't commented on, but he was most intrigued that the Port of Registry was Suva, Fiji.

'Aah, Fiji!' he said. 'How I would love to get to the South Seas!' So I kept him on the subject of the South Seas, and over a rum or two regaled him with tales of lithesome brown girls dancing under swaying palms on sandy beaches alongside sunlit lagoons. Every time he looked like getting back to business I would pour another rum. He asked for the cargo manifest, and after I had put him off with one or two more rums, he eventually insisted on seeing it.

Well! He nearly choked on his rum when he read the manifest. Thousands and thousands of cases of every type and brand of liquor you could think of.

'B-b-but Captain!' he roared, 'you have a very highly dutiable cargo here!'

'Oh, yes' I said, 'we tend to drink a bit in the South Seas, you know.'

'But Captain, you are lying in a non-Customs-controlled area. I must ask you to move your ship. There will be fearful trouble if head office knows about this.'

'Oh, that's no problem,' I replied. 'Anything to oblige. I'll just alert the chief engineer.' I poured him another rum and went off to alert the engineer.

When I came back he was still staring at the manifest, trying to get his eyeballs back into their sockets.

'I'm afraid there's bad news,' I said. 'The tide has dropped and we're sitting on the bottom. Nothing we can do.'

'This is terrible,' he said. 'We'll have to seal the hatches for tonight, but the trouble is tomorrow I have to report to Southampton. There will be real trouble. Unless of course if you sail tomorrow, then you'll be gone before they get my report.'

I assured him that whatever happened we would sail tomorrow; I certainly didn't want to cause any problems to a gentleman like himself. We finished the bottle of rum.

The Bay of Biscay was unbelievably calm and we made good time, arriving in the pretty harbour of Vigo on the eve of Good Friday. A number of ocean-going yachts were milling around and one of them came close by and called out 'Is Don Silk on board?' It was the manager of the yard that was to do our work and he was off on a race somewhere but would be back on Monday. This was a bit frustrating, as we hadn't appointed an agent, hoping he would organise that part of it for us. We were completely ignored by Customs and everybody else; we couldn't even get anyone to answer the radio. However, we were thankful for a good passage across the notorious Bay of Biscay, and after the cold of northern Europe the warmth was much appreciated. We did get a bit of attention when the girls took their tops off for a bit of sunbathing and we noticed the cross-harbour ferries coming much closer by us than previously.

There was plenty for the yard to do, fitting winches and boom-swingers, building accommodation into the forecastle with toilets and washrooms for deck passengers and crew. The deckhouse aft was cut in two and extended two metres. We lived on board while this work was in progress, with a big tarpaulin rigged over the top, under which we sat like Arabs in the desert, to the bemusement of the locals who would wander down to look at us.

Vigo is a major port. The part where we were berthed was amongst the fishing boats and we made many friends who introduced us to some local pubs and nightclubs which we would never otherwise have found our way into. English was very little spoken, but we soon picked up words and phrases in Spanish to get by, especially with the help of a bit of sign language. I did get stuck one day, in a hardware store, and I was having hell's own job to explain that I wanted a set of three-eighth-inch Whitworth taps and dies. Everyone wanted to help, but nobody had a clue what I wanted. It became a challenge, until someone was sent to get a Spanish/English technical dictionary, then I was able to ask for 'giramacos tres octavos Whitworth', a term I'll never forget, and almost certainly never use again.

Although we had done the hatch modifications in Marstal, it became necessary to open the hatch to do some welding under the deck where the winches were being installed. Having shipyard workers in and out of the hold all day was a worry, given the nature of our cargo, but nothing was touched; the cargo out-turn in Rarotonga was correct except for one bottle of Chivas Regal 12-year-old Scotch whisky, no doubt a record.

On one occasion we had all been out to a nightclub, and had been driven home by people we had met there. Back on board, Annette realised she had left her purse at the club, money and passport inside. Next morning it was delivered intact to the ship. But with all this honesty on the one hand, there was corruption on the other. Bob had a chuckle going through my expense accounts when he came to the entry, 'Bribe to Guardia Civil, 500 pesetas'.

As the job neared completion, the Spanish Marine Department started taking an interest in us. Where, they wanted to know, were the stability calculations that allowed us to put all this extra weight of steel on the ship? I didn't think it had anything to do with them, but they insisted it was their job to see that every ship sailing out of a Spanish port was in a safe condition of stability. I suggested they do the calculations themselves and tell me what was required, if anything. So they did. They looked at the new steel work and said, 'You have added three tonnes above deck. You must put three tonnes of ballast below deck.' I suggested we pump three tonnes of water into the double-bottom tanks, but they said no, I might pump it out again (now why would they think that?) but three tonnes of concrete would be okay.

We ordered three tonnes of ready-mix to be delivered. The forepeak tank was chosen as being the least bad place to put it; this already had ballast water in it which we were still trying to pump out when the concrete truck arrived. The tank turned out to have a faulty valve which we were unable to get at, so we sent for a portable pump. This wasn't easy to find, but eventually the fire-brigade arrived with one which was lowered into the forepeak tank by crane. The concrete truck continued to sit on the wharf with its big bowl going round and round. The firemen got down inside the tank and started their diesel-driven pump. It didn't pump too well either, but it sure produced a hell of a lot of smoke. What with the smoke and the fire-engine and the concrete truck, plus the yard supervisor's truck, and the fire-brigade supervisor's truck, and the crane standing by to hoist out the pump, it became quite a circus. Assuming there was a fire, there was soon a crowd, and the bigger the crowd got, the more people it attracted. The firemen inside the tank were getting overcome with fumes from their pump, so they had to be replaced with others wearing breathing apparatus. The crowd was getting its money's worth.

Finally all was ready to pump in the cement, and for the price of a bottle of Chivas Regal 12-year-old Scotch whisky we got the concrete truck driver to accidentally pump half of the cement into the harbour.

Once we sailed from Vigo we had a pleasant uneventful voyage to Rarotonga, the only stop being a brief one in the Canal Zone.

One of the first voyages after that proved to be the most eventful in the *Mataora's* history. It was to be to Pago Pago via Nassau and Pukapuka. Paranapa Ben was my mate, and I was doing the last trip with him before he took over as master.

We approached Nassau before dawn, and to our utter amazement the place was a blaze of lights, instead of the one or two kerosene lamps that one might expect.

'Looks like a ship,' said Ben.

'Yeah, looks like it's on the reef,' I replied.

Sailing day, Avatiu

And so it was. A Taiwanese long-liner high and dry, generators running, lights ablaze, and not a soul on board.

These Taiwanese long-liners, operating out of American Samoa, had long been in the habit of calling at Nassau and trading rice, sugar and cigarettes in exchange for coconuts, fresh pork, and certain other favours evidenced by the growing number of Asian-looking kids around. The Cook Islands Government was very much against it, but the Nassau people were very much for it, and the long arm of the law wasn't quite long enough to stop it.

Few of these boats were licensed to fish in Cook Islands waters, and those that were, were not permitted to call at any islands, unless entering a Port of Entry. Such calls contravened health and agricultural quarantine regulations, both of which were important. The Islanders have poor resistance to imported disease and, in the case of Nassau, a lack of medical facilities to deal with any outbreak. Also, American Samoa, where these fishing boats are based, hosts the rhinoceros beetle, scourge of the coconut industry.

The sea was calm and by the time the Nassauans and their Chinese guests woke up we had a line on the *Kou Yuon 72* and were doing our best to pull her off, but it was the wrong stage of the tide, and we didn't have enough power. A few hours later, while we were still trying, two more Taiwanese ships came over the horizon and started to nose in on our catch. It was almost as if they thought they should be doing the salvage job, not us. Men from one of them, the *No. 22 Shin Yuang Cheng*, swam to the stranded ship and were joined by still more Chinese from ashore. Our own sailors in Ben's charge were soon outnumbered by about eight to one and were too intimidated to prevent them cutting our towline.

The laws of salvage are quite clear, and having got our line on first, we had every right to her. It wasn't the time and place to be consulting our law books, but we had another, more effective card up our sleeve. As I endeavoured to manoeuvre into position to reconnect the tow-line I sent a boat over to the *No. 22 Shin Yuang Cheng* to fetch the captain so we could discuss the situation, which was potentially dangerous with three ships manoeuvring in very close proximity, all with single-screw, direct-reversing engines, and nobody able to anchor because of the depth of water. But he declined to come, and indicated he wanted our boat to take him to the *Kou Yuon 72*. (The Chinese ships had no boats of their own.)

Our passengers were taking a great interest in proceedings and none more than the Hon. Inatio Akaruru, the Honourable Member for Pukapuka and Nassau. Inatio in many respects was a typical Pukapukan; short of stature and stocky build, quiet and courteous, very much a gentleman. He had donned his suit and tie, ready to go ashore and impress his constituents, who hadn't seen him for years, when one of the Nassau boats arrived, bringing the captain of the *Kou Yuon 72*. The captain spoke some English, and I introduced him to Inatio, looking resplendent in his number-one gear. Inatio drew himself up to his full five foot seven and informed the captain that he represented the Cook Islands Government, and Her Majesty, the Queen of England (Liz would have been proud), and that he had taken possession of the fishing boat, which was here illegally. The captain could send his crew on board to get their clothes; they must then leave. There was an eyeball to eyeball confrontation; I had to admire Inatio's guts, but I reckoned it wouldn't be long before he would need a change of underwear. Among their three ships the Chinese could muster a hundred men, and if it came to a showdown we wouldn't have a chance.

In the end the captain backed down, and we took him across to his ship while the Hon. Inatio went ashore to attend to electoral business. In the meantime the *No. 22 Shin Yuang Cheng* and the other vessel, the

No. 3 Kuo Zong, had launched inflatable liferafts which they were using to offload frozen bait from the *Kou Yuon 72*, of which there was about 20 tonnes on board. (The fish holds were otherwise empty.) As they had no means of propelling these rafts, they were pulling them from ship to ship with long lengths of fishing line. We didn't mind them taking the bait as it was lightening the ship, besides we had no means of storing it. However, after they finished off-loading the bait they started dismantling equipment from the wheel-house and other parts of the ship, so we paddled Inatio over and he ordered them off, leaving our party in sole charge. There were a couple of confrontations with the Chinese, but we managed to keep them at bay until, with a little help from the tide, we pulled her off and departed for Pukapuka, our next port of call, 60 miles away.

The two Taiwanese ships, having picked up all the crew of the *Kou Yuon 72*, followed about five miles behind until we were about 20 miles from Pukapuka, when they closed in, one on each side, very close to the *Kou Yuon 72*, the crew lining the rail and brandishing knives. Watching through binoculars, it appeared we had three rather white Cook Islanders on board *Kou Yuon 72*.

It had been my intention to tow the ship to Pago Pago, which was to be our next port after Pukapuka and where the fishing-boat would have to be dry-docked for repairs, but it was obvious that such a venture would result in the Chinese taking the ship off us. I was having trouble with my radio and couldn't get through to Rarotonga, so it wasn't until we got to Pukapuka and sent our passengers ashore that I was able to send a signal to the Prime Minister and to Bob, telling them we were being harassed by the Taiwanese. (Actually all they wanted was their fishing-boat back, but I considered that a bit of unChristianlike covetousness.

I asked the CAO on Pukapuka to round up all the firearms on the island, which resulted in five shotguns, but two of them I sent back ashore as being more dangerous to the operator than the target. We thus became an armed merchantman, but still didn't feel all that confident. The lights of the Taiwanese could be seen on the horizon all that night.

Next day a reply came back from Prime Minister Albert Henry to say we were not to proceed to Pago Pago, but to bring the fishing-boat back to Rarotonga. This posed a problem, as we had enough fuel only to reach Pago Pago and not enough to get back to Rarotonga. (We were under the mistaken impression the Taiwanese were using a heavier grade of fuel.) In the end we decided to get the *Manuvai* to meet us in Suwarrow, 215 miles to the southeast, with extra fuel and a spare tow-line.

Back in Rarotonga things had been happening too. Wellington was advised of the situation and a Royal New Zealand Air Force Orion was diverted from Fiji to circle over us. The Taiwanese soon got the message and immediately departed for parts unknown. God bless the Queen!

At Suwarrow we anchored in the lagoon and were able to have a good look at our prize. There was little damage. We managed to get the rudder working, and Lance was soon reading enough Chinese to get the main engine running. She was a nice little ship of about 300 tonnes, only four years old, fully equipped, and had just come off dry-dock in Pago Pago. We were able to find the chart in use and saw where the captain had plotted his course directly from Pago Pago to Nassau.

The *Manuvai* arrived and Bruce Carnahan took the *Mataora* to Pago Pago while I took the *Manuvai* back to Rarotonga, accompanied by the *Kou Yuon 72*, under her own power, with Captain Ben in his first command, and Lance as engineer.

A couple of weeks later the Chinese owners arrived to negotiate the purchase of their ship. They were tough customers and tried to convince us the ship was worth far less than it really was, quoting all sorts of fancy prices for the cost of building a new ship in Taiwan. However, Bob had been to Taiwan negotiating the price of a new-building for ourselves, and was able to call their bluff. Eventually agreement was reached, and after paying a fine to Government in addition to salvage money to Silk & Boyd (whose coffers badly needed it), they were free to take their ship away. By the time our crew had got their share, all hands were hooked on salvage as a way of life. The guns went back to Pukapuka on the next ship.

It was about this time some of my friends started calling me Sinbad.

CHAPTER ELEVEN

THE SHOESTRING BREAKS

It was a big day in Rarotonga when the first DC8 landed in December 1972. Half the island turned out and the scene at the airport was a total shambles. Although the runway was finished, there was little else. There was no way of controlling the crowd. It rained in torrents, but nobody cared, although the terminal building was still without a roof. Customs and Immigration gave up; the passengers were pretty well all Cook Islanders anyway. One very important one was Patsy Silk, home from her second year at boarding school, where she hated every minute. After four years she came home never wanting to leave the island again and eventually married the chief pilot of Air Rarotonga, Munro Hockin, so he didn't leave either. Gary and Karen, on the other hand, spent their school years in Rarotonga and couldn't leave soon enough, Gary to settle in Queensland with his Cook Islands wife Mingi, and Karen to make a career in the New Zealand Army.

Once the airport was open and a few tourists started to come, some of the more hardy adventurous types sought passage to the outer islands. Usually these were younger people travelling on a budget, or expatriate schoolteachers wanting to see the outer islands at minimum cost, and they would want to travel on deck. Besides, hadn't they read about the romance of sleeping on deck under the stars on balmy tropical nights? However, after the nights turned not so tropical and not so balmy, and they had been drenched with salt spray and spewed on by fellow travellers, they felt the need to creep into the accommodation to use the facilities there, which would be already stretched to the limit by the cabin passengers. Some would have to be dislodged from the saloon settee so that breakfast could be served and, all in all, for the few dollars they were paying, we were better off without them. So we made it known that deck passage was only for locals; if Europeans wanted to travel, they would have to pay cabin fare. Well, that didn't go down too well either; now we were branded as racists.

Bob now compiled what we called our guff sheet. This set out in no uncertain terms just how bad it could be travelling on deck with Silk & Boyd; that it was really not recommended unless your forebears had been doing it for generations and you were impervious to heat, cold, wet, hunger, smells and violent motion. This didn't seem to deter anyone. In fact, there seemed to be a whole generation of masochists determined to undertake the ordeal, just so they would be able to tell their grand-children about it, but at least it cut down the complaints, and once people knew what to expect they accepted the situation and got on with enjoying the voyage.

But you could also have thrills and adventures travelling cabin class. Take the experienced Steve Jackson, an agricultural teacher. He had been ashore at Mauke for the day and came out on the last lighter when we had finished loading cargo. The hatches were battened down, the crates of chickens stowed on the fo'c's'le head, the pigs and goats in the scuppers, and we were just weighing anchor as the last of the passengers leapt aboard over the rail. They used to breed some mighty fine pigs in Mauke, and had some Large White pedigree stock from New Zealand. Steve unfortunately chose to leap over the rail right where a particularly large grandfather boar was having a quiet snooze in preparation for the voyage ahead. It would be hard to say who squealed the louder, Steve or the boar, but Steve came off second-best when the boar leapt to its feet and a long curving tusk tore through the muscle of Steve's thigh, leaving a hole you could put your fist into.

Steve couldn't stand the sight of blood, especially his own, of which there was a great deal, and he passed out on the spot. The pig seemed okay, so we attended to Steve, and by the time he came to he was well trussed up and stretched out on his bunk. It was several weeks before he could walk without crutches.

On another occasion at Mauke the last boat, coming out at the end of the day quite deeply laden with the last of the cargo plus pigs, goats and passengers, hit a breaking sea just outside the passage and turned over. The current coming out of the passage carried the upturned boat, and everything that floated, out to sea, including the people and the animals. A rescue operation immediately went into effect, with priority being given to a pedigree boar, also of the Large White variety. This very

Tarpaulins provide shelter for deck passengers

valuable animal was of such vast dimensions that not only was it barely able to swim but it was impossible to haul it into another boat. Helpers promptly leapt into the sea and assisted it towards the ship, where a cargo net was rigged underneath it so that it could be hoisted aboard.

By this time most of the floating cargo and animals had been hauled into other boats, while passengers were generally able to help themselves, except for Dick Chapman, the former unpopular Customs officer, who was now the unpopular Resident Agent on Mauke. Dick was of such vast dimensions that not only was he barely able to swim, but it was impossible to haul him into another boat. Helpers not so promptly leapt into the sea and herded him towards the ship where a cargo net was rigged under him so he could be hoisted on board. One of my more prized photograhs is of Dick and the Large White drying out together on deck.

Another victim of wildlife on board was an American named Don Ronaldo. The ship had called at Suwarrow during a Northern Group voyage and picked up quite a few of the huge coconut crabs for which Suwarrow is famous. A crate of these broke adrift in the night, and the

MATAORA
RAROTONGA—PENRHYN

1+3+80

On board the *Mataora*

crabs went walkabout. One got into Don's cabin and was quietly nosing around when Don, in his sleep, dropped his hand onto it. Like the pig, it acted defensively, and with its giant claw, which was bigger than Don's hand, grabbed one of Don's fingers in a vice-like grip. Don wasn't the fainting type, and his blood-curdling yell could be heard in the further-most parts of the ship. It sounded like first-degree murder, but in fact only the crab got murdered, for that appeared to be the only way he was prepared to release his grip. The resultant crab-meat salad was most appreciated, except by Don, who was convinced the exquisite taste was due to the portion of his finger that was missing. His was actually a nasty wound, with a broken bone sticking through lacerated flesh, but Don, being an old soldier, took it all in his stride — he'd been around blood and guts before. Not so one of his fellow American passengers, who, when she got back to Rarotonga, burst into print, condemning the ship, the captain, the medical facilities on board, and even the poor crab, who had already made the supreme sacrifice. We were thankful it wasn't *her* finger, or we'd have had a million-dollar lawsuit on our hands.

But still the passengers came. Richard Goodman, a Californian tour-organiser whose specialty was getting small groups of people into faraway places on adventure tours, reckoned a trip around the Northern Group would be an adventure. Well, there were plenty of people who wouldn't argue about that, but we found it hard to believe Americans would fly all the way from California, just to spend two weeks on the *Manuvai*. However, they did, and they all seemed to enjoy it. The first contingent of 20 flew from Los Angeles and joined the ship in Pago Pago for the trip to Rarotonga via the Northern Group. The first island was Pukapuka, Frisbie's 'Island of Desire', where they spent the day and a night ashore, feasted and entertained like royalty by the Pukapukans (who were getting paid by Goodman but who just loved to do it anyway). These Americans were mostly middle-aged or older people who had read everything they could lay hands on about the South Seas and had probably dreamed half their lives of one day getting there. Now here they were, a few days out of Los Angeles, on one of the remotest lonely atolls of the Pacific. They loved it, and so did the Pukapukans.

The word travelled ahead, and each island tried desperately to outdo the others in hospitality. Meanwhile, at each island, the ship loaded copra and picked up the usual passengers (who this time had no option but to travel on deck) and the tourists were able to revel in the knowledge that this was a genuine South Seas copra boat. The copra beetles were soon in abundance and, just to add to the genuineness, we had the boys let go the odd cockroach out of captivity now and again, while the engineers arranged a water shortage and a toilet blockage when the time seemed appropriate. On arrival at Rarotonga the tourists climbed aboard the next jet to fly home and tell their grandchildren all about it, while another 20 hardy souls joined the ship for the whole thing in reverse.

The only reason we couldn't keep doing these trips was the very demanding schedule they required. The ship had to be right on time at each end of the voyage, and what with working cargo at open roadsteads where you are completely at the mercy of the weather, not to mention diversions for medical cases or any other mission of national importance, we eventually had to tell Mr Goodman we couldn't accommodate any more tours — but not before Bob got some new phrases for his guff sheet, culled from the odd magazine article written by some of these hardy travellers:

'The *Manuvai*, a 143-ft relic from an earlier era of Pacific travel, foul smelling, roach infested, and entirely without amenities.'

'... deck passengers, crowded together on the hatches under an awning. Pigs run loose along the gunwales, squealing pitifully, and feeding off bits of coconuts.' (Now that writer should have been around when Steve tangled with the boar.)

But it was obviously all worth it to see '... these atolls of romance and fantasy, the most legendary in the Pacific, each one a handful of emerald chips scattered across the opal waters of a shallow lagoon, snugly tucked inside a coral reef which encircles them like a loose-fitting necklace.'

After the oil-price shocks of the seventies there was a lot of interest in developing sailing ships again, or sail-assisted ships. We did our own experimenting with sails on the *Mataora*. These were simple affairs, strongly made and fitted with a minimum of fancy gear. They worked well when used, but the trouble with sailing vessels is that the wind is not always in the right quarter, or if it is, it is either blowing too strongly or not strongly enough. Unless there are keen sailors on board, it is easy to imagine that the right conditions never exist. Much easier to rely on a good main engine and an auto-pilot — especially if Government is paying for the fuel. We were unable to get any Government interest in the project, other than to nominate me to attend a seminar on sail-

Mataora under sail

assisted ships, hosted by the Asian Development Bank, in Manila in 1985. The seminar was attended by representatives from all over the Pacific, with lectures by world experts, and we heard and saw many interesting ways of propelling ships with sails, but most of us left with the impression that there were easier and more effective ways of reducing fuel costs, such as more fuel-efficient engines, more efficiently designed hulls or better bottom paints. The sails outlived the *Mataora*.

With the advent of self-government the Resident Commissioner was elevated to the position of New Zealand Representative. After Ollie Dare, the position was filled by George Brocklehurst, an older civil servant from New Zealand due for retirement. A pleasant friendly type who never seemed sure just what his job was, George was very keen to make a trip around the Northern Group before he went back to New Zealand. Mrs Brocklehurst wasn't so keen to go, but there was no way she was going to let George go on his own, what with the stories she had heard about shipboard romances and the reputation Silk & Boyd's captains had for performing marriages at sea. So a cabin was booked for two VIPs and the crew did their thing of applying a bit of spit and polish, digging out clean linen and reducing the cockroach population to acceptable proportions.

Jim Little, who was the First Secretary at the time, was in charge of arrangements, and assured us that the Brocklehursts would be no trouble, so long as there was ample gin and tonic on board at all times. Just to make sure, Jim brought a case of each to the wharf, and, just to make sure it didn't disappear, Bob put the cases in his office for safekeeping until sailing time. They were so safe in Bob's office that they were still there after the ship sailed.

Bob was aghast at the enormity of the blunder. He wasn't worried so much about George, who was a good scout, but he trembled at the very thought of life on board for everybody else when Mrs B. discovered the loss, which wouldn't be long, and how it would likely get worse each day as withdrawal symptoms set in.

Racing up to the radio station he called Archie Pickering and told him to open the cargo hold and broach the liquor consigned to Manihiki, the first island. Archie had already stopped a broadside from Mrs B., and he told her the good news, but she was not to be appeased. She refused to deprive the poor people of Manihiki of their liquor, and preferred to go without for the duration of the voyage, which meant everybody suffered. Later at a cocktail party at Ngatipa before they left for New Zealand, Mrs B. personally served Bob and myself with water for our first drink. 'Just try drinking that for three weeks straight,' she admonished.

One day at the sailing club our good friend Ian Fogelberg introduced me to a visiting American couple, John and Mrs McDermott. Ian muttered something about 'he's the man to get you to Pukapuka', as he found urgent need to go to the bar, or other business. Assuming the McDermotts were old friends of the Fogelbergs, I expounded on the delights of Pukapuka, then, turning to Mrs M., I said facetiously, 'But you will find plenty to do in Rarotonga while John goes to Pukapuka.' She replied, 'But I'm the one who wants to go to Pukapuka. John gets seasick!'

I pretended to be aghast. 'You? You go to Pukapuka? But women don't go to Pukapuka! Only men go to Pukapuka. Good heavens,

Pukapuka doesn't need women, they have a desperate need for men. It's not called Danger Island because of its reefs, it's because of the voraciousness of its women! No, no, don't go to Pukapuka.' And more inspired nonsense in similar vein.

What I didn't know was that the McDermotts were travel writers, and had only met Fogelberg because he was manager of the Tourist Authority. They wanted to do a book on the Cook Islands, but otherwise had only a passing interest in Pukapuka. Now, because of my buffoonery, the Lady Navigator, as John called his wife, was absolutely determined to go to Pukapuka, on her own, and the more I tried to talk her out of it, the more determined she became.

Her trip was a disaster. She happened to be one of those people who should never go to sea, for she was chronically seasick for the whole of the voyage, not that the weather was particularly bad. Unable to hold down food, and scarcely able to sip water, she lost weight to the extent that her condition was of serious concern to the captain, indeed to all on board. When the *Manuvai* arrived back in Rarotonga she was almost a stretcher-case, and both John and I were filled with remorse at having let her go. The McDermotts' book, *How to Get Lost and Found in the Cook Islands* was a success and we became good friends, although the

The delights of Pukapuka

glories of travel on the *Manuvai* didn't feature all that largely in the guide.

When we had had our remaining liquor on board seized by Customs on arrival from Hong Kong, it left a bit of a sour taste in our mouths. I mean, we declared it all, and were quite willing to pay the duty on it, but the law was quite clear — only the Government may import liquor. This law was a carryover from the old colonial times, when the natives had to be protected from the Evils of Drink, and alcohol could be obtained only on a doctor's prescription. Everyone was sick enough to warrant two bottles of spirits or a case of beer a week, unless he had a birthday or something, in which case he might be sick enough to need four bottles of spirits or two cases of beer. Meanwhile the natives got even sicker, drinking horrible concoctions of bush beer.

Anyway, with the advent of tourism, the law became a pain in the butt, with poor unsuspecting tourists having their part-bottle of whisky or whatever confiscated by Customs on arrival. Eventually the Government was prevailed upon to change the law, which then read, in effect, that a passenger arriving with more than two bottles must pay the current import duty on the remaining bottles.

We thought about this for a while. There was clearly no limit as to how much a passenger could bring in, as long as he paid the duty on all in excess of two bottles. Now, the exorbitant price of liquor in the Cook Islands was not so much because of the duty (which was actually quite modest) but because of the very comfortable retail margins applied by the Government liquor store. So we rustled up a few friends and over a round or two of (duty-paid) drinks one Sunday we hatched a plan.

We picked Brett Porter to be the passenger. With a Cook Islands mother Brett was a genuine Cook Islander, even though he had spent most of his life in New Zealand. If the deal turned sour, he couldn't be evicted from the country. It was arranged that Brett would fly to Auckland, buy sixty thousand dollars' worth of liquor and have it shipped to Apia under bond. Silk & Boyd would despatch the *Manuvai* to Apia to uplift the consignment. Brett would travel on the ship as a passenger, and on arrival at Rarotonga declare to Customs, 'I have 20,000 bottles of liquor — I wish to pay the duty on all except two bottles.'

Of course it didn't work out quite so simply. Although every supplier in Auckland was sworn to secrecy, the word went out like a thunderclap:

'There's this Cook Islander in town with a suitcase full of money, buying grog like there's no tomorrow!' The shipment was hardly on the water before the Cook Islands Government heard about it, and was very quick to express its displeasure at our venture. However, the proposed importation by Brett was perfectly legal, and what could they do about it? What they could do, and they made quite clear they would do, was change the law before the arrival of the liquor, so it would then become illegal, and Customs would seize the cargo. At the same time, the Government didn't want to cause undue hardship to a poor Cook Islander wanting to make an honest buck (nor did it want to admit that it had cocked up with some sloppy legislation), so a hurried agreement was reached whereby the authorities would purchase the liquor before its arrival, at cost plus ten per cent, and take no further action.

The *Mataora* proved to be a good reliable ship. Her six-cylinder Brons main engine still had the original pistons and liners 30 years after she was built. We implemented our plan of a monthly service to Pago Pago and Apia, including Niue on the way. This service eventually became very popular and successful, but it was hard-going convincing the importers in Rarotonga that they should be buying some of their imports from countries other than New Zealand.

Until Tom (now Sir Thomas) Davis became Prime Minister, the private sector received little assistance or sympathy from the Government, which believed that anybody in business was automatically a millionaire and a thief. Although we had been self-governing since 1965, we were still using the New Zealand Customs tariff, designed in many instances to protect New Zealand's industrial development, protection that often resulted in poor quality and high prices. Because we were using the same tariff we were virtually forced, by our own Government, to buy from New Zealand, or else pay high import duties on foreign goods (such as 80 per cent in the case of clothing). On the other hand, things we had no use for, such as railway sleepers and torpedoes, were duty-free. Much of the tariff made no sense to us. Tom called the tariff a comic book and threw it out the window, much to the horror of the New Zealand Prime Minister. Suddenly we were able to shop world-wide; other countries could supply us on a competitive basis.

For some years we had been selling basic foodstuffs from the ships as we travelled around the Northern Group. It started because they were always running out of basic commodities and sometimes the ship would hardly be back in Rarotonga before they would be pleading for another voyage. At first we bought from the wholesalers in Rarotonga, but they seemed to resent us selling to their customers, so we started importing from New Zealand, and eventually we formed Import Traders Ltd to handle this trade. It became a thorn in the side of the big importers, who thought we should restrict our activities to shipping. The fact that shipowners throughout the Pacific were doing the same thing was irrelevant.

Import Traders soon took advantage of the new service from Samoa. We started buying flour from Australia and were able to land it cheaper than flour from New Zealand, and it was much superior flour. As soon as one baker started mixing Australian flour with his New Zealand flour, his bread improved so dramatically that his competitor had to follow suit. The more Australian flour, the better the bread, and it wasn't long before the bakers were no longer buying flour from New Zealand. People thought Import Traders had a monopoly on the flour but the trade was open to anyone; what we needed was cargo for the ship.

Having established the monthly link to Samoa, other importing possibilities presented themselves. Soon we were the principal importers of rice (also from Australia) and canned mackerel, from Japan. Timber from Western Samoa became an important cargo, and we were given the agency for Western Samoa's Vailima beer. We couldn't sell the beer of course, but we got a commission of five cents a bottle for helping to promote it, plus the freight of five cents a bottle for carrying it, and then five cents a bottle for carrying the empties back again, so for every bottle of Vailima we drank we were 15 cents better off. We couldn't afford not to drink it — plus it was good beer.

Eventually the service was accepted by other importers and it was surprising the amount of cargo that was trans-shipped through the Samoas from many different countries. Pacific Forum Line appointed us their agents in the Cook Islands, as did China Navigation, New Guinea Pacific Line and others. So successful were we that we eventually cut our own throats.

Hawaii Pacific Lines, a new company, started a service from Honolulu to the Samoas and Tonga with a small chartered container vessel. Avatiu Harbour was continually being developed over the years, and Hawaii Pacific's *Urte* at 90 metres long was tailor-made to fit the harbour, and the 300-odd tonnes a month we were moving from Samoa to Rarotonga

Loading the *Mataora*

was tailor-made to round off their service. The *Urte* was a beautiful ship for the job (if any container ship can be called beautiful) and provided a good service while it lasted, but the company went broke like several predecessors that had tried running a service from Hawaii to the South Pacific. There isn't the volume of cargo to make it viable. However, HPL hung in for three years, to everyone's surprise.

There was no way the *Mataora* could compete with a container service, and there was no room for her within the group, as trade had declined to the point where the *Manuvai*'s monthly service to each island was all that was needed. Pineapple shipments ceased at the end of 1980, while the shipping agreement with the Government expired in August 1981, although the fuel subsidy continued to be paid (presumably in preference to an increased freight rate).

The opportunity came to sell the *Mataora* when, due to a tightening of American environmental laws, the fish canneries in Pago Pago were required to dump more and more of their waste water at sea, rather than pump it into the harbour as they had done in the past. We fitted tanks in *Mataroa's* cargo hold coupled to a big sludge pump and sold her as a tanker. A new company, Pago Marine Inc., operated the vessel under contract to the canneries. The ship performed well for three years, and never missed a trip until the day the main sludge tank exploded in the hold, spraying hatchboards over the roof of the cannery.

Silk & Boyd had been operating ships in the Cook Islands for over 20 years now and although during that time we had seen more than a dozen other operators come and go, it was generally accepted that Silk & Boyd had a monopoly and, like the Government, had been there far too long. The service was lousy, there were complaints about passenger conditions, and why did they need a subsidy?

The Government set up a Parliamentary Select Committee to investigate us and report to Cabinet. People were invited to make submissions to the Committee which sat long hours over its two-year existence (for the members were getting paid in addition to their parliamentary salary). Although matters such as a proposed Cook Islands Port of Registry were discussed, basically it was a witch-hunt into the activities of Silk & Boyd, who were not allowed to be present to hear any allegations made against them.

The Committee set itself up as a judge between the shipping company and those complaining, and there was never any doubt in the mind of the Committee that the shipping company was guilty and it was a waste of time trying to prove it innocent. In fact the allegations made by the members of the Committee were generally much worse than any made by the public. One member claimed to have seen out-dated rations in the liferafts on board, which demonstrated remarkably good vision, since liferafts are only opened for annual inspection at an overseas servicing depot. Some thought the ships were too small, as they were always overloaded. Others thought they were too big, and too costly to run. Some thought they were too slow, and took too long to complete a voyage, while others thought they didn't spend long enough at each island. Everyone thought they were too old. Definitely freight rates were too high, as proved by the operations of the *Timo*, an even older vessel, which had recently arrived in the Group and was operating at lower rates and without a subsidy. (The reason the *Timo* was able to do this became obvious when, before the Committee finished sitting, she collapsed financially and was arrested for non-payment of debts, including wages, while the Northern Group Copra Growers Association, which had invested one hundred and twenty thousand dollars in the ship, saw their investment disappear over the horizon.)

Criticisms by the public mainly revolved around conditions on board for passengers, particularly deck passengers, who, in the words of one witness, were no better off than the animals they shared the deck with. Actually I thought most public witnesses were very subdued in their comments, except for one who swore on oath that Silk & Boyd had sold 4500 gallons of Government fuel. (The Financial Secretary was able to refute this when he explained that Government didn't own any fuel on the ships, it only reimbursed Silk & Boyd for fuel they used.)

After the barrel of complaints was apparently exhausted, Silk & Boyd were asked to come to the hearing to be questioned by the members. They were not impressed when I turned up alone. They seemed to think that the occasion was important enough that both of us should be there. I assured them that Bob would be only too happy to come along and answer any questions that I was unable to field.

On the subject of deck passengers I said I agreed that conditions for deck passengers were unsatisfactory, and while they might have been considered satisfactory 15 years ago when the *Manuvai* was purchased, this was now 1985 and the people deserved something better. *Manuvai* had been built to carry cargo in northern Europe, and there was no way such a ship could ever be made to carry 90 passengers in comfort in the tropics. The ship and others like her had been purchased in Europe for a song, to provide a shoestring service at minimum cost (whether the cost was met by the user or subsidised by the Government made no difference) and as such they had done a good job, but in this day and age the people were entitled to a bit more comfort.

The important thing to realise, I tried to explain, was that ships the age of the *Manuvai* were nearing the end of their economic life, and that there had been no ships like them built in the last 25 years. So the big question was, what should we replace them with, since any ships that size would already be 25 years old? The obvious answer was a new-building. A new ship would cost in the order of five million dollars, and believe it or not, Silk & Boyd didn't have that sort of money, and even if they did they wouldn't be building a new ship, for the money could never be recovered over the life of the vessel in the Cook Islands trade.

While people might think the present service unacceptable, the day was fast approaching when, unless action was taken soon, there would

The end of the line: *Manuvai* among the coconut trees on Nassau Island

be no service at all. The action needed was for the Government to seek aid money or a soft loan to have a ship built. Then it could decide whether to operate the vessel itself, or charter it to a private company, not necessarily Silk & Boyd, who, like their ships, weren't getting any younger either.

Certainly some members of the committee had the intelligence to understand what I was saying, but when it finally reported to Parliament, my suggestions were not included. The report, like others before it, was filed away and apparently forgotten.

The day of being confronted with no service came sooner than expected with the loss of the *Manuvai* on the reef at Nassau in December 1988. Travelling overnight from Pukapuka after three strenuous days working cargo in bad conditions, she was on auto-pilot, with the man on watch asleep. Although passengers saw the island dead ahead, no one realised there was nobody at the wheel until too late. The ocean-going tug *Raumanga* happened to be in Rarotonga and was immediately dispatched, but was not even halfway there when the weather packed up and salvage became impossible. It was the fringe of a cyclone and the weather was so bad that when the *Urte,* on passage from Apia to Rarotonga, diverted to pick up the passengers, she was delayed three days at the island before she was able to get them all on board. (Having no passenger accommodation at all, the *Urte*'s captain hit on the novel idea of housing them in empty containers on deck.)

We were able to charter the Sofrana Lines vessel *Moana II* to do a trip to pick up about a hundred people stranded in the Northern Group, mostly tere parties from New Zealand on holiday, and to pick up the *Manuvai*'s crew which had stayed in Nassau to salvage what removable gear they could. Nassau is a difficult island to work at the best of times, and more so in the hurricane season, when the reef is swept by persistent swells from the north and west. It was no different when the *Moana II* called. While loading salvaged gear with the ship's boat the mate got swept off his feet and drowned in the surf before anybody could reach him. This was a sad note to end on, but Silk & Boyd's shipowning days were over.

Cook Islanders living in the outer islands had come to accept a regular shipping service as a matter of course; in fact there was a whole new generation that knew no difference. Over the years ships had come and ships had gone, but suddenly there was nothing — nothing at all. People kept asking us, 'When are you going to get another ship?' and they didn't believe us when we said, 'Never.' Things became pretty grim in the outer islands with shortages of basic commodities, particularly in the Northern Group, which still had no air service.

With the Cook Islands at last a Port of Registry, and with the power of the New Zealand unions now greatly reduced, there was competition on the route to and from New Zealand, so much so that the Government felt obliged to license the trade, if only to protect its own investment in the Cook Islands National Line. There were to be severe penalties ('draconian' one judge called them) for operating without a licence. But no such protection was available to anyone who wanted to operate a local inter-island service. The Government's stated policy now was to leave the field wide open, with no restriction on the number of ships. Obviously there was little enthusiasm for offering to provide a service within the Cook Islands. In spite of our efforts to project the image of shipping as a fun game, nobody seemed keen to get into it.

We submitted a paper proposing a quick and long-term solution. This proposal contemplated a bigger, faster and better ship, of a type readily available in Europe, with 'tween-deck space that could be converted for passengers, as well as other advantages such as heavy-lift derricks, and the ability to carry containers and lighters. One such ship would provide a better service, catering for all the cargo and passenger needs of the whole group, but the service would be more costly; additional annual revenue of about three hundred thousand dollars would need to be found, either from increased freights and fares, or some other source. The banks agreed to finance such a vessel, but only if the Government gave exclusivity for five years.

The Government was unable to make a decision on the proposal, and meanwhile did what it could to try to charter vessels. The Fiji Government kindly offered one of its ships, the *Tabu Soro*, which in Fiji was often called *Tub of Sorrow*, for she had caused nothing but headaches for the Fijians from the time she left Norway in 1974, and further headaches while on charter to the Cook Islands, where she continued her habit of breaking down. On another occasion the *Wairua* was chartered from Fiji but she wasn't suited for the job either. Although freight rates were increased by 45 per cent, these charters were financial disasters for Government, and made the former subsidy paid to Silk & Boyd look like an offering in the church plate on a Sunday morning.

We even had the old *Timo* limping round the group for a while, and on yet another occasion the landing craft *Fotu o Samoa* was chartered from Western Samoa to bring a tere party from Pukapuka to Rarotonga for the constitution celebrations. This was even more disastrous, with the ship twice losing its way at sea and running out of food and water. Safety standards weren't just slipping; they were sliding downhill on greased launching-ways. It was like the 1950s again.

Not only were the people of the outer islands suffering, but the lack of shipping was causing a downturn in the economy of the whole group, as almost half the population lives in the outer islands. No business was suffering more than Import Traders, which had the major part of its business in the outer islands. Sales suddenly plummeted, while orders in the pipeline kept arriving from overseas, resulting in an overstocked warehouse and a critical cash-flow problem. It wasn't easy to suddenly reduce the size of the business, for we were now in the container age, and ordering less than a container-lot was expensive and sometimes impractical, while on the other hand ordering by the container-lot (FCL) often resulted in carrying stocks that took too long to turn over. This dilemma was faced by all the importers, for there were too many in the game, and it was a relief to the others when we decided to close down Import Traders. In any case, it was time for us to retire.

Two or three of the traders felt that the situation was sufficiently desperate to have a go at getting into shipping themselves; even if it didn't make any money it would help their basic businesses. We were consulted on the viability of such a venture, and after doing the numbers it did appear that with the high freight rates that now seemed acceptable, it could work, providing a suitable ship could be found at a reasonable cost.

I had recently returned from delivering a tanker from Liverpool to American Samoa for Pago Marine to replace the *Mataora* and it must have appeared as if I had nothing to do, so Brett Porter, the principal instigator, asked me to find a ship. Don Beer, another would-be shareholder in the venture, was to come with me. Since I had nothing to do, I agreed.

Correspondence with brokers proved the point we already knew, that there were very few of the little 400-tonners left in Europe; they were scattered far and wide. The trick was to find one still with some life left in her. Our first inspection was an ex-Dutch coaster, now trading between the Bahamas and Florida, named *Arawak Sun*. She had been in the

Caribbean for seven years, and a lot of money had been spent adapting her to her new trade, including air-conditioning and some superb cargo-handling gear, but seven years in the tropics had made its mark on a ship already over 30 years old when she got there.

While in Florida we learned of a similar vessel for sale, lying in the Miami River. Formerly owned by the Panamanian dictator Noriega, the *Sylvia G* had been seized by US Customs while drug smuggling from South America. An interesting feature was a false bulkhead that had been constructed in the cargo hold, about three metres ahead of the engine-room bulkhead, leaving a secret space for stowing illegal cargo. It had been cleverly done, with materials and workmanship exactly duplicating that of the original construction, but apparently not clever enough to fool US Customs officers; Noriega was now serving a 40-year jail sentence. The ship was in good condition, and was a tempting buy except for the complete absence of any certificates or documentation.

It seemed unlikely that we would find what we wanted in the Caribbean, so from Miami we flew to northern Norway where we looked at two ships, both of which had their good points. The cold climate and low humidity of these latitudes, coupled with the very high standard of maintenance typical of owner-operators in Scandinavia, is reflected in the beautiful condition of ships in the area, even those of 25 or more years of age.

In Copenhagen at the offices of Wonsild and Sons, the brokers handling these two ships, we met young Soeren Victor, the man in charge of this operation and already a friend of Brett. Soeren showed us what to me was typical Danish hospitality and I would have been happy to have spent a week there, but Don was having trouble adjusting to the climate and the cost of living, so next day we were winging our way to LA, Honolulu and Rarotonga, by which time our minds and bodies were totally confused as to what time or even what day it was.

Back in Rarotonga, while reviewing what we had seen and learned, we were given a stark reminder of just how grim the local shipping scene was. A 15-metre New Zealand crayfishing boat, which had inadvisably come to the Cooks to try to make a living fishing here, had been trying equally unsuccessfully to make a living carrying freight to the outer islands, a job for which she was hopelessly inadequate. In view of the desperate need for anything to carry freight to the outer islands, the authorities were closing their eyes to a certain recipe for disaster. The *Intrepid* was a stout little ship, well built for fishing off the New

Zealand coast, or travelling the 400-odd miles to the Chatham Islands, sensibly laden, but the way she was being overloaded for trips to the outer islands was absolutely ridiculous. (But then, stuck with a ridiculously low price-controlled freight rate, there was no way she could pay her way carrying any less.) Forgotten was the lesson of 25 years ago when the government fishing vessel *Ravakai* capsized with loss of life after being overloaded with deck cargo and passengers.

Heading for Mangaia on the night of 14 November 1990, in typical trade-wind weather, loaded down so that her decks were awash even before she left port, *Intrepid* began taking on water and, having no reserve buoyancy to speak of, there was insufficient time for the crew of five to do anything other than inflate the liferaft and jump into it as she went down like a stone. The wind blew the raft back towards Rarotonga, but they would have drifted right past the island had not a sharp-eyed pilot on a scenic flight sighted them about three miles off Ngatangiia and notified the police, who are the search-and-rescue co-ordinators in the Cook Islands.

As if there weren't yet sufficient ingredients in this recipe for disaster, the police allowed three of their officers to go out to the raft in a 16-foot open boat which one of them kept at Ngatangiia. On reaching the raft they compounded the problem even further when the *Intrepid* crew left their perfectly safe liferaft and boarded the open boat which, being overloaded, swamped in the rough seas, drowning the outboard motor and the hand-held VHF radio. The liferaft sailed off towards Samoa, complete with its supply of food and water, leaving eight men clinging to a swamped wooden boat.

Elgin Tetachuk and I were having a quiet glass of ale at Trader Jack's. Elgin's eyes, as always, were scanning the sea for signs of birds, for he pays for his ale by taking tourists fishing in his charter boat *Seafari*. 'Looks like a liferaft,' he suddenly said. We lost no time in getting down to Avatiu Harbour while Trader Jack rang the police, who by now were wondering where their three policemen were. We soon had some police on board the *Seafari* and with the help of the scenic-flight pilot, Simon Egan, who was airborne again, we were able to locate the liferaft, which to our surprise was empty, but it wasn't long before Simon spotted the men in the water, about a mile or so away.

We picked them up, except for two of the policemen, who, incredibly, had set off to swim ashore. This set off another search, resulting in them being picked up, which was fortunate, for they would never have made it. The current was carrying them away from the island faster than their ability to swim. We towed the boat back to Avatiu. It was all in the day's work for Elgin, whose tally now stood at 20 successful sea rescues, but it brought home rather forcefully the urgent need for a suitable and safe inter-island ship. It also brought home the need, demonstrated in the past, for surface craft to be able to communicate with aircraft in a search-and-rescue operation. We had managed only by talking to Trader Jack on the VHF, who then talked to the control tower by telephone, which then talked to the aircraft by radio. And speaking of Trader Jack's, we went back and finished our ale.

Even worse news came two weeks later with the loss of the 74-year-old brigantine *Edna* on the reef at Atiu on 28 November. Another ship unsuited to the trade, the *Edna* had been given a shipping licence when standards had already gone by the board (although standards had nothing to do with her going on the reef). Minister of Shipping Vaine Tairea was quoted in the *Cook Islands News* as describing her loss as the 'twelfth case of inter-island shipping where there has been some breakdown or other since we became the Government last year'.

We reviewed what we had seen and learned of the various ships we had inspected. All things considered, the *Ovoll* in Kristiansund, Norway, was the ship to get, so Brett got an option on her and asked me if I would bring her out. I said I would, since I had nothing to do.

Edna on the reef at Atiu

CHAPTER TWELVE

THE MYSTERY SHIP

I got some more pages put in my passport. I still didn't like flying, but I seemed to be clocking up as many miles as a Cook Islands politician. It was January 1991 when I reached Copenhagen again. The owners had agreed to deliver the ship from her home port in Norway to the little port of Assens in Denmark, where she was to be dry-docked and the sale completed.

It had been decided to do a minimal amount of work in Assens — the important thing was to get the ship into service as soon as possible — but we did sandblast the hull right up to the bulwarks, and the steelwork looked immaculate. In a phone call to Brett I suggested we paint the ship all white — she would look tremendous. He agreed. I asked about a name. He said, 'I want her named *Marthalina*, after my mother.'

The crew were to be all from Rarotonga. First to arrive was Wes, or to give him his full name, Waisale Ravuso Wainiqolo, our Fijian engineer who had spent ten years on the *Manuvai*. Then came Bud Sheedy, an American retired in Rarotonga, and a close friend of Brett. A tall, quiet, likeable guy, Bud is a gourmet chef and turned out superb meals. Wade Swoboda was to be my first mate. A former Silicon Valley whiz-kid, he had drifted into Rarotonga on a yacht 20 years ago. Wade was still an electronics wizard but had opted for a lifestyle in which he believed in working only sufficiently to support the necessities of life.

With Wes, Bud and myself all over 60, and Wade well into his fifties, it was starting to look like a home for ancient mariners, and I was glad to see Paul Henry arrive just in case there was some real work to be done. Paul was young and energetic, able to turn his hand to almost anything, and was always right there wherever the action was. Like his father,

Hugh, Paul was gregarious and always quickly surrounded by friends wherever we went. Although only five in number, we were a good team and got on well with one another. Not that I had ever had any problems in the past, but this voyage was going to test our patience and tolerance of each other in no small measure.

Work went smoothly at the yard. Some small bottom repairs were done, modifications made for carrying additional water, all surveys completed, new certificates issued where necessary, registration completed, instruction books in English obtained for all machinery and electronics, spares obtained, plus charts, pilot books, light lists and radio signals. We came off the floating dock on 29 January 1991, and all hands were looking forward to a quick voyage home. Nobody thought it would take a year.

Meanwhile Soeren Victor had been looking for cargo for us and came up with a consignment of rocket motors from Zeebrugge, Belgium, to Kaohsiung, Taiwan. This meant going via Suez and adding a couple of weeks to the voyage, but it was good freight and would pay for the delivery. Brett asked me to make sure that everyone was happy about carrying a cargo of this nature; everyone was.

The Gulf War had started, and many people were incredulous that we proposed heading that way, particularly with such a cargo, but it seemed to me that by the time we got that far, the war would be over. If not, the Canal would probably be closed, but we would face that problem if it arose. As it happened, the Gulf War caused us hardly any inconvenience. It was a different war in another place, hardly making the international news, that was to become our undoing.

We left Assens with a good deck-load of snow and picked our way down the channel by radar. The fog accompanied us all the way to the Kiel Canal where, at night, and in a driving snowstorm, we passed from the Baltic to the Elbe River and the North Sea. On the river ice floes were 10 centimetres thick and to avoid damage to our new paint we tried to keep close behind bigger ships where we could.

At Zeebrugge our cargo of rocket motors was ready for loading. Packed four to a case, there were 2750 cases, making a total of 101 cubic metres. We were all pretty ignorant as to just what rocket motors were, but we were to learn all about them later. Basically, they could be described as missiles without warheads. As cargo, they were explosive, but from a military point of view they were useless without the other half.

Marthalina

The shipper, Andre Braet, was a sad-looking old Belgian who special-ised in shipping arms and ammunition anywhere in the world. He was a lover of old traditional ships, and thought the *Marthalina* was a little honey. We had a good view of the loading operations from the warmth of his office, and a tot or two of rum added even more warmth, in contrast to the snow and sleet outside. I got to know him well before the voyage was completed, and always appreciated his wry sense of humour.

It was nearing midnight when the loading and the paperwork was completed. Harbour regulations demanded that we sail immediately, something not to look forward to with a gale-force southwesterly wind blowing. In fact the pilot wasn't keen on taking us out, but we had no option, and in the end reached a compromise with him and dropped him off just inside the breakwater. It wasn't very pleasant outside, but the ship had a much easier motion with 100 tonnes of cargo in the hold, and in any case the storm soon passed. By eight o'clock next morning it was fine and sunny with a calm sea as we passed the white cliffs of Dover. The weather favoured us all the way across the Bay of Biscay, down the coast of Spain and Portugal and through the Strait of Gibraltar.

Our voyage down the Mediterranean was a dream. Fine days, with the wind always behind us, the main engine running like a Japanese watch and giving us a steady 240 miles a day. Our course took us past Malta and I went fairly close in to have a look, not that there is much to see. The hills were just as low and barren as when we had called there in the *Port Chalmers* in 1948. Apparently we were a bit too close in for the Maltese, who sent out a helicopter to chase us off. What an inhospitable part of the world!

At Port Said we anchored offshore to await our turn to go through the Canal. Every day more grey ships arrived from the west, full of war material for the Gulf. The war had just finished, but the supply line, it seemed, couldn't be stopped. By the time we entered Port Said there were a dozen of them at anchor, awaiting orders. We used to listen to them chatting to each other on the radio and they sounded really cheesed off, sitting there on their way to a war that was already over. We also learned from them that we had been extremely lucky with the weather, as ships coming behind us had taken a real beating.

After three days enjoying the balmy Mediterranean breezes we got orders to enter port in preparation for the transit. Officials arrived with the usual mountains of forms to be filled in, plus two electricians to mount a searchlight on the bow (we had to accommodate and feed these electricians) plus three line-handlers and their two-and-a-half tonne boat (we had to accommodate and feed them too).

The passage through the Suez Canal is weary and boring unless you particularly like sand dunes. We were a little crowded with the extra people on board, all of whom were trying to sell us all kinds of souvenir junk. The ship was like a Cairo bazaar. The pilot spent much time telling me how underpaid he was, and how impossible it would be to feed his family without the gratuities which captains customarily gave their pilots.

When planning this voyage, careful consideration had been given to bunkering ports, as not every port welcomes ships carrying explosives. Colombo, Sri Lanka, was right on the way, and a reputable agent there, McLaren Shipping, had advised us that there were no problems calling there for bunkers with such a cargo as ours. We appointed McLarens our agent and advised them that our estimated time of arrival would be 21 March.

The weather was again kind to us for crossing the Indian Ocean and we did in fact approach Colombo in the early hours of the twenty-first. After contact with the pilot station we anchored outside the breakwater.

So far the voyage had proceeded remarkably smoothly, but somehow I had a premonition that we were due for a change of luck. I worried through the night about possible infringements of a minor pettifogging nature that I might unwittingly make. I completely overlooked the fact that we were arriving in a country at war with itself; a country where people were killing each other by the hundreds, often with smuggled, illegal weapons; a country where, only a week or so before, a Cabinet Minister had been killed by a car bomb.

Just before 1100 hours we were told to proceed to the harbour and pick up the pilot in front of the pilot station inside the breakwater. The pilot was a pleasant young fellow who gave helm orders to take us to our berth at the far end of the harbour. Halfway there, he said, 'What's your cargo, Captain?'

'Ammunition,' I replied.

Obviously he hadn't been informed, and both of us were surprised. He immediately stopped the ship and called the harbourmaster, who gave his okay to proceed to the berth. The pilot explained that there was no problem entering Colombo with explosives, but it was necessary to advise the authorities 48 hours beforehand, as special security has to be arranged. I said we needed only about four hours in port. Once berthed he gave me his form to fill in with the usual details of the ship and a description of the cargo. A copy of the manifest was attached to it.

Within a short time the officials arrived, a rather large party of them. First was the Customs boarding officer and a young man from McLarens, Sanjeewa. There was some discussion between the pilot and Sanjeewa about McLarens not having notified the authorities about the dangerous cargo, the pilot saying it was a serious matter.

The health officer was a lady, and I got her forms filled out first; no sickness on board, nobody died on the voyage, et cetera. Then came the Customs declaration, a very large form of several pages, printed in Sinhalese, with a translation into English in very small print underneath. It was an imposing document, and struggling through it I came to the part where the quantity of cargo carried had to be described in each of 14 different categories, each category subdivided again into cargo for discharge and cargo in transit. Reading the form was difficult enough, understanding it more so. There appeared to be about five of the categories where it might be appropriate to enter our cargo, for instance: Dangerous Cargo (it was certainly that), Explosives (equally appropriate), Firearms (could be), Ammunition (certainly), Chinese Crackers (I suppose so) and so on. While I was puzzling over this the Customs officer said, 'If you have only transit cargo you don't need that,' and leaned over and put a large cross against the whole lot. He said, 'Just put the total tonnes at the bottom,' so I wrote in '101 tonnes' and gave him the form after signing it. There were a couple of questions I'd missed and he answered them by writing an appropriate 'Nil' in the spaces provided.

Other officials followed, and had their forms filled in and helped themselves to copies of the crew list and manifest, of which I had a generous supply on the table. Last in line was a Port Security officer who was concerned about the dangerous goods part and went off to seek further instructions. He was soon back with more forms and a request that I write a formal letter asking for permission to bunker at this wharf while loaded with explosives.

Meanwhile the bunker barge was already alongside, but they didn't have a small enough hose to fit our connections, so it was being arranged to bring the fuel by road tankers. I took advantage of the delay to call on McLarens. This involved a 30-minute drive through Colombo's traffic, more hair-raising than the Monte Carlo Rally. The manager, Ivan Dias, a small sprightly 60-year-old dressed in the Rarotonga expatriate's uniform of the fifties — white shirt and shorts, long white stockings — made me welcome. I explained the delay with the bunkering and asked if he thought we might get permission to stay overnight at the berth. He rang the harbourmaster — and stopped an earful of abuse. How come this ship had entered the harbour with a cargo of explosives without prior notification? The harbourmaster wanted the proper documentation done immediately, or the ship wouldn't be allowed to sail at all! Ivan apologised for the oversight, of which he was unaware, and promised to attend to it right away. The harbourmaster then apparently relented and we got our permission to stay overnight, which would be a good break. It turned out to be a slightly longer break than we needed.

Back at the ship I found that Customs officials had arrived to say that the agent hadn't advised them in advance as to the nature of the cargo, therefore there would be an investigation, and meanwhile our clearance to leave was cancelled. I was naïve enough to believe that because our documents were squeaky clean, the problem would soon solve itself. Perhaps there would be a small fine, which our agent would of course attend to.

Bunkering finished, we got cleaned up and headed shorewards for the evening, stopping first at the Seamen's Mission to make a call to Brett, but the operator advised it was not possible to call the Cook Islands from Sri Lanka. After a pub or two we got back to the ship about 2300 hours to find Bud entertaining a police inspector and a director of Customs. These gentlemen were later joined by the director of CID and the head of Intelligence. Big brass. We found out subsequently that news of this shipload of ammunition had got to the ear of the Prime Minister, who had phoned the chairman of the Ports Authority to 'sort it out'. It took some sorting out. I finally got rid of them at 2am and hit the sack feeling that we were perfectly in the clear and that every move we had made had been done by the book. Meanwhile we had been put under guard by police, Customs and Port Security, the last armed with automatic rifles.

First thing next morning the Navy arrived with two truckloads of Marines all carrying AK 47s. The show was starting to look pretty impressive. Then three carloads of chauffeur-driven big-wigs, top brass from Ports Authority and Defence Department, and others unidentified. Much snapping to attention and saluting by the Marines. It was turning into a pantomine.

Sanjeewa came to tell me I had to go with him to the harbourmaster's office, but when I tried to go ashore the Ports Authority guards stopped me. I asked them to call their boss, but they had no means of communication. I tried the Navy, but they wouldn't even speak to me — I was obviously the enemy — so I called the harbourmaster on the radio and explained that I was unable to accede to his request as his guards wouldn't let me. He sent a car with a plainclothesman and more guards to escort me to his office.

I found the harbourmaster a most pleasant and courteous gentleman with little more hair than myself, and we got on fine. He explained that the situation had got a little out of hand and through no wish of his own he was obliged to furnish a full and detailed report of it to higher authority. It took most of the afternoon to make this report which was taken down in longhand by a secretary who was short on English and not very good on the typewriter.

It was 1800 by the time I got back to the ship which was still bristling with guards and guns. Wes and Wade had been taken away for questioning by Customs, and I had just reached into the fridge for a cold one when the bastards arrived back to fetch me as well. With one on either side of me and one in front with the driver, they weren't taking any chances as we drove to the Preventive Office, still within the confines of the port.

The scene of the interrogation was on the second floor where I was to spend many frustrating hours in months to come. And what a filthy dilapidated place it was, probably last cleaned before the British left.

And talking of the British, the chief investigating officer was a big muscular man with the face of a pugilist and a blustery, military bearing, even a touch of the regimental sergeant major in his manner of address. It would not have surprised me to learn he had done training at Sandhurst. I always felt I knew where I was with him — in the gutter. We nicknamed him Boof-head, but not to his face.

His fellow interrogator was a balding, higher-ranking Customs officer from another office. He had an unpronounceable Sinhalese name and we always referred to him as Tangata Vavia for his look-alike back home. He had a smooth, roundish, pleasant-looking face and a ready smile which could easily trap you into thinking he was on your side. The Sri Lankans have a peculiar way of shaking their heads, not horizontally as we would to indicate no and not up and down as we would to indicate yes, but in a rocking manner from side to side. Tangata Vavia did this to excess, and I never for the life of me got to know whether it meant yes or no or possibly 'I don't know'. I didn't really like referring to him as Tangata Vavia, for his look-alike back home was a pretty nice guy whereas this one was a dangerous piece of work. We eventually referred to him as Noddy.

They wanted to know not only about the voyage, but the circumstances leading to the purchase of the ship. They were obviously very sceptical that I had had to go halfway round the world to buy a ship for the Cook Islands; there must be plenty of ships closer than that. As for having to come to Colombo for bunkers, that was even more suspicious. After a lot of questioning they said they wanted to see the layout of the vessel.

Once on board they lost all interest in any layout, but went straight to the bridge. They wanted to see the charts I had used on this alleged voyage, and I had to describe in detail the routes taken and the courses steered. This was easy, the used charts were all stacked in order in their drawer, course lines were still drawn on them and substantiated by the log book. It all looked watertight to me. Then they wanted to see the charts from Colombo to Taiwan, and they too were readily available, stacked in order in their drawer. Then what about the charts from Taiwan to the Cook Islands? Well, we hadn't got those yet, we didn't yet know what our route would be after Taiwan. Wasn't that suspicious! Back at the Preventive Office the questions went on for several more hours. I was getting tired and irritable and hungry. They had cold sweet tea and biscuits brought to me, and at one stage a couple of bananas. I was starting to have visions of a few years on this diet before I was finished.

Out of the blue Boof-head suddenly asked, 'Who is Soeren Victor?' You could have knocked me over with a feather. How did they know his name, and what else did they know? I explained as well as I could that Soeren worked for Wonsild & Sons, the brokers for the sale and purchase of the vessel. Boof-head said they knew that, but who was he, what was he like? Had I met him and how well did I know him? I said yes, I had met him and his family but knew him only in connection with this business of the ship and the cargo. He was blond and blue-eyed and looked like thousands of other Danes. He seemed an honest upright citizen as far as I was aware; I had no reason to believe otherwise. At this, old Boof-head appeared to get most incensed, and exploded, ' I think he's just another of those filthy Danes like the rest of them shipping illegal arms around the world!'

There was no stopping him, and he went into a tirade as to how they knew about this cargo before we even left Zeebrugge, how it was obviously meant for the Tamils and we never had any intention of taking it to Taiwan, or if we did it was only to bring it back in by some other way, and how would I feel if I'd had my friends and relations killed by those people up there?

Noddy asked in a more reasonable tone, 'When did you last speak to Soeren Victor?'

I said it was a couple of weeks ago. He was now on holiday and another man was looking after his desk.

'Now isn't that another coincidence?' said Boof-head. 'Do you know where he went for his holiday and where do you think he is right now?'

'Probably in Sri Lanka selling rocket motors,' I said, rather stupidly perhaps, for the humour seemed to be lost on them, and Noddy asked if I wanted that to go into the record. (Much later we learned that 'Victor' was the name of a well known leader who had died in battle for the Tamil Tigers. Another coincidence, as Boof-head would observe.)

Next they produced a photocopy of the Customs declaration form with its large cross against the description of cargo. That had completely gone out of my mind, and I suddenly realised its implications. No amount of explanation would satisfy them. When I tried to explain that it was the boarding officer who had made the cross, I was ridiculed. Wasn't that my signature at the bottom? I had made a false declaration and that was that. They wanted me to sign a statement to that effect. After much arguing, it was obvious I was going to be there until I did sign it, so I did so, and they sent me back to the ship.

It was 0200 hours and I spent an hour on the radio trying to get through to Brett via the local coast station, but although the operator seemed to be doing his best, I gave up after an hour or so. No sooner had I laid down to sleep than the security guards woke me to say one of our lines had parted, and after sorting that out I couldn't get back to sleep for worrying where this ridiculous situation was going to end. It was important to get word to Rarotonga and at six o'clock I was on the radio again, and finally got Brett after three-and-a-half hours.

It was now Saturday and the pressure was still on. Wade had a session at the harbourmaster's office and Bud and Paul were taken to the Preventive Office for about four hours. The director of CID came back for a couple of hours and I found myself getting pretty short-tempered as we went over and over the same ground. The lack of privacy on board was getting to us and I blew my top when I found one of the guards asleep on top of his rifle on my settee, boots and all. This seemed a good opportunity to do something, so I got on the radio and got put through to the head of security at his home. Within 20 minutes there was a flying squad down to sort things out and we got the guards removed to the wharf for a while after that.

On Sunday morning a large detachment of both Army and Navy arrived — lots of top brass and many in civvies. They wanted us to open the hatch for them so they could see the cargo. They wanted to 'take a few samples'. By the size of the gang of wharfies, plus a crane and a fleet of trucks, they were obviously going to take more than a few. A large fire-fighting tug stood by, plus the army bomb squad. There wasn't much to be done but co-operate.

The first pallet of four cases landed on the wharf. Everybody crowded round. They wanted us to open one of them, so Paul got a pinch bar and snapped the straps holding the lid. He didn't realise the case was lying on its side and when the lid fell off the rocket motors rolled out at his feet. Talk about a lot of people stepping back in a hurry! What a coup if they had gone off: all the heads of the Army and Navy in one go.

During the unloading Ivan Dias turned up. I wasn't very pleased with him. I felt that the omission by McLarens to advise the authorities of the cargo prior to our arrival had caused this whole shemozzle and, in spite of promises to do so, he hadn't even visited us since the shit hit the fan.

Ivan said he had been trying to visit us but had been refused access. He now introduced to me a tall, distinguished-looking gentleman who presented his card as J.B.L. De Silva, solicitor, and explained that he had been appointed by the Cook Islands Government to represent myself and my crew, and that he was available at any time of day or night. I was to call him to report any further developments. (It was many months later that I learned that even he was suspicious of our bona fides, due to the prevailing conditions in the country at the time, and the publicity in the press and on TV about the 'Mystery Ship in Colombo Harbour, found to be loaded with illegal arms'.)

This was good news. It would have been already Saturday afternoon in Rarotonga when I had got hold of Brett, and here we were less than 24 hours later and we had a Government-appointed lawyer acting for us. I thanked God for a prime minister able to make quick decisive actions. Imagine if he had set up a parliamentary select committee to make recommendations! Things were obviously being taken seriously back home, and it was good for morale to know we weren't on our own in this godforsaken hole.

The stevedoring operation was pitiful. What took five hours to load in Zeebrugge took 14 hours to discharge in Colombo. They were still at it at midnight when a squad arrived from Naval Headquarters and started dismantling parts off the main engine. There were so many of them crowded into the engineroom that I couldn't get near, but in the wheel-house a man in civvies acknowledged he was in charge. I asked him what authority he had to dismantle the engine. He pointed to one door where a Marine stood with an AK 47 at the ready, and then the other door where there was another Marine similarly armed. He said, 'How much authority do you want, Captain?'

I called Jebba De Silva and he said to co-operate and give them whatever they wanted. There didn't seem to be much option. During this conversation I had turned off the speaker and was using the handset, so that others couldn't hear what was being said. I was conscious of someone standing close behind me, and it turned out to be the head of CID. He asked me who I had been talking to and I told him. After this we were fairly sure our radio calls were being monitored, judging by electronic switching noises we could hear in the background.

When everyone had finally gone I lifted the ration on the grog, which on the voyage had been three cans of beer per man per day. By daylight we had sunk a case of beer, two bottles of rum and a bottle of akvavit, and felt much better for it. I didn't feel quite so good at noon when I was woken up to greet the Honorary Consul for New Zealand, Norman Gunewardene, who had come to inquire into our well-being. Nevertheless, it was good to know that the wheels of officialdom were starting to turn on our side. Norman was of great moral support in the ensuing weeks. Since he was on a first-name basis with many influential officials, he was able to tell us a lot of background information we would not otherwise have been privy to, but he had a delicate diplomatic path to tread. New Zealand, while sympathetic, did not wish to make any representations at this stage that implied that the New Zealand or Cook Islands Governments prejudged my innocence, and by implication the guilty intentions of the Customs officials. Norman's visit prompted me to call the US Embassy to report that I had two of their nationals on board who had been relieved of their passports. They were already aware of the arrest of the ship and promised to keep an eye on the situation.

The next day De Silva came aboard and we spent some hours going over events to date. During his visit we had a team from Customs

A dhow in Colombo Harbour

rummaging the ship; they seemed to be looking for anything that might resemble the nose cone of the rocket motors, but they also went through every piece of paper they could find, looking for documentation of some sort. The radio log was examined in minute detail, and I was asked about some of the calls recorded there. One in particular was to 684-699-1054; who was that to? I said to my friend in American Samoa.

'Oh yes, you were in American Samoa the week before you left for Denmark.' So they had not only thoroughly examined my passport, but memorised it as well. During the day we each had hand-delivered to us an 'invitation' to attend a Customs Inquiry at 1000 hours the following Wednesday, our sixth day in Colombo.

Mike Mitchell, our lawyer from Rarotonga, arrived, and after great difficulty got permission to visit the ship, under guard. We spent some hours going over the chain of events, with the guards trying to listen at the portholes, until Paul accidentally turned the hose on them while washing down the upper deck. Mike had gone through the Customs Act and felt we had only to prove the legality of the cargo to have the inquiry dismissed. The lawyers were doing their best to get the Taiwan Government to come forward and claim it. This they seemed reluctant to do, so we would have to ask for an adjournment.

Just to cheer us up, Mike referred to a clause in the Customs Ordinance stating that 70 per cent of the value of any goods seized, or fines imposed, would go to the investigating officers and informants.

We spent the next week confined to the sweltering heat of the ship, along with our guards. We were subjected to further interviews, and two more extensive searches, one by Customs and one by the Air Force, both looking for 'the other half of the weapon'.

The inquiry resumed on (appropriately) April Fools' Day. Heading the inquiry was the Presiding Officer, referred to always as 'His Honour' and accorded all the respect and deference of a judge — for instance, everyone stood to attention whenever he entered or left the room. We found out he was just another Customs officer, a little long in the tooth. Assisting him at the top table were Boof-head and Noddy, the latter having the title of Prosecuting Officer, which seemed strange as nobody was being prosecuted yet.

Seated down either side of the room was an impressive array of legal counsel representing the shipowner, the Cook Islands Government, McLaren Shipping, the Belgian shipper and Sri Lankan Customs. Each lawyer had at least one assistant. Also present were Brett Porter, Andre

Braet and Norman Gunawardene. And of course the suspects — myself, Wade and Wes from the ship, while from McLarens we had Ivan Dias, manager, Sanjeewa Kotalawela, the boarding officer, and Pratapasinghe, the clerk who had failed to notify the authorities of the impending arrival of the ship. Entrance doors were locked and manned, and the only windows, which faced the main road through the port, were barred. A struggling air-conditioner at the judge's end of the room did its best.

It took all day Monday and half of Tuesday to get through the first witness, Mr Rajapakse, the Deputy Director of Customs who had interviewed me that first day on my return from the agent's office, and who had withdrawn our clearance to sail. Small, lean and rat-faced, his fixed false smile displayed several gold fillings. Constantly clutching his cellular phone (presumably waiting for another tip) he had a long story to tell of how, after the clearance to sail had been issued, he had received a tip from an informer that there was something suspicious about the *Marthalina*. He refused to name his informer or describe the nature of his suspicions. He had found Captain Silk to be a suspicious character, and when questioned as to how he arrived at that opinion, stated, 'Oh, body language'. (Something I'm going to have to watch in future, obviously.)

The next witness was the Customs officer, Sumunapala, who had boarded the ship and granted the inward clearance on arrival (and also issued the clearance to leave, we subsequently learned). He requested to be examined in Sinhalese, although I had found his English adequate. Perhaps he needed time to think while questions were being translated. The declaration form signed by me was produced as exhibit 'A' and passed around. This was the form where he had put a cross against the description of cargo, which in effect could be taken to mean 'No cargo', although the total cargo at the bottom was shown as 101 tonnes. I had been in a sweat over this, as it could be his word against mine as to who had made the cross. It was passed to De Silva, whom I was sitting next to. This was my first opportunity to see the original, as I had been shown only a photo-copy at the Preventive Office.

There was the fateful cross, clear for all to see. But done with a black pen, whereas the rest of the form had been filled in with a blue pen, except for a couple of words 'NIL' (referring to mail and passengers), also done with a black pen, and in a peculiar distinctive lettering where the bottom stroke of the 'L' was very elongated. I immediately pointed these features out to De Silva. Under cross-examination Sumunapala was asked by De Silva why the 'X' was done with a different coloured pen, and also about the two words 'NIL', which were in a different style of writing to the rest of the form filled out by Captain Silk. When confronted with the form, the Customs officer stated that these words 'NIL' appeared to be written in a hurry, that Captain Silk had shouted at him and seemed agitated.

Our lawyers had subpoenaed the log book from Customs, wherein boarding officers make their report when they get back to the office. It was pointed out that the handwriting of the numerous entries made by Sumunapala matched the black words 'NIL' on the form. When confronted with this, Sumunapala said he couldn't see the difference.

On the fourth day of the inquiry Sumunapala was again in the box (actually it was just a chair) and he began by making a statement regarding the black pen and the different writing. It seemed his memory had been refreshed for him since the previous day. He said that during the filling out of the form the captain had gone into another room and come back with an assistant who had helped him fill out the form. De Silva leapt shouting to his feet, calling him a shameless liar, and put it to him that his statement was totally false, really roasted him in fact. Then he turned to the judge and said if this sort of evidence was going to be admitted, it was a sad day for Sri Lanka, and he felt ashamed to be a Sri Lankan, et cetera, et cetera — the tirade went on for about five minutes and was quite some performance. Under further cross-examination Sumunapala was almost reduced to tears; certainly he was reduced to English, for he said to the judge, 'I haven't done anything wrong. It's not me that's on trial here, it's Captain Silk!' I almost felt sorry for him. The lying little turd.

The inquiry dragged on for days. A major from Army Ordnance, bristling with importance, brought one of the famous rocket motors into the room as an exhibit, and proceeded to give us a lecture on field artillery. He explained how the rocket motor was harmless without its warhead, but nevertheless nobody seemed keen to get too close to it.

Meanwhile Brett had done a tremendous job going around the various officials and getting the written approval of each one for the crew to get daily passes to go ashore. He was appalled at the magnitude of this apparently simple task, but also surprised at how easy it was to talk to people in High Places. These passes allowed Bud and Paul to get away during the day, and all of us to meet in town in the evening, where we could relax in Brett's and Mike's rooms at the Hilton and review the day's proceedings under conditions somewhat more favourable than those on the *Marthalina*. We had to be back on board before the passes expired at midnight.

By the end of the first week we were getting pretty depressed. McLarens' senior clerk, Pratapasinghe, had explained that he knew all about the cargo and had slipped up in not making the statutory declaration prior to arrival. He had been in the job 19 years and this was the first occasion he could recall having made such an omission, which he said was just a simple human error, nothing sinister in it at all.

Ivan Dias produced numerous exchanges of correspondence between Wonsilds and McLarens, showing full prior knowledge of the cargo. He stated that this cargo was the second of two shipments to the same consignee, the first having passed through Colombo just a few weeks ago on the Danish ship *Tiger*, but the prosecutor objected to any mention of the *Tiger*, the objections always being upheld by His Honour, who never struck me as having a mind of his own. Mitchell, accustomed to legal proceedings in New Zealand and the Cook Islands, was furious at the way things were being conducted here, but was powerless to act, not having a ticket to practise law in Sri Lanka.

Over the weekend De Silva managed to pull some strings in order to have the documents relating to the *Tiger* cargo admitted as evidence to show that our cargo was just as legitimate as that carried by the *Tiger*. This seemed important to us at the time as the whole thrust of the inquiry appeared to be to prove that we had tried to cover up the nature of the cargo.

There was prominent coverage in the media with continued reference to the 'Mystery Ship *Marthalina*' and how the 'diligence of the Customs Department' had exposed this illegal cargo of arms. Interpol, it was said, had been asked to investigate the European end. Meanwhile, McLarens' staff were being ostracised in their own villages. It wasn't hard to deduce that the propagandist feeding this garbage to the newspapers and television was Rajapakse.

The second week saw Dias and Sanjeewa in the box. Sanjeewa turned out to be an excellent witness. He produced the arrival report that I had filled out for him, clearly stating the nature of the cargo, and written incidentally with the same blue pen. He also stated that the pilot had spoken to him in front of Sumunapala about the ammunition.

Wes was called as a witness and was questioned at length about the repairs done at Assens. They were still trying to build a case that there was something sinister about the voyage. When asked why he wanted fuel at Colombo, he replied, 'We needed it.' No further questions.

Wade's turn came next and he was led step by step through the whole voyage with particular emphasis on loading at Zeebrugge. This was all time-consuming and not getting us anywhere. Meanwhile, De Silva's assistant, Denzil Gunaratne, had been doing some scouting around on the side, and had located the police officer who had boarded the ship on arrival and was prepared to produce the police report form filled out by me, showing where ammunition had been declared as cargo, and also his report-book from the police station, showing where he in turn had reported the cargo. He was to bring the report and the book to the inquiry on Thursday morning. He showed up on Thursday morning but without the report and without the book. He explained that these had been uplifted by the CID the night before. De Silva was furious and asked the prosecution what was going on, and what were they trying to cover up. An order was made to produce them, and when they finally arrived they did show that the cargo had been correctly declared, and with the (by now) famous blue pen.

Then my turn came. The statement that I had made and signed at my interrogation on 23/3/91 was read out. Considering the circumstances under which it was made and the deluge of subsequent events and interrogations, it wasn't surprising that I couldn't remember just what I had put my name to, but I need not have worried, for having had nothing to hide I had told only the truth. Nearly all the statement concerned the events prior to arrival at Colombo: the inspection in Norway, the purchase in Denmark, the dry-docking in Assens and the voyage out. There was very little relating to the non-declaration of the cargo, just that I had admitted that the cargo had not been declared, not a word about my explanation as to how the declaration form had been wrongly completed. Under examination by the prosecution I was asked the same old questions. As I had nothing to hide it was easy to tell the truth and their questioning really didn't get them anywhere. In the end Noddy and Boof-head seemed to get themselves all confused and were arguing in whispers between themselves and with their lawyer, until they finally gave up and said they had no more questions.

Under further questioning by De Silva I explained how the Customs officer, Sumunapala, in an apparent endeavour to assist me, had himself completed the form and put the 'X' in the space describing the cargo, and the word 'NIL' in some other places, all with his own pen which was a different colour to mine. I further said that all this had been explained at my interrogation, which took five to six hours, but they wrote down only what they wanted, which took five minutes to read out. I got a bit worked up at this stage, and asked His Honour to place himself in my position: I arrive in a strange port for the simple purpose of bunkering the ship. I make a stupid mistake with the Customs declaration form, which I have already admitted on 23 March. As a result I have my ship detained, the cargo taken away, my crew put under constant armed guard, itself a frightening and intimidating experience for someone from the Cook Islands, where nobody carries arms. In short, we are treated like criminals, but no charge has been laid against us.

It was a good performance, and I was sorry I had been unable to shed a tear or two, but Brett said it would have been superfluous. I was shaking like a leaf at the finish. Our lawyers also congratulated me. What I had said had obviously come from the heart, and had more influence on His Honour than all the hours of testimony, they said.

The following day was Friday before Hindu New Year, a long weekend, and we had hoped to finish, as there were only two witnesses left — the pilot and the policeman with his record book — but neither was available and the inquiry was adjourned. There seemed to be a changed attitude towards us suspects, possibly a result of my outburst the day before. His Honour went out of his way to greet me, and later ordered shore passes to be issued to all the crew for the whole period until the inquiry resumed the following Tuesday.

There was a feeling of optimism at last. McLarens turned on two cars with drivers to take us all to Kandy, where we put up at their first-class hotel with accommodation and meals on the house. It is hard to describe the relief at getting away from the ship, away from the stupid inquiry, and out of Colombo city. It was a beautiful drive to Kandy, a delightful resort 750 metres above sea level, famous for its temple wherein is housed the Sacred Tooth Relic of the Lord Buddha, and for its botanical garden where there is an incredible collection of tropical and temperate flora, including an orchid house with the largest collection in Asia. We were in a relaxed and jovial mood, and felt that at last the inquiry looked like going in our favour. We got back to the real world on Tuesday.

The pilot, Captain Kappitipola, gave evidence to the effect that I had informed him of the nature of the cargo on the way into port, how he in turn informed the harbourmaster by radio, and how he had discussed the cargo with Sanjeewa from McLarens in the presence of the Customs officer. He produced the form I had filled out for him, describing the cargo, with a copy of the manifest attached.

The policeman with his record book gave evidence, already described, and then Denzil pulled another witness out of the hat, someone I had overlooked. This was the Port Security officer who had also boarded the ship on arrival, Mr Balasubramanium, whom we called Muhammed for short. Muhammed was a Tamil, a big old guy with a friendly open face full of crooked teeth. He produced yet another report signed by me, describing the cargo, and also a letter from me requesting permission to remain at the wharf with explosives on board, for the purpose of bunkering. He said that in addition he had notified the Dangerous Goods Division of Port Security about the cargo. Unfortunately he gave his evidence in Sinhalese, but what he did say was that everybody knew about the cargo within an hour of the ship's arrival, and what the Customs people were feeding to the press about subsequently 'detecting' the cargo was just so much bullshit. This resulted in a shouting match between him and the prosecutors, all in Sinhalese, with Boof-head using his RSM's voice at full parade-ground power, but he wasn't able to gain any ascendancy over Muhammed, who stood his ground. Poor old His Honour just sat there with a bemused look, lost in a fog of irresolution, chewing on his spectacles, until order was restored.

That wrapped up the inquiry so far. His Honour now had to go away and think it over, and decide what charges were to be laid, if any, and what penalties would be imposed, if any. We were to wait with bated breath until he announced his findings the following week. Also waiting with bated breath were the Customs officials involved, who stood to gain 70 per cent of any fines imposed.

Meanwhile we had a certain amount of freedom under the system of shore passes each day. The pass was supposed to enable us to proceed directly from the ship to the nearest gate, and vice versa. Once off the ship, nobody seemed to worry what we did between the ship and the gate. I found Colombo city unattractive, but the port itself was fascinating. Nothing was more fascinating than the magnificent sailing dhows from India. Built entirely by hand and by eye, they hardly had a piece of iron in them, and about the only navigation equipment was a compass. The larger ones were almost the size of *Marthalina* and I spent many hours on board admiring their massive construction and talking to their hospitable

Tamil crews. One captain invited me to do a trip with him, an invitation I rather wisely declined.

I was accosted by a security officer coming ashore and asked to show my pass. He knew exactly who I was, and all about *Marthalina*. He thought I had done a foolish thing, visiting this dhow, because it was well known these dhows, which came from Tuticorin in the Tamil area of India, were smuggling arms for the insurgents in the North. I shouldn't be seen associating with them. However, for $20, plus my camera, he offered to refrain from reporting me to his superior officer. I suggested he take me to his superior officer so I could get a receipt for my $20, and for the camera. He declined, but it wasn't the last I heard of the incident.

His Honour went away and thought about it all right. What he thought was that I was guilty of four offences under the Customs Ordinance and one under the Explosives Act. In the case of McLaren Shipping, Ivan Dias, Sanjeewa and Pratapasinghe each was guilty of separate offences.

Charge No. 1: I was guilty of illegally importing arms under the Explosives Act. *Penalty:* forfeiture of the cargo.

Charge No. 2: Guilty of knowingly using a ship for the importation of illegal cargo. *Penalty:* forfeiture of the ship.

Charge No. 3: Guilty of importing illegal goods under section 129 of the Customs Ordinance. *Penalty:* forfeiture of Rs 316,093,800.

Charge No. 4: Making an untrue declaration under section 28 of the Ordinance. *Penalty:* forfeiture of Rs 100,000.

Charge No. 5: Failing to furnish a manifest of cargo. *Penalty:* forfeiture of Rs 100,000.

These charges were serious enough, but at least they weren't pursuing the notion that I was smuggling arms for the Tamils, so I wasn't going to face a firing squad.

Having been charged with these offences, I was given a week to make submissions as to why I should not receive the maximum penalties as stated. The lawyers were going to be busy. On the bright side, there were no charges against any of the crew, and they all had their passports returned, although they were unable to make use of them as yet, as they needed visas to enter the country before they could get permission to leave it. In any case, they all decided to stick with me. It was comforting the way we had been able to live in complete harmony throughout the discomforts and tensions and demoralising events of the past few weeks, on top of an already long voyage. I was extremely grateful to have such a team.

Denzil and De Silva, with Mitchell's help, prepared 27 pages of submissions on my behalf. The inquiry was reviewed and analysed step by step. It showed clearly how there had never been any attempt on my part to conceal the cargo, or falsify the nature of it, nor did I have any reason to do so. The charges were dealt with one by one, and the appropriate legislation referred to.

Charge No.1 referred to the importation of illegal cargo. Our argument was that the cargo was not imported. If, lying in the hold of a ship within the confines of the Port of Colombo, in transit to another country, the cargo could be defined as having been imported, then this must apply to every cargo consigned to another country transiting in Colombo. If their case is that the cargo had not been declared, then reference to the Ordinance clearly shows that the captain or his agent has 24 hours to produce such a declaration, or to amend a previous declaration, so even if the declaration, made to the boarding officer, Mr Sumunapala, is considered untruthful or unacceptable, they must accept Rajapakse's evidence that when he boarded the ship a few hours later the captain answered all questions put to him truthfully and promptly, and gave a full description of the cargo on board, together with the manifest. It was also noted that the declaration form provided is headed 'Preliminary' in English and Sinhalese.

Charge No. 2 referred to knowingly using the ship to import illegal cargo. We had already disputed the fact that the cargo was being imported, illegally or otherwise. Alternatively, to invoke the second part of this section of the Ordinance it would be necessary to prove that the vessel was used with intent to defraud revenue. The prosecution never put a case to this effect; although it was the unstated allegation that the cargo was for the northern terrorists, and the captain's interrogation clearly indicated this. Now that the Taiwanese government had formally claimed the cargo, such doubts should be dispelled.

Charge No. 3 dealt with the same 'illegal importation' as charge No.1 but under section 129 of the Customs Act rather than the Explosives Act, and we used the same argument as in charge No.1 that no evidence had been submitted to the effect the cargo had been 'imported'.

Charge No. 4 referred to the making of 'an untrue report'. Our submission was that it was a 'wrong' declaration, rather than an 'untrue' one. The word 'untrue' connotes an element of deceit, or wilful with-holding of the truth. Against this the word 'wrong' does not have this deceitful connotation and will include bona fide mistakes, as pleaded by the captain — 'a stupid mistake' were the exact words he used. His Honour's attention was drawn to a proviso in section 32 which gives him the discretion to permit the master of any ship to amend obvious errors, or to supply omissions from accidents or inadvertance, by furn-ishing an amended report.

Charge No. 5 arose out of the alleged failure of the captain to produce a manifest when he made his report. As stated earlier, the master is allowed 24 hours from the time of arrival to do this, and he did so when he gave the manifest to Rajapakse at 5.30pm on 21 March, the day of arrival. It was also brought to His Honour's attention that when De Silva cross-examined Sumanapala (the boarding officer), he pointed out that of 21 consecutive arrivals recorded, masters of 10 vessels had not produced their manifests at the time of making their report, and some manifests were produced up to four days after arrival, and in the case of one ship no manifest was produced at all. His Honour's attention was further drawn to the casual attitude hitherto adopted in the reporting of shipments of ammunition transiting Colombo. In the case of the MV *Tiger*, the lethal cargo discharged in Colombo had been declared under question No. 7 (f) as 'inflammable cargo eg acids, chinese crackers, sulphur, lucifer matches, lubricating oil, etc.' The rocket motors in transit on the *Tiger* were declared under this category and accepted by Customs.

Our case looked foolproof; in fact I thought it made the prosecution look ridiculous. Nonetheless, it was a tense period waiting for His Honour to deliberate over our submissions. The Cook Islands Government had by now spent a vast sum on my defence, for which I was grateful and, even though I suspected the Government was more concerned about the release of the ship than it was about the fate of its captain, I hoped the expenditure wasn't going to be wasted. The owners, too, had been faced with their own colossal expense, and were having grave financial difficulties. If the ship and/or cargo did become forfeit, the implications didn't bear thinking about. There were commitments to the banks to be met, and the matter of insurance was a very grey area. The Belgian suppliers, too, were worried; their contract called for delivery of the cargo in Taiwan in two weeks' time, a date that was fast approaching impossibility. Andre Braet looked even more worried, as his reputation as a shipper of explosives was on the line. The Chinese remained inscrutable. But there was no point worrying. At last our lawyers were able to relax and take the time to show us another side of life in Sri Lanka, and of their own personalities.

Both Denzil and De Silva went out of their way to introduce us to a range of friends, met mainly at their favourite club, the Sri Lanka Sports Club. Very British in style, the club is a purely Sinhala club, started by the Sinhalese for the very reason that British clubs did not entertain their membership at that time. Jebba claimed to be the first 'black' man to be admitted to membership of a British club, not that he was very black, and nowadays there wasn't a white face to be seen, not even carrying a tray of drinks.

They both got a lot of mileage out of introducing us as being from the 'Mystery Ship' *Marthalina*, which everyone had read about, and it was good to be in their distinguished company in the circumstances, for the press had had no more good to say about us than it had to say about the Tamil Tigers. The people at these clubs tended to be older, professional types, and were genuinely distressed and embarrassed when told the real story of the shabby treatment that had been meted out to us. It would never have happened in the days of the British, they would say. Those were the days, when everything worked!

Denzil and De Silva were opposites in many ways. People called De Silva 'Jebba', which we thought was a corruption of his initials J.B.L., and it wasn't until we learned that his name was actually Jebba that I felt comfortable calling him by his first name. Tall, athletic, serious, he was of such a fair complexion that one could be forgiven for assuming he was of part-European descent. Denzil Gunaratne, on the other hand, was such a jovial friendly character it felt unseemly to call him by anything other than his first name. Short and rotund, he was as black as a duty-free shopkeeper from Cummings Street, Suva. As lawyers, they earned our tremendous respect. As people, they became good friends. We were in good hands. In some respects it was a bit like being in the islands, the friendly atmosphere and spontaneous good times. Denzil took us home on the spur of the moment and we met his delightful wife, who didn't seem at all fazed about a sudden demand to feed a dozen people. A piano stood in the living room, so in no time Mitchell was thumping out rollicking tunes with everyone singing and having a party, Cook Islands style. On more than one occasion I recall waking up at Denzil's place in the morning; nobody seemed to take offence or even think it out of the ordinary. I decided perhaps I might like to return to Sri Lanka for a holiday some time — but then what if I ran into Boof-head, or worse still, Rajapakse? That would ruin any holiday.

The day came when we all assembled again back at the Special Investigations Unit to hear His Honour's verdict. It was a hushed room while he read it out. Each of the charges was read at length, followed by the penalty to be imposed.

In brief, I was found guilty on all counts, and had the maximum penalty imposed, which amounted to forfeiture of the ship, forfeiture of the cargo, and fines totalling three hundred thousand rupees (about seven thousand five hundred US dollars. Maclarens were also found guilty; Dias, Sanjeewa and Pratapasinghe were each fined a hundred thousand rupees.

The room sat in stunned silence and disbelief. I asked how long I had to produce the money, and His Honour said, 'twenty-four hours'. I tried to explain how impossible it would be to get money from Rarotonga in such a short time. 'Then Captain Silk can go to jail until the money arrives.'

Wade immediately left for the ship to call Rarotonga, while Dias found a phone that worked and called his office to bring some money to at least pay their fines. While we all waited for the results of these two missions, De Silva went through the motions of filing an appeal to the Director General of Customs, who has the power to reduce or cancel fines or penalties.

Premadasa arrived from McLarens' office with several large paper bags stuffed with rupees. Customs officers were called in to count it all, while Noddy and Boof-head and the rest of them sat goggle-eyed at the mountain of paper money in front of them, 70 per cent of which would soon be theirs, personally. To my surprise and relief there was sufficient to pay my fines as well as McLarens'.

Custody of the ship was given to the Navy. The Army already had the cargo, and Customs had the money. The Navy wanted to evict us from the ship, and we were only too happy to oblige, but until we got immigration visas we had nowhere to go. I went to Boof-head's office to get my passport back. He claimed at first he didn't know where it was, then later changed his story to say that it was in a safe in another office, but the man who had the key couldn't be found. Deeply worried and inwardly boiling with rage, I went back to the ship, only to find more trouble. A large oil slick had come into our corner of the harbour and we were accused of pumping our bilges. This was patently absurd; it wasn't even the type of oil that a ship like ours would be carrying. Anything I said didn't make any difference, charges were going to be laid, there would be an inquiry … just what I needed.

I called the friendly harbourmaster. He was quickly on the scene, with his deputy. He agreed with me, the oil couldn't have come from us. The way the wind was blowing it had obviously come from a Greek ship which was lying upwind of us, and which had been leaking oil since going aground on the breakwater a few days earlier.

Then there was the incident of the flag. Since they had taken my ship from me, I didn't see that it was appropriate to continue flying the Sri Lankan courtesy flag which had been up since we entered port, so I pulled it down, perhaps a bit unceremoniously for some nit-picking officials who happened to be watching. A police officer arrived, and I had to make a statement. And the security officer who had caught me on the dhow was still threatening to report me (I still had my camera, and the twenty dollars).

After having carefully watched my crew for the last six weeks for any sign of cracking up, I suddenly realised I myself might be the first candidate to do so. Leaving Wade in charge, I got a taxi to the Central Railway Station and boarded the first train. It happened to be going to Anuradhapura, 200 kilometres to the north.

CHAPTER THIRTEEN

SNEAKING OUT

A young Sri Lankan made an effort at conversation with me. I would have preferred to be left alone, but he seemed a decent enough chap so I talked to him for a while.

As far as I was aware, I was the only white face among about 2000 passengers, so I supposed I was a bit of a curiosity. Of course he wanted to know where I came from and what I was doing in Sri Lanka and so on. Determined to avoid any association with ships, and the *Marthalina* in particular, I said I was a wheat farmer from Australia, and long before we reached our destination I had improved his education, and my own, on the subject of wheat farming in Australia.

Nearing Anuradhapura in the evening, my new found friend, Dudley, came again and chatted to me, saying that if I didn't have accommodation arranged, he had an uncle who let a few rooms and he would be happy to take me there. It was only a hundred-rupee taxi-ride and if I didn't like it, that was all I had to lose. It sounded like the usual come on but it turned out to be a nice comfortable place at very moderate cost. They already had one guest, a Westerner, who was in the sitting-room reading a book. I said 'Gidday!' in my best Australian wheat-farmer accent. He said, 'That sounds all right!' Another Australian, for goodness sake. Of course he wanted to know what part of Oz I came from and, as I still had my friend of the train with me, I had to carry on the duplicity.

'Oh, Gulgong,' I said, 'the town on the ten-dollar note!' He hadn't heard of Gulgong and wasn't aware that that was the town pictured on the Australian ten-dollar note, so rather than get caught out, I was able to tell him quite a bit about Gulgong, on which I was an authority, as we had built up a friendship over the years with our supplier of flour from there.

Next morning Dudley showed up with a spare bicycle and together we set out to visit some of the many shrines and monuments for which Anuradhapura is famous, many of them dating back as far as the 4th century BC, for this was the first capital of a thriving civilisation even before the enlightenment of Buddha. In fact the most holy object in Anuradhapura is the Sacred Bo Tree, grown from a piece of the original under which Buddha received his enlightenment, and brought to Sri Lanka in 230 BC.

Our tour included a visit to Dudley's place to meet his mother, who spoke no English but soon rustled up a cup of tea and some fresh fruit. Then I had to meet his sister next door, and her young children, and take photos of the whole family. Really friendly people, and I accepted an invitation to stay with them. Of course they didn't know they were consorting with a convicted criminal and smuggler of illegal arms.

I spent several days mentally unwinding in Anuradhapura, staying with Dudley and his friends, seeing the sights by day, and drinking arrack by night. One night we went to a political rally to hear the Prime Minister address a huge crowd. I didn't know how good his security was, and I made sure not to be anywhere near him or his official party. It seemed peaceful enough. They were having what appeared to be the equivalent of local-body elections, and as Dudley was involved in the house to house distribution of propaganda, I got invited into numerous homes and drank gallons of tea. All political discussions were in Sinhala or Tamil, and I never even got to know which side he was on. When I left he refused to accept any payment for his services as a guide, or the use of the bicycle, but I was allowed to make a small contribution towards the family food bill.

The thought of returning to the stench and heat of Colombo, with its beggars and bureaucrats and corrupt officials, wasn't particularly appealing. They were probably managing without me, happy to have my passport. I decided to see a bit more of the country.

Travel by bus is something not to be missed by the hardy adventurer in Sri Lanka. Most of the long-distance buses are of the small minibus 28-seater Japanese type. A 28-seater holds about 56 Sri Lankans, but it's not easy to get a head count. The cost is cheap, the comfort non-existent. The drivers are suicidal maniacs, always driving in the middle of the road, swerving to avoid oncoming traffic at the last possible moment or braking suddenly to avoid the odd ox-cart or wandering buffalo. However, all this is not sufficient to keep the passengers awake in the sauna-like atmosphere inside the bus; those standing drop over those seated, or even to the floor.

I travelled on many of these buses all over the country, except for the trouble spots of the north and east. One memorable journey was the 72 kilometres from Kandy to Nuwara Eliya, a tea-growing centre at 2000 metres, which took four-and-a-half hours. This bus driver had a refined addition to the usual tortures of Sri Lankan bus travel in the form of a cassette player and loud-speaker system over which he played Sri Lankan or Indian music, I'm not sure which, but to my untuned ears it was a screaming, screeching, caterwauling at many decibels per square centimetre. Fortunately he was too busy at times, wrestling with the wheel and the gear lever, to turn the tape over when it ran out, so there were periods of relative quiet and harmony, listening only to the roar of the diesel engine and the protesting groans of the gears and the whole drive-train.

Just when I was starting to think the road couldn't possibly climb any higher, or the bus accept another gear change, there in a broad valley lay Nuwara Eliya. It was like driving into Scotland. The air was cool and fresh and there was yellow-flowering gorse on the hillsides. The post office with its clock tower could have come straight from an English provincial town. Other buildings boasted gabled roofs and bow windows, with immaculate lawns and gardens of rose bushes. Tall macrocarpa trees lined some of the roads and there was even an 18-hole golf course in an idyllic setting, with a club-house built like a colonial hotel where I was served tea and scones on a silver tray by a white-coated waiter. I decided the Rarotonga Golf Club had a long way to go.

At a little store on the edge of town the shopkeeper let me a room and his wife provided meals. I inquired if I could hire a motor-bike, and learned there were no such facilities, but the shopkeeper said the town boasted two motor-bikes and he managed to persuade one of the owners to hire me his for the following day. It was a Suzuki trail-bike, in good order, and just as well, the places it took me.

I had a map of sorts, but it was of limited use, for, although it was printed in English, the signposts were all in Sinhala or Tamil. However it did give me an idea of general directions. I had read of a place called World's End, where you can stand at the top of a 1500-metre cliff and see clear out across the coastal plains to the south. It wasn't shown on my map but the shopkeeper had given me an idea where to find it. By late afternoon I had travelled many kilometres in different directions trying to get to the general area of World's End, but there just didn't seem to be any roads going the way I wanted to go, the way always being blocked by impassable mountain ranges.

At a little village I asked an old bloke to show me on the map where we were, and he pointed to the name Belihul Oya. I said I wanted to go to Nuwara Eliya, which was the quickest way? He looked at the bike, looked at me, looked back at the bike and said, 'That way,' pointing to a track leading off through the bushes directly towards the base of an escarpment at the top of which could be seen a tea factory in the distance. The escarpment looked almost vertical and about 1500 metres high. I realised I was looking at World's End from the bottom up. The old guy assured me that if I followed the track, I would arrive at the tea factory, and after that it would be easy. It looked absolutely impossible. There was no sign of a road or even a track anywhere up that massive face, but I thought I might as well see where the track led anyway.

Surprise, surprise, it did lead to the top of the escarpment, by a hidden tortuous route, switchbacking up the sides of narrow concealed gullies and hugging cliff faces where crampons would have been more appropriate than a Suzuki trail-bike. It was many years since I had ridden a motor-bike, and I had never tackled anything like this. I thought of turning back, but the thought of going down that track was even worse than continuing up. I could have done with more horsepower to cope with the grade, and certainly a couple of lower gears to handle the roughness of the track. It occurred to me that if I hurtled over the edge I could be waiting a long time for someone to find me, and Rawene Hospital was far, far away. The worst bit was the last few hundred metres, and I was glad to get off and rest the bike against a crude sign which warned travellers that this was the Devil's Staircase, and to please use extreme caution.

There was no sign of the tea factory, but the track turned into a road, albeit a rough one, leading through a large tea estate which went on for many kilometres, through country still rising in altitude. Soon there was habitation, with clusters of workers' huts, and children goggle-eyed at this apparition on a motor-bike appearing out of the mist from the direction of the Devil's Staircase. Possibly the Devil himself, they might have thought. The mist got thicker and colder as the road got ever higher, surely 2000 metres (700 feet above sea level) by now. My hands felt frozen to the handlebars, but I pressed on, not wanting to get caught in the dark up here. At last the road began to descend, and it was a magnificent downhill ride through many kilometres of tall gum trees to reach the little railway siding of Ohiya. I was back in Nuwara Eliya soon after dark, and spent the night sleeping in what dry clothes I had and shivering under two blankets.

From Nuwara Eliya the bus dropped down 300 metres in 15 minutes to reach the railway station of Nanu Oya, a fascinating six hours from Colombo, and for ninety-eight rupees the greatest travel value ever, even if the only seat you get is the carriage step with your feet hanging outside. Leaving the tea plantations where the rolling hills are carpeted with dark green tea bushes, manicured by hand every three weeks, you enter tropical rainforest. In places the track runs along narrow valley floors with rice paddies and terraces on one side and jungle on the other. Then you might go through a tunnel and suddenly you find you are no longer on the valley floor but clinging to the side of a mountain with another valley floor 300 metres below.

Feeling mentally refreshed, I arrived back in Colombo to find the wheels of bureaucracy grinding exceeding slowly and the wheels of justice ground to a halt, if indeed they had ever ground at all. The ship was handed over to the Navy. My passport was at last retrieved with a 30-day visa stamped in it. We decided we might as well go home and lick our wounds.

Back in Rarotonga we were celebrities of a sort, but certainly not heroes, for the country was still without a shipping service to the outer islands, and the ideal ship for the job lay wasting away in Colombo Harbour, over 11,000 kilometres away.

In the background there was much going on at diplomatic level. Prime Minister Geoff Henry (now Sir Geoffrey), to whom we were exceedingly grateful already, continued to press the matter in letters to the Prime Minister of Sri Lanka, and was preparing the ground to send a representative of government to Colombo to talk directly to the Prime Minister (or any appropriate Minister) as one sovereign state to another. A diplomatic approach was also made to the Chinese Ambassador in Wellington, who admitted that China had actively pursued a policy of preventing the sale of arms to Taiwan, but he promised to take it up with Beijing. Sir Robert Muldoon, on holiday in Rarotonga, happened to ask me how shipping was going these days, and was appalled when I told him the story of the *Marthalina*. Although the National Party was back in power in New Zealand, Muldoon was not Prime Minister, in fact he had declined any portfolio, and was unaware of what had happened. He took the matter up personally with President Premadasa as a former colleague among the Finance Ministers of the Commonwealth.

We will probably never know what effect these and other efforts had, but in October word came from Colombo that they were prepared to release the ship on condition that the owners withdrew their court action against the Sri Lankan Government, and paid a further ten thousand US dollars by way of 'mitigated penalty'. Mike Mitchell flew to Colombo to confer with Denzil and De Silva to make sure the offer was genuine and there were no hidden snags attached, particularly in relation to the cargo. Mike reported back that yes, we should come and get the ship; the additional fine was unpalatable, but it was peanuts compared to the cost of any alternative. Although litigation through the courts might eventually succeed in recovery of the ship, plus fines as well, and perhaps even damages, the company did not have the financial resources to fight such a case, and anyway it would take so long that the ship might not be worth much when we did get it back. As for the cargo, the Sri Lankans

Avatiu Harbour

would keep that, which was a relief as far as I was concerned, for with all the publicity attached to it, and the determination shown by certain quarters to prevent it reaching its destination, it would be foolhardy to try to continue the voyage with it. Having had it seized by an unfriendly power, I felt we had no further obligation to deliver it.

Brett and I flew to Colombo to complete the paperwork. The crew were to follow a week later. It was one of those flights where we lost luggage and missed connections, and we weren't in the best shape by the time we arrived in Colombo in the middle of the night. In order to not draw attention to myself I was travelling on a round-trip ticket like any tourist, for I had a gut feeling the bastards might still be after me, so it was a rather spine-chilling experience when I was recognised in the queue at Immigration and whisked off to a special room and relieved of my passport. However, all was well, I was getting special treatment to speed my passage through officialdom, thanks to the super-efficiency of McLarens, whose man, Premadasa, was there to meet us.

Mitchell had already laid all the groundwork and seemed to be on good terms with the Attorney General, who appeared to be the one pulling all the strings to get the ship away, and through whose intervention we got access to the ship to see what condition she was in. She was moored to a dolphin near the breakwater at the far end of the harbour, still under 24-hour armed guard by the Navy, and with all doors and access hatches sealed by Customs, so it was quite an exercise getting the ship opened for inspection. Although the seals appeared to be intact, the ship had been broken into and quite a bit of damage done, particularly to the liferafts, both of which had been opened and ratted. However, the worst damage had been caused by the ship having been in collision with one of the Ports Authority barges which had broken adrift in a storm.

We met with the lawyers in the Attorney General's office to draw the necessary documents for the release of the vessel. There was to be no compensation for any damage done to the ship; we had to accept her 'as is' and sign a document absolving the Government from any responsibility, as well as withdrawing our court action which was already in place, plus guaranteeing to not sue the Government on any other occasion in the future. Also we would indemnify the Government against any claims the owners of the cargo might bring against it — and of course pay the 'mitigated penalty' of ten thousand US dollars. Having agreed on all points, we were to meet again the following day to sign the documents and pay the money.

At the meeting the following day we were informed that the rules had changed. Now we were to take the cargo with us; actually not all the cargo, but about 85 per cent of it (presumably they had used some). Our lawyers explained that this was something that we would first have to discuss with the owners of the cargo.

It seemed we were back to square one, and meanwhile the rest of the crew were on their way. Talking to the Taiwanese proved fruitless, as they had by now wiped their hands of the whole thing, closed their Colombo Trade Mission in disgust, and lodged a claim with their insurers for seventeen million US dollars. Trying to talk to the insurers in Taiwan wasn't easy either. As it happened, they had reinsured the cargo with another company in the United States. It was getting pretty complicated, so Mitchell and De Silva flew to Taiwan and had meetings with both the insurers and the reinsurers, but to no avail — nobody wanted anything to do with the rocket motors. Then we thought perhaps the shipper in Belgium could divert them to another buyer, but neither he nor the manufacturers were interested. What we didn't realise, and learned by chance, was that a Lloyd's surveyor had been sent from London and a survey of the cargo had found that it had deteriorated and was now worthless. No wonder the Sri Lankans wanted to get rid of it, and the sooner the better. Obviously they were in a dicey situation themselves if the insurers decided to sue for the value of their cargo.

It was an impossible situation. Even assuming the cargo was still safe to carry, where could we take it? As long as the ship was loaded with rocket motors for Taiwan, that was the only place we could go, but it was no use going there if the consignee wouldn't accept them. We could dump them at sea, but then we'd be in worse trouble trying to prove we hadn't delivered them somewhere else. One way or another, the insurers were going to be after someone's blood.

The lawyers wrote to the Attorney General, pointing out that we had come back to Sri Lanka in good faith, prepared to meet their conditions, that these conditions had been changed after our arrival, that we had explored every avenue but were unable to meet the new conditions because of circumstances beyond our control. Furthermore, the owner, the captain and the crew had already undergone severe financial hardships and mental anguish, and the captain had already paid penalties totalling three hundred thousand rupees, penalties totally disproportionate to a wholly innocent and human error. If we were to be stuck with the imposition of this new condition taking 85 per cent of the cargo we would have no alternative but to proceed with the action already instituted, and pursue the claim for the value of the vessel.

The weeks dragged on, with everybody getting more and more depressed. Brett was just about ready to call it quits, and in desperation flew to Belgium to plead help from the shipper or manufacturers. Meanwhile, with a bit of help from the Attorney General we got permission for the crew to make daily visits to the ship so we were able to keep occupied doing a bit of much-needed maintenance. It was my job each morning to go to the Customs Preventive Office and wait (up to an hour) for an officer to be assigned to accompany me to the ship. I detested these visits: Boof-head and Noddy didn't seem all that pleased to see me and were no doubt pissed off that their watertight case of detection had turned sour on them and they had been caught out trying to make a fast buck in an unsavoury manner.

Just when we were about to give up, the miracle happened; they agreed to release the ship without the cargo. No sooner did we get advice of this than we got word that the insurers would arrest the ship as soon as she was released from Customs, so once again it looked like being back at square one. However, by now the Attorney General seemed to be very much on our side, and a great subterfuge was entered into, whereby we were to be allowed to bring the ship alongside for the purpose of stocking up on fuel, provisions and mechanical equipment needed to set sail. The crew would be permitted to take possession of the vessel and the release would be effected upon payment of the fine and withdrawal of the court action. Thus we could do everything necessary to prepare the ship for sea, during which time nobody could serve a writ on us, for she was still under control of Customs, then at the last minute we would wrap everything up and shoot through. Just to make sure everyone co-operated, the Attorney General wrote me a letter, with copies to the Director General of Customs, the secretary to the Ministry of Finance, and the secretary to the Ministry of Defence, stating that we were free to do whatever necessary to get the ship ready for departure. This letter was to be of immense value over the next few days, overcoming many bureacratic hurdles.

Friday 20 December was to be a public holiday (one of the 146 they have each year) and as it would be a long weekend we figured that if we arranged for the release of the vessel towards the end of the business day on Thursday, and sailed that evening, we would be well on our way before anyone got around to getting a court order to stop us. McLarens had to be taken into our confidence, as they had to arrange the clearance, but otherwise very few people knew of our plans. Anyone asking was told, 'Oh, we are still waiting for Customs to release the ship'. The insurers had instructed their lawyer to have the ship arrested immediately upon its release, but even they weren't able to find out. It seemed that almost everybody was on our side at last.

The lawyers paid the 'mitigated penalty', signed the documents, and the ship was released, together with the Customs clearance to sail, a document I was pleased to be able to produce when we arrived in Darwin. But it seemed that God had one more trick to play on us. The heavens opened up in the most torrential downpour. It was almost totally dark long before sunset, except for long almost continuous flashes of forked lightning, sometimes several at the same time in different parts of the sky. The whole city of Colombo virtually closed down and all shipping movements came to a standstill. Obviously we weren't going to get arrested that night, so I ordered a pilot for 0600 hours next morning, by which time it was fine and calm, and as we sailed out of Colombo Harbour amidst all the floating debris brought down by the previous night's floods we were treated to the most magnificent sunrise.

I decided to call Soeren Victor in Copenhagen with the good news. This was the first time we had used the radio since our return to Colombo. The same operator came on, and when I said it was the *Marthalina* he wanted to know if it was the same captain as nine months ago, and when I said yes and that we were now on our way home, he said, 'Congratulations! I think you've been here eight-and-a-half months too long!' I thanked him for his tremendous help in getting calls through to the Cook Islands during that difficult period.

There was a sense of euphoria on board as Wes cranked the main engine up to full power and we headed off down the coast, anxious to put as many miles between us and Colombo as possible, as quickly as possible. There was a hilarious episode when Wade found he had locked himself out of his cabin, and we had to lower him over the side in a bo'sun's chair so he could reach in through the porthole with a boat-hook and get the door open. Not so hilarious was the cry of 'Fire' shortly after — but it wasn't too serious. The crows had built a huge nest inside the funnel and once this was consumed, that was the end of the fire. Much worse was to come from the engine-room department that afternoon, when we lost the ship's entire electrical system in one great brilliant flash.

We were about ten miles offshore and 90 miles from Colombo. We stopped and held a council of war, summing up the options. The ship was still mobile; we would be without lights but we could get by without lights at a pinch. The gyro compass would soon stop, but there was a spare spirit compass that we could lash in place, and we could steer by flashlight while the batteries lasted. We would in any case be steering by hand. We would be without radar, but that was no big deal. Our GPS would die when the batteries gave out, but we had a sextant, so that was okay. There would be no running water or sanitary system, but that wouldn't kill us. When it was all boiled down, we could if necessary get the ship to Australia. But then from a seaman's point of view it didn't make sense to set off on a 3500-mile voyage with the ship in this condition when help was available at Colombo, 90 miles away.

I decided to head back towards Colombo and that night I called Ivan Dias. I gave him a list of equipment we needed, all of which should be readily obtainable in Colombo. But should we come back to Colombo, I asked, or should Ivan get it delivered to us down the coast? He suggested that hanging about down the coast would arouse suspicions, better to come and anchor amongst the ships outside Colombo Harbour where nobody will notice. 'In any case, it's quite safe. Everybody knows you've left for the Cook Islands.'

We anchored outside the harbour on Saturday morning, informing the pilot station that we didn't need a pilot, we were just waiting for spares to be delivered. Just after lunch a launch came out with the spares, and shortly after there was a call from Ivan, asking if we had the spares on board yet. He sounded very agitated, which was unlike Ivan. I told him the spares had just arrived. 'Get out of there!' was all he said. I needed no second bidding and we were under way while still weighing anchor. With binoculars trained on the harbour entrance behind us, and the main engine doing more RPMs than it had seen for years, we were once more heading down the coast. This time we didn't stop until we anchored in Darwin.

The reason for Ivan's panic back at Colombo was never explained until we reached Rarotonga. The lawyer for the insurers had got word the ship was at the anchorage and called the pilot station to get a boat out to it. The operator on duty happened to be a good friend of Ivan

Dias, whom he called: 'Hey, Ananda is trying to get out to the *Marthalina!*'
'Stall him off!' shouted Ivan. It was close enough.

Our first contact with Rarotonga was through Perth Radio on New Year's Day. I talked with Brett about the possibility of the insurers having a bailiff waiting for us in Darwin. Although we had cleared Colombo 'for the Cook Islands' it wouldn't have been too hard for anyone to figure out that we would need a bunkering port on the way, and that that port would logically be Darwin. Brett, having heard from Ivan of the close shave back at Colombo, recommended calling at some small port elsewhere in Northern or Western Australia, but with our limited range and lack of charts there was little choice. We investigated the possibility of rendezvousing with a bunkering vessel offshore, but none was available. So Darwin it was, and with some trepidation we entered Darwin Harbour.

The harbourmaster told us to anchor and await the next tide, when a pilot would take us to our berth. The tide came, but not the pilot. The harbourmaster advised that the pilots were terribly busy, and we would have to wait for the next tide. This seemed odd, for there were very few movements in or out. Then Customs advised they would clear us while at anchor. They came aboard in force, armed with sniffer dogs, and did a thorough rummage of the ship, opening up everything, including ballast tanks. As a search team they would leave the whole of Sri Lanka's armed forces and Customs for dead. It was by far the most thorough search of a ship I had ever seen.

The pilot arrived for the following tide, and his first words were, 'Is this the *Marthalina* I've been reading about?' We assured him it probably was, but what had he read? He was a Sri Lankan, and had received the newspapers from home and couldn't believe what had been reported. We said we could scarcely believe it ourselves. Then the agent came aboard with the current issue of the *Daily Commercial News*, with more reporting about the *Marthalina* as part of a front-page feature on the various calamities befalling Cook Islands-registered ships, something we needed like a hole in the head.

Nevertheless, the stopover in Darwin was a pleasant break. What a contrast to Colombo, without a beggar or any garbage in sight! But we weren't there to enjoy the sights, and as soon as stores and bunkers were loaded, we were once again on our way. Tropical Cyclone Mark was

Avatiu Harbour, Rarotonga, as it is today

lurking in the Gulf of Carpentaria, but obligingly moved inland as we passed by, giving us a pleasant lift through Torres Straits. We continued down inside the Great Barrier Reef and out into the Coral Sea, where Cyclone Betsy conveniently passed to the south of us after creating havoc in Vanuatu, giving us more westerlies to hurry us on our way towards Rarotonga, where we arrived on 29 January 1992, exactly one year after coming off the floating dock in Assens. Rarotonga had been hit by Cyclone Val the week before, and there was a fine mess to clean up at home — but that was all right; now I had nothing to do.